Emilio Castelar, Amelia Elizabeth Hyde lady Arnold

Life of Lord Byron

And Other sketches

Emilio Castelar, Amelia Elizabeth Hyde lady Arnold

Life of Lord Byron
And Other sketches

ISBN/EAN: 9783337416713

Printed in Europe, USA, Canada, Australia, Japan

Cover: Foto ©Thomas Meinert / pixelio.de

More available books at **www.hansebooks.com**

LORD BYRON

AND OTHER SKETCHES.

BY

EMILIO CASTELAR.

TRANSLATED BY

MRS. ARTHUR ARNOLD.

LONDON:

TINSLEY BROTHERS, 8, CATHERINE STREET, STRAND.

1875.

[The Rights of Translation are Reserved.]

LONDON :
SAVILL, EDWARDS AND CO., PRINTERS, CHANDOS STREET,
COVENT GARDEN.

PREFACE

TO

THE ORIGINAL EDITION.

By JOSÉ ROMAN LEAL, of Havana.

"He chose a great and honourable work, and laboured to bring it to perfection."—THALES OF MILETUS.

THE coincidences of life are so curious, that the work of combined calculation will assimilate better than the product of improvised circumstances.

Castelar, whose meridional imagination is one of the most exalted of this century, under the melancholy influence of the heavy atmosphere which hangs over the Saxon city, turned his thoughts to Lord Byron—a genuine descendant of that race; and having confided some of these reflections to a native of New Castile, eighteen hundred leagues from his own country, under the ardent rays of the sun, which bathes in its light the luxuriant vegetation of the tropics, the writer of these lines sent across distant seas a greeting of affectionate admiration to the author of those brilliant pages, which are worthy of being immortalized in gold and marble.

b

He does not, however, think himself entitled on this account to write a prologue to the work of the most daring and brilliant literary colourist of our times — like the announcement of a shopkeeper painted on the drop-scene of a theatre. Nor does he fall into the folly of wishing to unite an obscure name without any literary pretension to that of the universally-celebrated Republican author—an orator unparalleled in this age for eloquence and poetic power; for feigned modesty is more offensive than ostentatious arrogance. Obscurity has its honours in a prudent silence, and in the precise and just estimation of things at their proper value.

But from all places, and in all times and circumstances, one friend may salute another, and send him in his salutation a share of his joy or of his sorrow; thus helping him to withstand the moral changes of his feelings or his ideas, often as fatal as the currents of winds and of rivers, and of all that is agitated in this manifold and living nature, in which the great and the little are mingled, and complete that marvellous conjunction which we call harmony.

Whoever has felt within his breast the furious waves of passionate desires—whoever has dreamed of fantastic delights, and awakened to contrast them with cold and naked reality—whoever has asked the love of his country, and been looked upon disdainfully, and at length been cast from her with contempt—whoever has sighed for intimate friend-ship, and has seen buried in the hungry jaws of death the friends of his childhood—whoever has ardently longed for the ineffable joys of home, and his family has denied him its pleasures—whoever, in a terrible disgust of life, has sought to deaden his pain, and suffered himself to be drawn into the whirlpool of sensual pleasures, the inevitable consequences of which are remorse, shame, and opprobrium—whoever has endured sorrow without consolation—whoever has wept without being under-stood—he only can draw near to salute the tomb of Byron.

But Castelar is in a very different position. He, an upright man, an aristocrat by education, a demo-crat by origin and by sentiments, gifted with fine tastes, opposed to all habits of disorder, a loving son, an affectionate brother, a faithful friend—Castelar cannot find in the crystallized remains of the Saxon poet the shadow of a mortifying or shameful recollection.

Those remains are for Castelar the worm-eaten leaves of the sad lawsuit which, having failed in opposition, demands the solemn opening of the re-cords to comply with the imprescriptible right of defence. And Castelar, rebutting the charges, accom-plishes his high mission as an advocate of great causes. In order to justify Lord Byron, he deals with the painful history of the nations of Europe, which is the prolonged Calvary of a civilization destined to give considerable, though posthumous, fruits.

Lord Byron is the Jeremiah of the present age; Lord Byron is the Œdipus in an unexampled struggle against the fatality of old institutions.

He loves the impossible, and appears inconstant because he never finds fault with the ideal. Wounded by disenchantment, he attempts everything—actions the purest and the most sensual; tastes the most exquisite and the most debased. He desires glory, and receives but contempt; he feels grandeur, and yet rolls in the dust of littleness; he exalts melancholy, yet wastes his life in bacchanalian orgies; he has the most extreme ideas of mental independence, yet submits to the humiliating domination of tyrannical women; cries out against the pride and the despotism of privilege, yet is himself remarkable for arrogance; pretends to be above the emptiness of ceremonious customs, yet decks himself with frivolous satins and laces, representing in his own person the weakest part of the civilization which has exhausted all the eccentricities of fashion, from the capricious costumes of Heliogabalus to the embroidered robe of Louis XIV.; he desires, in fine, to scale Olympus, but is unable to keep his equilibrium, his lameness forbidding him.

Is not, then, this new Œdipus the simple personification of his age, if not the abstract of a gigantic civilization, full of cancerous ulcers?

Our civilization is that which, loving science, approaches the juridical age, and appears inconstant because it accumulates systems upon systems. Disappointed by abuses, it grasps at everything without being able to realize its constant ideal—peace and justice. It desires a gentleness of manners, a purity of style, a delicacy of taste, and yet allows itself to be dominated by a devouring cupidity, withdrawing itself from the discomforts of resistance to the greater disorders of feudalism, to the catastrophes of paper-money and of fraudulent bankruptcy. It dreams of glory, yet loads the cannon to destroy misery; understands greatness, yet seeks an evil reputation, leaving to parasites the government of the people; admires seriousness, yet debilitates its frame with bacchanalian revels and idle spectacles; protests against the rigid exclusiveness of castes, and constructs a society made up of a hierarchy of uniforms—an old habit of historic dotage, which extends even to the man of the people, covering with clasps and crosses the bosom of Cambacérès; has the most exalted idea of independence, yet cannot inspire respect for the law without the appearance of the police; labours and struggles to attain prosperity, and sees rise at his feet, like the ghost of Hamlet, the terrifying spectre of pauperism. Alas! the daring sons of the Caucasus place their feet on the coldest and most sterile zone of the earth, and wounded by the thorns, like the Saxon poet, suffer more pain and fatigue every day from their cruel lameness.

The superior genius of Lord Byron conquers everything but the vulgarity of the intelligences which surround him.

The supreme power of civilization which, torn from the Cyclops and Sestrigones, received its baptism in the Greek Areopagus, has been the means of determining nearly everything except the geological problem which we have under our footsteps.

The Gracchi are impossible in Rome; where poverty makes a merchandize of a vote, there will not be wanting a Pisistratus. Luxury, alternating with misery, will always recall the Capitol or the hovel. Without doubt misery is not repulsive to the poor except for its privations. Instruction is of small moment to those who have not the means of subsistence. Education alone elevates or degrades us. Where there is ignorance and brutality there must be abasement. Tiberius could not have existed unless the people had been abject. The nobility of the future will be the aristocracy of education. These social differences are not determined by the ceremonies of the antechamber. Ceremonious customs alone declare castes.

Not even the eminent author of this book can

overcome that which stifles thought in Europe, by loading the moral atmosphere with so many recollections stamped upon the memory, so many interests created in the shadow of privilege, so many old prejudices deep-rooted in the conscience, and feels—according to his own expression—a little affection for the tyranny of custom, which is a sort of worn-out dike, raised by society to prevent an overflow.

The Saxon poet found only in England a gloomy and frigid sky ; dry, skeleton trees, without leaves or flowers ; the country all harsh, frosty, and bitter, and goes in search of other spots more pleasing, seeking repose and consolation in the melancholy of ruins, in the sublimity of grand memories, in the luxuriant vegetation of the valleys, in the freshness of the fountains, and in the purity of the heavens. His soul pined for nourishment, and finding inspiration in his travels over the still warm ashes of the Hellenic people, he wrote the beautiful cantos of " Childe Harold," gave an immortal work to the world, which at one bound raised him to the heights of the English Parnassus.

Thus the indomitable son of the Caucasus, flying from the snows, which deny him necessary food, crosses the Oregon, climbs dangerous mountains, and finding a fertile plain, which invites him with grateful fruits, writes in glowing words which kindle the world, an immortal page in the wondrous way of the Pacific.

When genius traces the path of human intelligence it erects from epoch to epoch a monument of wisdom. The people, in order to indicate the chart by which history advances, construct here and there an architectural monument. Nature, anticipating the steps of humanity, erects monumental mountains in each zone. Thus nature unites and works with man.

Nature is the majestic theatre in which is unfolded the great tragedy of the thoughts, of the labours, of the sorrows of this gigantic protagonist preceding social catastrophes and geological deluges. As time moves onward she ornaments the world with rocks and valleys, rivers and torrents, seas and plains, according to the greatness of her space. She immortalizes beforehand the glorious periods of succession in the process of ages, raising an obelisk to the eternal memory of the origin of civilization in the Himalayas, to the unfolding of art and science in the St. Gothard, to the hope of the future in Chimborazo.

The second act of the great drama is fruitful in accidents. The subject is the emancipation of art and science, counting among their martyrs Galileo, Telesio, and Campanella. Among metaphysicians, Locke and Descartes, initiators of the idea which proclaims the rights of man. Among publicists, Montesquieu and Filangieri. Among philosophers, Kant, Hegel, and Krauss. Among soldiers, unknown herds, who voluntarily join the conscription; and at the head of critics appears Voltaire, initiator of the periodical press in the "Encyclopædia." But after cruel sacrifices, after long vigilance, after grievous torture and bloody struggles, on definitely attempting the problem for which so many fought and suffered, how many have met with degraded poverty on demanding a morsel of bread which the sterile zone, exhausted in its productive efforts, denies them!

Without doubt, neither the elevation of the idea, nor the sublimity of the subject, nor the quality of the personages can admit of an unfortunate conclusion. But the magnitude of the situations demand a more extended scene and greater magnificence in the decoration. For the new Prometheus, personified in Maury, has no room in the narrowness of the ancient world, being destined to surprise the mysterious revolutions of the winds, to reveal the secret motives of currents, to throw the sounding-lead into the stormy deep, and to establish the epic artery of thought in the bottom of the sea.

If Lord Byron had contemplated this splendid spectacle, he would have understood how fruitless is a warfare with tears, and how fruitful is the stupendous struggle with nature, which extends from Behring's Straits to Cape Horn; this great power which stretches forth its hands to the venerable mother, armed and provided with the marvellous uses of steam and electricity, made serviceable by man. Living in the centre of modern life, and with lively recollections of his country, the poet would not have been able to extend his anxious vision from right to left, from Baffin's Bay to Patagonia, without discovering in those vast monolithic temples, sphinxes, statues, pyramids, and obelisks, evidences of the art of distant ages, and which also attest a constituted right, a legitimate interest, a historical difficulty, an obstacle of preoccupation opposed to the triumph of new institutions. In this colossal theatre there are no other monuments than those of the wondrous vegetation whence the torrid zone, superabundant in raw materials, feeds the industrial spirit of the colder zone; whence the pure springs, the flowing rivers, the impetuous torrents fertilize the valleys; where the fruits are spontaneous, the cotton-plant scatters its down, the golden grain of the corn falls in seed to the rich earth, the sugar-cane renews itself; and where, showing their outline against the sky, are rich groves of ancient trees with precious woods; and chains of rocks, with mines of gold and iron, coal and silver. Here nature invites to this glorious struggle against her, to bore mountains, to shorten distances, to gain the shore and dilate the breast with hope, breathing the pure and vivifying air that ripples the immense plain of the ocean. This is the hoped-for theatre of civilization.

If Lord Byron had beheld all this, he would not have sunk into scepticism.

Castelar, on the contrary, a man of faith and of knowledge, hopes and consecrates all his force, all his faculties, the powerful and irresistible enchantment of his eloquence, to the cause of progress, in any direction that he sees or expects some of these manifestations; for, in fact, this is the cause of humanity. In the work of progress are included all ideas, all sentiments, all sorrows, all difficulties, all the degrees of civilization; and in this Lord Byron is the synthesis of these varied elements, united together by the force of European peoples, in the critical and supreme hour of anguish, of shock, of confusion, which manifests itself in a penetrating cry of heart-rending, though sublime doubt, like a momentary eclipse, which, by the law of contrast, makes appear brighter the flood of light of this intellectual prodigy, which gives neither truce to the thoughts nor peace to the hand.

Such is the epopee of the intelligence in the Olympian battle.

Sublime subject, to which science cannot refuse her number, her barometer, or her quadrant; neither can the lyre refuse her chords, poetry her rhyme, nor architecture her keystone!

May Castelar continue to accomplish his high mission on the earth, engaged in the defence of an important cause; whilst the humblest of his best friends sends him a remembrance of affection and admiration in these unconnected lines, earnestly hoping that the book which contains them may leave in the mind of the numerous readers the sweet impressions that are felt at this moment among all his admirers, and particularly by his friend,

JOSÉ ROMAN LEAL.

CONTENTS.

THE
LIFE OF LORD BYRON.

PART THE FIRST.

ONE day, about the hour of sunset, I wandered through the long walks of Hyde Park, and as I passed on, memory brought before me my recent visits to the Bay of Naples and the Lido of Venice. I thought lovingly and almost tearfully of the far-distant horizon of Cadiz, where the pure sky and the waters commingle, presenting to the eye a feast of colours. And I thought of the groves of Elche, where the palm-trees, shaken by the gentle zephyrs of evening, make a melancholy music in harmony with the sadness of the surrounding desert.

English landscape is altogether different from such scenes, and often as it has been described by great poets, I had never succeeded in picturing to myself its reality. The soil is green, damp, and porous; the sky is of a sombre grey, shadowed by heavy masses of clouds, sometimes whitish and sometimes approaching to dark violet, from out of which filters a pale and undefinable light, like that from a colossal moon. The trees, which rise to an immense height, are covered with a rich verdure, and the grace and beauty of their fantastic outlines are half lost, half revealed, by the clouds which lend them a mysterious veil.

In the distance the oriel window of Westminster Abbey and the Gothic towers of the Houses of Parliament, seen through the capricious and moving vapours, appear less like solid edifices than dissolving pictures traced by the hand of some genius in the watery air, and ready to float away among the clouds.* The different aspects of Nature in the north and in the south is something surprising. In the glowing light of the South a line becomes a landscape; in the twilight of the North a building fades into a shadow. Perhaps for this reason the Greeks, who were the great interpreters of southern intelligence, made their monuments small and low, leaving to the sun the task of elevating and extending them on his golden wings; whilst the English, the great interpreters of the North, have made their monuments colossal, that they may penetrate with their pointed spires and massive angles the heavy atmosphere, and dissipate the darkening shadows.

This is not the country for the plastic arts. A

---

* Probably Señor Castelar speaks of St. James's Park, from which Westminster Abbey and the Houses of Parliament are visible.

marble statue, which the ardent sun of Italy gilds
into the warmth and colour of life, is here soon transformed into a shapeless mass of coal. And if one
passes quickly from the contemplation of the snowy
ornaments of the Chiaja of Naples, half hidden among
groves of olives and laurels and lighted up by that
brilliant sunshine which is reflected in the azure
waters of the Tyrrhene Sea, on beholding these
sooty figures of London, one is both shocked and
astonished, for they offend the eyesight and upset all
one's ideas of good taste and of the fine arts. The
statues of the South preserve that which in them is
eternally beautiful—the outline ; and the people of the
North lose in their sculpture that which in themselves
is eternally great—the soul. These countries are not
those of the arts, but they are the homes of spiritual-
istic poetry. Here, like Sir Walter Scott, we may
awaken the heroes of past ages, here we may penetrate into the innermost recesses of our being, as
penetrated Shakspeare—that immortal diver into the
oceans of the soul. On arriving at these northern
shores a stranger at once feels the influence of the
climate upon his peculiar temperament. If he be
strong and nervous, he is induced to labour ; if enter-
prising, he inclines to commerce ; if philosophic, he is
led to think ; if he be a dreamer, he becomes a poet.
In these countries, or in others where the atmospheric
influence is similar, have been written the creations of
Swift, of Hoffman, and of Richter. The grosser part

of us—our body—seems to be lost amid such scenes, like an angel in the immensity of the heavens.

This is the land of Byron! One's thoughts must turn to such a man on visiting his birthplace. And why not study his life on beholding his country? What do not the children of this sickly and unsettled generation owe to his tenderness and susceptibility? Now a sudden revelation of our doubts, then a bitter lamentation in which to express our sorrows, as if his mouth were the fountain from which flowed the stream of our lives, the riches of our ideas. The genius of Byron, which appeared at the beginning of this century, is like a funeral torch sculptured on our cradles. Let us reflect upon the life of one so extraordinary and so gifted, and afterwards examine his works, and learn to appreciate his talents. The sublime conjunction of the forms of antique sculpture with modern ideality is chiefly embodied in the countries of the North.

His family is of Scandinavian origin. His genius sprung from the foam and the winds of the Northern Ocean, borne on the leathern barques of the Normans. His ancestors, wandering southward and beaten by the hurricane, after passing through France, were carried on the pinions of their uneasy ambition to the farther side of the Strait. Among the companions of William the Conqueror was the head of the Byron family, who afterwards became one of the territorial lords of Nottingham. The richest and

most beautiful estate possessed by them was that of
Rochdale, which came into their possession in the
time of Edward the First. His forefathers wandered
through icy deserts and northern forests, replete with
poetry and mystery. They struggled in the immensity of distant seas with the roaring waves and the
unchained winds; they went, inspired by the simple
faith of the Middle Ages, with the lance in hand and
shield upon the breast, to look for the Sepulchre of
the Redeemer amid the burning sands of the East;
they fought like gallant cavaliers with the French in
the field of Cressy; they dwelt in magnificent
castles, protected from their rivals by their fortified
towers, from their vassals by the gibbet, and from the
king by their privileges. This hardy race slaughtered
monks in England in the reign of Henry the Eighth
to serve the heretical party, as they did Arabs in the
desert to serve the Church and to gratify Richard
Cœur de Lion. Afterwards they entered boldly into
Parliament, defending their seignorial rights and aristocratic prerogatives, and contributed without their
own desire or knowledge—as did all the British
nobility—to found the basis of modern rights, always
aided by that exalted genius and that individual
independence—their hereditary patrimony from the
ice of the Polar seas. But when the estates of this
distinguished family descended to the great poet,
Byron, they were encumbered, almost engulfed in
ruin. This decline commenced in the time of James

the First, when one of his predecessors gave himself up to the extravagances of Court life, and to support this lavish expenditure he heavily mortgaged the property. Another Byron served Charles the First faithfully all through the troubled reign of that monarch, and still more contributed to the ruin which the Civil Wars completed. Old eagles, when they have no longer feathers to warm their nests, seek shelter in tottering towers, often the homes of the lizard, and the sport of the winds of winter. There, in misery and solitude, they are proud as in their strength and glory.

In 1750 this family burst for a time through the shroud of poverty and forgetfulness. The grandfather of the poet suffered a shipwreck so remarkable in its dramatic details as to awaken the attention of all England. In 1765 one of his uncles—he who bore the hereditary title to which the poet afterwards succeeded—killed, in a quarrel rather than a duel, one of his relations, and suspended from the tester of his bed as a trophy the homicidal sword, in order that the sight of it should continually sting his conscience. The House of Peers, summoned to judge the case, absolved him, but he was condemned by public opinion. Retired to his castle, he isolated himself like an imprisoned wolf, shunned all company like a bird of the night, by day chased the wild boar, by night tamed crickets, teaching them by skill, patience, and punishments to perform certain movements, and ever showing a hatred of humanity, a most ungovernable temper, and extravagances which bordered upon insanity.

The father of Byron was twice married, the first time for love, the second from motives of interest. He stole his first wife from her husband, Lord Carmarthen. From this resulted a lawsuit, and from that a divorce. The divorce was followed by a marriage with the wife of his victim. The fruit of this union was Augusta, the elder sister of the poet, and by him most tenderly beloved. Becoming a widower, Byron's father was married a second time, to Catherine Gordon. From this marriage sprang the great poet, begotten in sorrow, born under a decaying roof-tree, made wretched by continual matrimonial dissensions. Byron's father married in order to live luxuriously upon the fortune of his wife, who was passionately attached to him. In two years he dissipated her property, and to conceal their misery from their neighbours they set out for France. Lady Byron, no longer being able to endure the indifference of her husband, which increased with the privations of poverty, returned to London, wounded in her fondest affections, despairing of the future, still devoted to her husband, but finding her love a poisoned fountain of sorrow. Under these melancholy circumstances the poet was born, described by Goethe in his poem as the son of Faust and Helena, fallen from the heavens to the mire, but preserving his mystic wings; in his hands his golden lyre, and all the splendour of divine beauty in his Olympian features. Byron observed that the marriages of his family produced but single fruits. "Beasts of prey, tigresses and lionesses," said the poet, " bring forth seldom." The birth was difficult and dangerous, as if he dreaded the sea of life, which he was to ruffle with his passions, to darken with his scepticism, and to stir gently with the sweet zephyr of his sonnets. Torn at last from the bosom of his mother, which had well-nigh been his sepulchre, he entered the world, which seemed to scorch him ; for this being, destined to fly towards infinity, had one foot contracted. Thus he was a cripple in childhood. This stormy fireside, this rebellious birth, this spendthrift father, this assassin uncle ; this mother embittered by disappointment, the sweetness of whose sex had been pierced by the thorns of her sorrow ; this blood, boiling and agitated like the troubled seas over which wandered the Normans ; this cradle, rocked by despair and watered by tears ; this decay of an illustrious line, which threatened extinction in its lost representative ; this accidental lameness, to which the cruel shaft of ridicule made him keenly sensitive ;. all these influences, acting on a naturally sensitive nature, inspired the eternal elegy embodied in his verses, like the continuation of the first bitter cry of his existence.

There lives but one creature who can soften such sorrows, and smooth the roughest pathway—a mother. God has given her that she may put a drop of honey

with her pure kisses into our cup of aloes. God places
her near the cradle that the wings of her love may
hide from our infant eyes the darkness of the horizon
in which we must hereafter combat and conquer death.
He wills that her hands should fold ours for their first
supplications, and that her smile should be the dawn-
ing of the infinite for our aspirations. She is virtue,
charity, the tender part of the heart, the melancholy
note of the soul, the foundation of purity and innocence, which always exists among the folds and windings of the lowest of humanity. When you feel a
benevolent impulse, the desire to dry a tear, to assist
an unfortunate, to divide your bread with the hungry,
to give your own life for that of your neighbour;
close at hand, like the guardian angel who inspires all
good, is the beloved shadow of your mother. Reason,
books, the schools, the father, these give us ideas;
our sentiments are always given by the mother, she
forms our characters.

Catherine Gordon might have sweetened by careful
training the gall of her son's existence. The Titan
needed the chisel in the tender hands of his mother
to smooth away his defects and angularities. But
Lady Byron, proud, eccentric, and capricious, had no
other passion than that of love for her husband, and
stung by his indifference, she seemed even to hate the
child whose constant presence kept alive her love and
her misfortune. The father, virtually divorced, went
home merely to deceive his wife and to preserve

appearances, and seldom looked at the boy, telling him sternly how much he disapproved of him, and giving him a frown or a blow for sole token of endearment. Byron endeavoured to conceal these painful facts, but the whole history of his life hangs upon them. In 1791 death deprived him of his father, who, though given up to dissipation and insane passions, possessed certain qualities, set off by a remarkable and a manly beauty, which commanded admiration. Both his wives were devotedly attached to him. The first, who deserted a wealthy husband for his sake, killed herself by accompanying him to the hunting-field, when her delicate health made violent exercise dangerous. The second, the mother of the poet, loved him to the last with unshaken fidelity, and mourned his death with all the abandonment of sorrow.

The youth thus strangely educated, had at least one fountain of inspiration—the Bible. The study of the Prophets invigorated the poetic character of his nature. Their rugged genius is visible in some of his works, severe and steady as the simoom, monotonous as the desert, but solemn as immensity, and sublime as the idea of the Almighty; their semitical genius, expressed by Isaiah in his admirable works, is reproduced by Michael Angelo in the majestic features of his Moses, whose venerable beard, descending to his breast, seems to be stirred by the breezes of Sinai. With these scriptural inspirations were mingled those of the country—of mountains; for his mother took him from

London, where he was born, to a retired spot near Aberdeen. There, before the dawn of day, while the shrill cry of the cock replied to the melancholy song of the lark, he went out alone, under the pretence of hunting, exercising his body and gratifying his spirit of adventure by wandering on the brinks of precipices, on the summits of mountains, through caverns where still is heard the voice of the gods of his fathers, seeking inspiration in the grand spectacles of Nature, and joining the wail of his poetic nature to the voice of the universe. To these rural inclinations he owed his agility in all athletic sports. He excelled in the chase, understood the use of arms, was a good swimmer and horseman, and was skilled in all gymnastic exercises, could run well, and pitch the bar or throw the ball. When he was compared with Rousseau, in his private life, he compared his own robust frame and the debility of the philosopher of Geneva; the awkwardness and feebleness of the latter and his own vigour in all manly sports; the aristocratic and elegant habits of Rousseau with his own simple and careless toilet.

In a body so vigorous, a character so energetic, and an imagination so exalted, the early development of love was a natural occurrence. In the first years of youth one loves unconsciously, and before the instincts of Nature are fully awakened, but later on, when we experience a profound passion, we know that we have loved before. Then we remember that in boyhood we preferred to play with one girl above all others, that by her side we felt happy, most happy; that in her absence our eyes looked for her, and were not satisfied till she appeared again; that we went to her soon and left her late; that we thought of her in our innocent bed, and at our awakening that we asked for her, and were sad till we had found her, our greatest desire being to meet herself, and our greatest grief to bid her farewell. Byron has admirably expressed this psychological phenomenon, saying that he had loved before he understood the name or the meaning of love. The worship of Dante for Beatrice was a passion of this kind, the child whom he saw smiling in her infancy, crowned in her girlhood with a death garland, and afterwards by the stars of Heaven.

Mary Duff was the Beatrice of Byron, his first love at the age of twelve years. His mother laughed at him, the parents of the girl and the friends of both houses ridiculed him, but Byron continued to love her sadly and seriously, without being himself aware of his passion, and with all the tenderness and purity of childhood. When she gave him her miniature—a likeness of her ivory skin which the snow envied, of her rosy cheeks, her bright ringlets falling upon her shoulders, her deep azure eyes—the young poet told her in one of his first verses that he would prefer the painted and inanimate beauty of the picture to all living loveliness, except that of her who had placed the image on his heart.

This uneasiness of temperament, this precocity of sentiment, this too-early unfolding of life ; the study of the Prophets, which formed his taste for the lofty and sublime ; the pages of history, which moved him to converse with the heroes of past ages and almost to summon them at will; the premature love, which smiled upon his boyhood like a tree which flowers before the spring ; his solitary walks to the tops of mountains to see the sun rise before other mortals, and to watch the flight of the clouds and of the eagles, to listen to the roar of cascades and of the wind in the forests; all these were symptoms of that feverish infirmity of the soul which is called genius; of that infinite thirst for the ideal which is never assuaged, of that deep melancholy felt by all great natures, a sorrow without relief or cessation, which implacably pursues its victim; a restlessness engendered by the immense difference between a wish conceived and a desire realized; between beauty imagined by the mind in its purity, and beauty obscured by words or by manners ; an evil persecutor from which all great natures suffer, and of which they die ; their glory, but also their tormentor.

Byron, that mental invalid, of independent character and original genius, educated in the free bosom of mother Nature, was at a very early period of life constrained to move in a society in which the native energy of liberty is tempered by the severity of custom. It is often noticed that wherever liberty is great, fashion and custom are imperious. Wherever the curb of the written law is deficient, the restraint of conventionalities is placed by the tacit consent of the people.

There is no part of Europe in which an individual is more free, his home more secure, his conscience more respected, his speech and his opinions more independent than in this Great Britain—the continual object of our admiration; but nowhere are the customs of society more tyrannical. The *sans façon* of the Frenchman, the carelessness of the Spaniard, the ease with which we suppress all ceremonials, the lightness with which we overstep all distances, the familiarity of our conversation and manners, are not known in England. Yet do not imagine I lean too much to Spanish customs. I would give some of those which level classes in exchange for a little of the English liberty, the like of which I have never seen either in France or in Spain. I love equally Liberty and Equality; 1 cannot conceive them separated; I believe them to be, not conditions, but essentials of justice. But separate them, and compel me to choose between them, I take Liberty. In France there is more Equality than in England. In England there is more Liberty than in France. I decide for England. Here, without being an English citizen, I find myself in my house, under the protection of the English laws, which are as rigorously executed as the laws of Nature. In France I find myself at the mercy of the commissary of the district, and I know not whether

the *concierge* who opens the street-door belongs to the
secret police. There is no monster more terrible than
an arbitrary Government. A tiger may rend my
flesh; a despotism lacerates my conscience. But
we should understand that liberty is not a gratuitous
gift, or an object for sport or luxury; it is obtained
by maturity of judgment, and consolidated by a
great severity of manners. The trifling sacrifices
which are exacted by society are abundantly compen-
sated by the dignity so desirable for a people, and as
gratifying as the voice of a tranquil conscience for individuals. Thus English liberty finds its natural
counterpoise in the rigidity of customs, which are
imposed, without the necessity of law or authority,
by social power. It is most difficult to explain
this idea to men who are habituated to live under a
despotism. In my numerous travels through Europe
I have met many Russians, and among them all
I found but one who was not progressive. He
strove to prove to me a very singular thesis—namely,
that St. Petersburg is more free than New York. I
ought to say that the Russian was a prince, but a
musician. The reason he gave in support of his
theory was laughable; in New York people are not
allowed to play the violin on Sundays. And indeed
it would be impossible to make the people of the South
understand how the Sunday is observed among Anglo-
Saxon nations; the cities seem dead, the intercourse
of the inhabitants is restrained for twenty-four hours.

The southerns could never understand English manners and ceremonies ; the bells at the doors, the reverences at the rubric, the complicated forms of address, according to the rank of the person spoken to, in fine all those innumerable small fetters with which instinct disciplines Anglo-Saxon individuality, to withdraw it from anarchy, and to prevent disorder.

Here we have the young poet, naturally independent, educated among the mountains, and early placed in the midst of a severe and ceremonious society. Here Byron, who believed himself superior to all his surroundings, was obliged to bend his head and his back, to conform to the habits of those with whom he mingled. His true home had been the ocean cave, from whence he had often seen the stars arise, or the clouds form themselves from the vapours of the valley ; where he heard the raging of the wind as it tossed the branches of the pine-trees, or the rushing sound of the waterfalls, the howling of wolves,* and the sharp cry of the eagles. His greatest pleasure hitherto had been to leap and run, as if seeking to deny his lameness, exercising his strength after the fashion of the ancient clans of Scotland ; to address, like the bards, his songs to the winds, and send them on the wings of the air ; to wander in rocky defiles, and bathe his imagination in the silver rays of the

---

* Señor Castelar is evidently unaware that the last wolf in Scotland is said to have been killed by Sir Ewen Cameron of Lochiel, in 1680.

moon; to climb to the peaks of mountains, as if to approach infinity—that infinity which awed his own soul, as it must overwhelm all human greatness. This extraordinary being—a savage by nature, a mountaineer by habit; from his sublime genius a poet, and for these reasons incomprehensible—found himself amidst the most mechanical society in the world, and, as it were, tortured and torn to pieces by the teeth of its wheels. Destiny, which appeared to smile upon him, gave him, by the death of his uncle, the hereditary dignity of Peer, and then punished him by compelling his obedience to English manners. He assumed his new rank with much satisfaction: not comprehending that it would hereafter become a fetter.

From the humble elementary school of Aberdeen, where he learned his letters and the Latin language, he passed to that of Harrow. A life in common with others could not be congenial to one of his temperament, which, like the peak of a lofty mountain, sought for solitude. The discipline of the college suited still less his native freedom of character. Its pleasures were to him annoyances, its tastes and habits were repulsive. Above all, he suffered terribly from his unfortunate lameness. The various cures to which he was forced to submit were worse than the infirmity, and the ridicule to which these exposed him was more painful than the remedies. Even his mother mocked at the lameness of the young nobleman, who would not be able to mount the tribune—that pedestal of the English aristocracy—without staggering like one intoxicated.* These contrarieties drew into his soul the torrent of bitterness afterwards poured forth in his verses—a gall mingled with the leaven of the life of that age. Whenever he could lay aside the course of study marked out for him, and read for his own pleasure, he devoured books of travels and shipwrecks, as a true descendant of the Normans and a worthy son of Britain. With these he warmed his imagination, mingling the raging of his internal tempests, the fever of his passions, the lightning of his ideas, the sunbeam which pierced his temples, with the boiling waves, with the unchained hurricanes, with the battles of the winds and the waters, with the dashing of the frail planks against the rocks, with the despairing cries of the shipwrecked.

Under such circumstances, and in such a position, it is easily conceived that his first translation was the Prologue of Prometheus, born, like himself, with the celestial flame upon his brow; like him chained to earth, struggling with the pride of the gods and the ingratitude of men. At the same time, that sensitive intelligence which pervaded his whole being was condensed in his head and heart. He loved with exceeding tenderness his friends at college; he hated his enemies with all the fury of passion.

---

* Señor Castelar seems to think that speakers in the English Houses of Parliament ascend a tribune or rostrum, as in Spain and other continental countries.

And as, notwithstanding his aristocratic descent and the haughtiness natural to his order, he was always strongly imbued with reforming and progressive tendencies, he detested the tyranny of the strong, and enthusiastically desired the emancipation of the weak. He generously interposed to protect the new arrivals at Harrow from being persecuted and annoyed by their companions. According to old custom in public schools, on a certain occasion one of the elder and stronger pupils had determined to inflict a number of blows upon a younger and weaker boy. When engaged in this cruel task, Byron came up running, and throwing himself down, he exclaimed, "Let him alone, and I will bear the second half of the beating."

But to these noble impulses of the heart the greatest extravagances were united. He did not understand that genius can only unfold its wings for lofty flights, and that men of exalted imagination—like those birds which soar the highest—seem out of their sphere upon the earth. His lameness irritated him almost to madness, and his moral deficiencies affected him sadly. An artist, and a student of the plastic art, he loved to imitate the repose of antique statues, eternally dignified in their perfect beauty.

Alas! what statuesque serenity can be given to a cripple! No arrangement of his costume could be made to hide his bodily imperfection. Disgusted with English taste in dress, he clothed himself richly, after the Oriental fashion, in silk embroidered with colours, and adorned with gold or silver lace ; a turban studded with jewels, a red belt with knives and pistols of marvellous workmanship—thus imitating the heroes of the Eastern legends, of whom he had read so much, and whom he afterwards described in his verses.   He dressed in this manner, especially in his first vacation, about the year 1802, in Bath, where he commenced those orgies in which he wasted so much of his life, and consequently so much of his genius—for with Byron to live was to think, to imagine, to create, to compose.

Without the safeguard of maternal love, the friends of his childhood might have succeeded in calming his impetuous temper by their wise counsels, and, above all, by their own example.   But unhappily all his early companions—those who were possessed of prudence and moderation, and who would have exercised a beneficial restraint upon his ardent disposition—all these were prematurely removed by death, and left him abandoned to the whirlwind of his passions, the storm of his own fantastic conceptions, which shut him in from others, and prevented him from hearing the voice of society.   Byron had deeply lamented these friends. As he said himself, if tears could sometimes disarm Death, and force him to release the beloved ones he has stolen, they would return again to comfort us.

But though death robbed him of his friends, and though destiny willed not that maternal tenderness should be as sweet for him as for the rest of humanity, he might nevertheless have been saved by that wonderful passion—love. But every event in the life of the man was singular and tragical. The object of his first childish affection died, passing away like the fantastic figures sketched on a fevered imagination. Unfortunately, he became enamoured of Miss Chaworth, a lovely girl, but belonging to a family hated by his own relations. His uncle, the head of the Byron family, had killed the head of the Chaworth family, the uncle of the young lady. This caused a feud between the houses, similar to that which separated Romeo and Juliet, and a corpse lay between the hearts of the lovers. In boyhood, Byron feared to stay a night in the house inhabited by Miss Chaworth, lest the portraits of her ancestors should descend from their frames, go into the armoury, take down their weapons, and strike the last and only representative of the hated race whose sacrilegious hands had spattered them with blood. But when she walked abroad, when he saw her under the shadow of the grand old trees, on the fresh grass of the lawn, pressing it lightly as the mist of the morning, around her an aureole of beauty and of purity, like that of the silver moon; the azure heaven of her eyes half concealed by their long lashes—his whole being was subdued, as the ocean is calmed at the soft kisses of the breeze, and his impetuous and poetic nature was hushed and conquered by reality. Doubtless these touches of harmony were needed in the life of the poet, in order to elevate his genius to the great general principles of his time, to teach him to sing of events like Homer, to paint the passions like Shakspeare, or to unfold ideas like Calderon, to describe the sciences like Goethe, as well as his own sentiments. Who can say whether, if captivated by love, overcome by the enchantment of a pure and happy affection, Byron would not have been the objective poet capable of giving us the cyclical poem of our age, instead of being the subjective poet, who has bequeathed to us the fragments of his palpitating and bleeding heart?

The beautiful heiress of the Chaworth family was then sixteen, two years older than her devoted lover. The boy began to think like a man, wished to marry, and by this union to bury for ever all ancient animosities; to join old houses and estates, to mingle two English races which had originally sprung from the same root—from heroes, navigators, orators; worthy to bear his name into those two agitated elements of British greatness—the Parliament and the ocean.

With a simplicity equal to that of the " Confessions" of Rousseau (who is the eternal model of the art of confidences), Lord Byron describes his interviews among the hills crowned by a diadem of trees, his little voyages on the lakes, above all, one in which the boat containing the two young people was separated from the others, and entered first into the mouth of a cavern so low that they were obliged to recline in the floating conch upborne by the crystal waters, the soft murmur of the breeze expressing the love the boy dared not reveal by the light of a glance, or the sadness of a sigh.

The girl sometimes made him suffer cruelly. His lameness prevented him from dancing. But his beloved danced with all his friends, who had the privilege of encircling the waist which Byron could not approach without a nervous trembling, as if he had been struck by lightning. Whilst the happy girl waltzed, the jealous boy struck his heart, fearing that its violent beating would be heard through the saloons. And though he had never formally declared himself, he was understood. She knew well how to sound the abyss of a look; and he was even so far understood that she gave him her picture as a love token.

But one day he was nearly driven mad. He happened to be unperceived by a group of young people, among whom was Miss Chaworth, when the conversation very naturally turned upon love and lovers. Her friends mentioned Lord Byron, his beauty and talents, and the sighs and glances which they had observed directed towards Miss Chaworth. Without being in the least disconcerted, and with all the serenity of perfect indifference, she uttered this cruel sentence: " You offend me in thinking I can possibly be interested in that boy—that cripple."

In those two words she had expressly defined the two great gulfs which, according to the poet himself, separated him from happiness—his youth and his infirmity: that terrible defect, the first of his misfortunes, the most bitter of his sorrows! But to hear this from the lips of his beloved, to hear it when least expected, to hear it in the moment in which his most cherished projects were unfolding themselves like a vast panorama before his exalted imagination; just as he was about to throw himself at her feet, to show her the bottom of that heart, veiled hitherto by a profound reverence, to listen to that terrible death-sentence for his enamoured soul, panting with its tender aspirations. Alas! it was like reaching the threshold of heaven, half beholding its glory, then falling to the abyss of despair!

The youth was henceforth transformed; alone in his sorrow, stripped of his hopes, plunged into despair, into a night of thick darkness, and with no other confidant of his anguish and agitation than the sombre atmosphere whose vibrations repeated his heart-rending lamentations, which his stubborn will vainly tried to stifle within his bursting breast. His desperation was equal to his love. Rushing from the house, he ran into the country, without knowing whither he was going; all sleep fled from his burning eyelids, all tranquillity from his tortured soul. The world seemed to him to be empty: empty the heavens! He would have welcomed death, and in order that death should satisfy his great desire, he wished for non-existence.

In 1805 the one so deeply beloved was married to

Mr. John Musters. The love and the anguish of he poet are easily seen in the short and simple verses consecrated to this sorrowful event. Instead of painting his passion in glowing colours, the intensity of his love bordering upon insanity, the beauty of his beloved sufficient to excite his most lively devotion, the triumph of the favoured rival who knew her without understanding her, who wedded her without loving her, trampling under foot the heart of the poet, wounding all its fibres, torturing it with the poison of his own success, burning as molten lead and lasting as eternity — instead of giving himself up to all the furies of an unrequited passion, of a desire impossible to accomplish, of a love without hope—he is content to say mournfully that he will visit no more the hill, the scene of their interviews; the trees, witnesses of his protestations.

Thus was concluded the boyhood of Byron, and his youth commenced. He had passed from one period to the other by disenchantment, as he afterwards entered from nothingness to life through sorrow. At the meeting of the line which separated two great segments of the circle of his existence, an overwhelming grief possessed him. His fortune was valueless, his illustrious name was odious, the hangers-on who accompany all greatness were wearisome; society embarrassed and restrained him like the walls of a dungeon; glory was impossible, his friendships were dead, his love in the power of a happy rival. In this melancholy condition of mind, to return to his mountains, to wander alone in gloomy solitudes, to plunge into the blue waters, was his desire; or if not, to take the wings of the dove, to fly unceasingly, to mount and mount to infinity; to lose sight of this troubled world, and to search afar in the heavens for the peace he found not below.   Forced to leave Harrow, his school, he took a sorrowful farewell of all its surroundings— of the meadow, where he had fought with his companions; of the gloomy hall, in which he listened to the reproofs of the peda_ogue; of the theatre, in which he performed, thinking to eclipse Garrick; of the cemetery, where he went to mourn over his deceased friends, and to carve words cut with sobs in the marble or on the trunks of trees, to look at the last rays of the setting sun, to linger among the mysteries of life and of eternity among the shadows of evening.

This reckless desperation of Byron, which commenced so early, was destined to continue through life, and to become his moral infirmity.   Some attributed it to the gloomy climate of his country, others to the delicacy of his nerves and his peculiar temperament, others to the age in which he was born, and whose brazen gates, heated in the fires of the Revolution, enclosed this Titan at his birth, who rose rebellious against restraint, sometimes weeping like a child, and holding imploring hands to the heavens, supplicating a faith, a belief!

The poet cannot be the representative of his age,

like the philosopher or the orator. The philosopher, after having examined and purified his doubts, composes a system dictated by reason, fixed and verified by logic, and thus embodies a new idea or a distinct principle. The orator raises his voice to the height of his own conscience, and consecrates himself to a cause, to a reformation. To do this he is obliged to concentrate his powers, to discipline his character, to group his ideas around one capital subject; to be consistent and logical, not only in his discourse, but in his life. The philosopher is not an artist; inspiration is not a divinity. The orator is more artistic than the philosopher, but his art is subordinate to thought, and ought to follow his reasoning. To deliver an oration is not to recite; it is to reason, to convince, to persuade. Beauty and harmony should be the auxiliaries of ratiocination, designed to attain its speedy triumph. But the poet is a mysterious, undefinable being, who escapes from analysis and dogma, and soars from our sight like the bird of the mountain, the lark; when quitting her nest of clay, she mounts to the ethereal heights, and watches the first streaks of morning, whilst all other creatures sleep profoundly in the shadows, unmindful of the coming day. Poets are harps, which respond to every zephyr; lakes, whose shades vary with every passing cloud; their faculties are incomprehensible as prophecies, as presentiments, as dreams. The most antagonistic ideas struggle in their brains, and flow in wild disorder from their pens. The genius of the poet advances with the restlessness of a torrent; now it is peaceful, now clamorous; again it wastes itself among dark and rocky defiles, in foamy cascades, or seems to sleep gently; as a murmuring streamlet to repeat the stars of the night; and at last enters as a great river into the unfathomable ocean of eternity. By closely examining the mind of a great poet, we can almost understand the conscience of his epoch; we can behold all his fluctuations, his sorrows, his aspirations, his crises of reaction, his progressive impulses, his internal combats, his conceptions. Victor Hugo has been at times a Bonapartist, a romancist, a teacher, a believer, a rationalist, a free-thinker, and a democrat. But when you would seek the legend of this age, all that we have thought, all that we have felt, our moral failings, our abhorrence of slavery; the hopes we have conceived from the proud triumphs of mind over matter; how we imagine society ought to be constructed, and how we propose to reform it; our conception of the different epochs of history; our poem of progress, so much of which is written with the blood of humanity; our doubts, our fears, and our faith, fostered by the exaltation of martyrdom; if you would comprehend all this—read, study Victor Hugo.

And Byron resembles him. The sublime disorder of his genius is like the grand confusion of Nature. By the side of a snowy peak, on which the rays of light fall and are reflected with countless scintillations, there is an unfathomable abyss; close by an arid plain there is a grove perfumed by all the flowers of the earth, and filled with harmony from the songs of all the birds of heaven. These contrarieties are visible in the poet, for his work bears a relation to the universe; his conscience is doubt and faith, affirmation and belief, the whole of his epoch. Let us leave him now at his entrance into youth. Later we shall see him in his life; we shall admire him in his works.

L ET us now consider the second period, and the most critical, of the life of Lord Byron. I will not weary the reader's patience by naming the numerous biographies which have been written of this remarkable man. They would form a library in themselves. Writers of all classes, poets of different styles, psychologists, annalists, doctors, painters, politicians, phrenologists, all curious inquirers into the secrets of human nature, and into the history of the beginning of our century, feel an interest in the actors of those events, and write something about the strange being who passed before them like a whirlwind of ideas, and left behind him a chorus of immortal songs. Among this crowd of authors there is one who always believed in the mind and character of Byron—Thomas Moore, his friend and confidant. But Moore's book was written when the anger of England against the poet, who was to give her so much glory, was at its height; so that it was necessarily the biography suited to that particular period, and was deficient in the independence which is essential in order to secure the consideration and respect of contemporaries. And doubtless the "Life of Byron," by Moore, reserved and wanting in courage as it is, is the commencement of a rehabilitation of Byron's character.

In these later days we look with much impatience for a work on the life of the poet, a book which shall be, so to speak, monumental ; a book which would throw a new and a brighter light on this great mind, and be for it almost a resurrection. Let us imagine the sort of biography Laura would write of Petrarch. All literary people acknowledge the happy influence exercised by a beautiful Italian lady on the inspirations of the English poet. This lovely woman, merely from having caused some calm and happy moments in the turbulent and feverish life of Byron, raised herself in the estimation of this age to the choir of immortal women.

Lately I eagerly searched for her poetic spirit by the green waters of the Grand Canal of Venice, among the groves of her columns and the Grecian fretwork of her marbles, amongst those undying figures left by the pencils of Paul Veronese or of Titian ; and in the cemetery of Pisa, under the cypresses, upon the holy earth of Jerusalem which brings forth roses beautiful as those of Jericho, celebrated by the prophets ; between the grand oriel windows, where are the marble statues which weep eternally on Grecian monuments, the angels of Giotto and of Orcagna, forms of which the wings folded in graceful beauty seem

to move gently in the soft air; there I could almost
hear the sighs of that mysterious woman wafted by
the breezes of the Tuscan Sea, laden with the cadences
of the Arno and the deathless verses of Byron. It is
well known that the Vaucluse of their loves was not
a fountain shaded by olive-trees, but the solitary
graveyard in which the terrors of the Last Judgment
are displayed in all the mystery and all the solemnity
of eternal silence, interrupted only by the lament of
the bells from the adjoining leaning tower, or by
the echo of the orisons and religious canticles from
the basilica, by the rustling of the trees, or the
hum of the insects which transform into new tissues
of life the ashes of the dead.

While there I thought of one of the books which
exercises the greatest influence over my thoughts, and
inspired my boyhood with poetic dreams—the great
work of Quinet, " Ahasuerus." I could not forget the
verses in which the loving women of the story
snatch aside, in the moonlight, the white shroud
and behold souls without bodies, thoughts without
forms, a sort of spiritual butterflies. Wings of light,
beautified with ideas, hover over the brow of the
poet with their mystic inspirations. There among
that choir was Sappho; she who quenched in death
her loving thirst in the waters of Leucates; there
Heloise, in whose bosom human nature began a
new existence, under the sackcloth and ashes of the
Middle Ages; there, she who was spotless as the first

innocent love, the mysterious nymph whose features bore some resemblance to the virgins of Raphael, the star which turned to gold the bitterness of a stormy life, beautiful as none other, and adorned by the splendours of eternal sunshine : the Beatrice of Dante.

Among those immortal women Quinet numbered the Countess Guiccioli, as one of the loveliest forms in which inspiration has ever been clothed upon earth. And indeed that woman, who met the poet half-way in his career, when almost maddened by wild passions and desperation, when faith and life were nearly extinguished; she who smiled upon him like the moon between the clouds of the tempest, and soothed him with her tears, as the gentle rain calms the stormy ocean, and inspired him with tender verses, whose sweetness and pathos are equalled by their grandeur; she who incited him to deathless actions, such as the struggle for the emancipation of the Greeks, the memory of whose deeds shall be cherished among the heroisms and the noblest sacrifices of history ; that woman is one of those sublime Muses who pass over the world singing, like a flock of white mystic birds, over its sorrows and terrors.

I always thought that the Countess Guiccioli, after having smiled upon Lord Byron at Venice, after having brought him to Ravenna, after pensive meetings and wanderings with him along the banks of the Arno, beneath the dark green pine-trees of Pisa,—I thought she would have expired the day after Byron died upon the Grecian shores. What more remained for her on earth? Why live when the mysterious nightingale who sung at her side would return no more? No more chant those cantos, not alone to empty air, whose vibrations repeat and dissipate them in a short moment, but transmit them to space and bequeath them to immortality! I could never have believed that death would have snatched away the great Poet and spared the Countess. I thought that their souls would have mingled, so that they would have lived the same life and in the same heaven, like two stars of a constellation which are never separated, and that from the beginning of time look upon each other lovingly in the immensity of space.

Heloise would never have descended to posterity had she harboured another thought than that of Abelard. To exist through all time it was needful for her to die in the ocean of her tears, on the cold stones of the cloister, having lived in continual widowhood. Her tenderness endures as much as the learning of her lover, for the heart of Heloise contained an infinite capacity for loving, as the heart of Abelard was capable of inspiration and of reasoning. Hatred and violence separated the lovers, but now their bones rest together and mingle in the sepulchre, in the undying warmth of the flame which animated them during their lives.

But what then did the Countess Guiccioli? She lived. And not only did she live, but she married a wealthy nobleman and Senator of France, the Marquis de Boissy. And not only did she marry, but, on becoming a widow, she wrote a book upon Lord Byron, in two thick volumes, with the best intentions probably, but tedious like all diffuse apologies. I have gone over the twelve hundred pages of her work without finding any new information, or even a single ray of inspiration. The heavens have refused it to this rich marquise, this wife of a French Senator, who covers with bright flowers and with shining silks the skeleton of her lover! The Countess wronged her first husband for the sake of Byron. Such a fault could have had but one excuse—the eternity of her love. How did the Countess Guiccioli wear her perpetual mourning? Calling herself the Marquise de Boissy, after the death of her husband, she wrote an interminable book upon Byron, a monotonous and wearisome apology, instead of the lyric poem which should emanate from an enamoured heart. Certainly she would have written a book of another kind if she had shut herself up in her moral widowhood, and worn her mourning till God had called her hence, if, weaving a wreath for the poet, she had sought for the fragrant violets of the cemetery of Pisa, instead of the false flowers of Parisian *salons*.

In contemplating the life of Byron, we feel even greater sympathy for his misfortunes than sorrow for

his untimely death.　We left him in the early part of
his history, when he was leaving the school of Harrow
to enter the University of Cambridge.　Time passed
on, and in the year 1808 we find the boy has become
a youth.　If, in the beginning of his career, he had
been less unhappily circumstanced, he would doubtless
have been less vicious as his life advanced.　Childhood,
like the seed, takes root in the earth, from whence it
shoots forth powerful branches of life, mingles with the
exterior world, and is penetrated with the spirit of the
family; it is a continuation of the nine months which
precedes birth, of the two years during which the infant
hangs on its mother's breast; and as the maternal
milk is its aliment, as the maternal blood is its life and
substance, so the maternal education is its horizon, is
its heaven, is the blood and the nourishment of its
soul.　In the second period of human life these harmonies cease, this subjection is broken; the life goes
forth — almost always overflows from the paternal
abode, spreading itself far away from its source, like a
torrent loosened by the warm thaw of spring.　The
young are usually opposed to their surroundings; they
are full of vitality, excitable and rebellious.　The
passions shoot forth like flowers, they burst the bud
and expand.　Youth is a great infirmity, and has its
continual excesses which time squanders.　It looks to
the horizon, beholds it extended to infinity, but sees not
the shadows which darken it, nor the tempests which
thunder in the distance.　The life of the family de-

velops into friendship, the agitations of love take the place of tranquillity, and the passions are substituted for innocence. When we grow older, and as we advance on our journey of life, then the serpent appears to drive us out of Paradise. One must have a singular memory to be able to recollect those supreme days between youthful innocence and the tumult of the passions, that first ebullition of the blood, that first voluptuousness of life which must end in so much bitterness, if not sweetened by the honey of virtue. In our first years we need maternal love. But in the second period of life—that of youth—we need a wife to love with chaste affection, and to keep us safe and happy. If we meet with such a one on the threshold of life, our felicity is assured, and passion is like a refreshing dew, expressing itself in vague reflections, in ideal aspirations, in a species of poetical religion, which has, indeed, its troubles, like all greatnesses of soul, which kindles the whole of life like a fire, but which, like the fire, invigorates and spreads its beneficent warmth to infinity.

Lady Byron was a most loving mother, but she was not a tender mother; and she could not sympathize with the early moral necessities of her extraordinary son. His second love, Mary Chaworth, who touched even the depths of that privileged soul, even she cast him aside for an ordinary man *who was not lame.*

The domestic troubles of his own home, the constant quarrels between his parents, his hot and excitable Norman blood, the terrible family history which he often heard repeated, the lonely castle in which his early years were passed, the Scottish mountains scorched by lightning, and echoing with the roaring of torrents and the cries of eagles—all this gave to the solitary and impetuous youth born for Titanic struggles an energy so much the more extraordinary, that it did not burst all bounds in its determination to overcome whatever opposed it.

The University of Cambridge was another incitement. The extreme laxity of discipline permitted a corresponding looseness of morals, and this unrestrained freedom of life degenerated into licentiousness. Byron had strange eccentricities, the result of his warm temperament, deliriums of that moral fever called genius. At times, for instance, he dressed himself in the most absurd and fantastic fashion. He was greatly afraid of becoming corpulent, consequently he scarcely ate anything except meat and vegetables, but notwithstanding his own temperance, he gave Babylonian feasts, in which the image of Sardanapalus—afterwards so majestically evoked by his poem—seemed to appear amidst the exhalations of wine.

He kept near him a bear in chains, and asked those present to confer on this formidable creature the degree of doctor. On another occasion he persuaded a woman with whom he had become acquainted to disguise herself as a jockey, and to follow him on the public promenade. He took an insane pleasure in describing his life as a whirlwind of vice, and spoke of his conscience as a dead body devoured by corruption. He organized a sort of monastic association with some of his companions, and drank out of a skull mounted in silver. This circumstance was the origin of the popular belief that the skull was that of a woman to whom he had been attached, and who was supposed to have been murdered. He was skilful in the use of fire-arms, was an accomplished horseman, and swam three miles in the river Thames.

His favourite dog became attacked with madness. Unmindful of his own danger, he nursed it as if it had been his brother; and when it died preserved its memory in an epitaph as tender as if a portion of his heart had expired. At eighteen years of age he found himself ruined, and his future income in the hands of unprincipled usurers. At eighteen he had fought three duels : one of them, because he had been called an atheist. At eighteen he had already composed a volume of verses, and on taking possession of his property he invited his friends to orgies, where he had an ox in imitation of the ancient Homeric banquets, where he made libations of wine as in Asiatic festivals, and where they wrestled and fought like Roman gladiators, concluding with scenes of riot and debauchery. Amongst the guests at these entertainments were some young men who afterwards caused a political revolution, like that made by Lord John Russell in the matter of electoral reform ; and one of those social revolutions, which rise to the height of the greatest works of humanity, like that of Sir Robert Peel, who opened the storehouses of the world by giving free trade in corn to the people of England, till then compelled to feed on the scraps which fell from the tables of the aristocracy. Notwithstanding the malicious pains taken by many to picture Byron as a monster capable of all crimes and vices, it was only at this particular epoch that his life was really vicious. Yet nevertheless, on examining it scrupulously, we find his vices arose more from recklessness than from a deliberate intention to do evil; rather from a bold and daring disposition, than from a love of wrong-doing.

The enthusiasm of art might have been able to replace with some advantage the defects of his early training, and his unfortunate attachment. One absorbing passion would have left in his heart no room for corruption to enter, and no time to waste in dissipation. An infinite pleasure in labour, the slow elaboration of some great work, a continual contemplation of some beautiful ideal, extinguishes all desire for the voluptuous pleasures of sense. Sensual gratifications cannot compare with the pure delight caused by great artistic creations, or grand scientific conceptions. The fine arts gave to Michael Angelo, philosophy to Kant, mathematics to Sir Isaac Newton, a chastity as complete and spiritual as a cenobitical virginity. Their affections were immaterial, their beloved ones were ideas, their offspring the statue of the Night, the criticism of Reason, the calculation of the Infinite. Byron belonged more to humanity than these men of genius, who were isolated representatives of thought; statues, so to speak, animated and enlightened by immortal ideas. Byron was born to love and to be loved. But certainly his rare talents, his perception of the true and the beautiful, the admiration which he really felt for purity, the inspirations of his poetic imagination, and the greatness of his heart and soul, should have preserved him from those degrading intimacies and base pleasures, which intoxicate for the moment, but which leave after them an enduring remorse and disenchantment.

But he was unfortunate even in his love of literature. He sought for fame prematurely, and met with bitter censure and disappointment. Those only who have been born with an author's vocation will be able to understand the jealous impatience with which the youthful writer watches the appearance of his own works. And after the publication, with what eagerness he collects the different criticisms upon them! How carefully he weighs all opinions! Self-esteem magnifies their merit in an absurd manner. But this very anxiety for public applause is a proof of mistrust in his own powers, an assurance that conscience overrules all passion in the human heart, even self-love. It often happens that approbation is conceded to mediocrity, and denied to extraordinary merit.

There is something incomprehensible in every great nature; with every grand quality the sublime is mingled, and sublimity fatigues us with its incalculable weight, above all when we cannot comprehend its greatness. I have often seen people who, after a long contemplation of the vault of the Sistine Chapel, that masterpiece of Michael Angelo—with its legions of Titans, of prophets, and of sibyls—that wondrous painting which reaches the extreme boundary within which humanity can represent ideas, mounting to the highest summits of art. I have seen that from the study of such a work they draw no other result than a bad pain in their necks. And nothing is more easy than to malign that which we do not understand, Besides, there are literary schools just as there are political schools, which deny everything that does not adjust itself to their own particular constitution or idiosyncrasies. Calumny and assassination appear to them to be fair weapons, if used against the enemy. Above all, those who for a long season have been celebrated themselves, fancy they should have a monopoly of fame, and cannot suffer any competition, nor pardon the young author about to succeed them. They have imagined one particular type of critical belief; they have formed, as it were, a church after their own fashion; they excommunicate all heretics, and not being able to burn the whole body, they burn the blood.

Lord Byron presented himself with his first volume

of poetry before that Sanhedrim of criticism, the celebrated *Edinburgh Review*. That respectable publication poured molten lead upon the cradle of the poet.
Never was criticism so harsh, so implacable! The
youthful aspirant to the temple of the Muses did not
even reach mediocrity. According to his critics, his
ideas neither rose nor fell to the same level; they resembled stagnant water. He excused himself indeed
by speaking of his youth, and this minority was too
plainly visible from the beginning to the end of the
work, as the inseparable companion of his style. He
happened, like most other people, to write a great
many miserable verses in the interval between leaving
school and leaving the university. He should have
remembered, however, that to be a poet, a little sentiment was necessary, and also a little imagination.
The imitations of Ossian and Homer would not pass
as good exercises in a class of rhetoric, and were
unworthy of publication. In short, the critic boldly
declared that the young nobleman was not born to be
a poet, and he ought, therefore, to leave this enchanting art to those of taste and talent.

Lord Byron felt this cruel blow with all the nervous
sensibility peculiar to poets. The keen edge of that
first criticism froze his very soul. Blood and gall
seemed to flow from his lips. In his bitter rage and
mortification he turned against his country and against
all his contemporaries, whose names were more or less
famous. All the Satanic qualities with which he was

supposed to be endowed were called out of the depths of his heart by this satire—cynicism, irony, sarcasm, anger, hatred, and the thirst for vengeance. The immortal cripple—like Vulcan with his red-hot hammer—ascended the English Olympus, and spared none of the statues of the gods. Some he called narrow-hearted traders, and not inspired poets; to others he said they had chosen an idiot for the hero of a work, and after having read it one knew not who was the greater fool, the author or the person he described. To these, he says, they have fought a duel with pistols charged with powder; to those, that they have dressed Camoens in English lace; to a certain noble lord, that his dinners are worth more than his translations; to a celebrated historian, that he writes because he must eat, and eats because he writes. He is severe upon those who bring their daughters to crowded ré-unions of the dissipated and worthless, demoralizing them by immodest dances, as well as ruining themselves at the gaming-table, expecting to gain everything from these Babels of vice—the money or the wife of their neighbour.

Imagine what effect such satires would produce in a society where modesty is so scrupulously respected, and where there is so much chastity of speech and manners! Imagine how the wounded turned against that burning genius, whose hands had pierced them so ruthlessly! A cloud of injuries surrounded the poet. This unfortunate satire contributed not a little

to increase the implacable hatred of his contemporaries. At first Lord Byron published it anonymously,
but eventually he affixed his own name. He declared
that he would give in London as much satisfaction as
should be desired. But when all confined themselves
to murmurs, without any attempt to challenge him,
he exclaimed sadly, "The age of chivalry is over!"

Among those who had been most hardly treated
was his relation, Lord Carlisle, who had formerly been
his guardian. But the noble youth never repented of
this proceeding. On the contrary, in one edition of
his works, he excused himself for having once dedicated a book to this individual, on the ground of his
own inexperience, and declared that all the blood of
all the Howards could not ennoble a clown, nor make
a sage out of a simpleton. The cause of this bitter
vengeance should be understood, for it is intimately connected with one of the aspects under which
we should regard the poet—that of an orator; and
also with one of the most important acts of his
existence—his entrance into the English House of
Peers.

Lord Byron had asked the protection and assistance
of Lord Carlisle in order to be duly presented in that
assembly. Nothing was more natural than his desire
to sit in that great oligarchy, which, at that time
especially, resembled the Roman Senate, and which,
from its world-wide influence, warmed and excited his
poetic imagination. Like all men of remarkable

genius, he had a longing for greatness, an unquench-able thirst for glory; and the grandest, the most intoxicating of human glories, is the glory of the orator, who, without shedding one drop of blood, without staining his laurels with the fatal trophies of the warrior, can from the tribune conquer the souls of his hearers, and force them to mingle with his own. No spectacle can compare with that of the orator, who should be at the same time a philosopher, a poet, an artist, a musician, a tactician; one who can draw from the depths of his intellect the hidden treasures of thought, clothe and shape them into beauty, and (with a creative power which, like the fiat of the Eternal, brought forth the worlds) by a miracle of his intelligence and his will, and amidst the deafening applause of the people, lay invisible fetters on all hearts, making them slaves of that magic whose supernatural power is one of the most profound mysteries of the spirit. The restless, excitable soul of Lord Byron already imagined scenes in which his brilliant fancy should triumph over all his enemies by the mere magic of his words, and benefit mankind by the purity of his ideas.

The man whom his enemies represent as being indifferent to all human sorrows, and sceptical as to all good; a despiser of his fellows, and an enemy of God; altogether given up to the gratification of his own vanity and his unbridled vices, had in the depths of his own great soul an altar reserved for the religion of the oppressed, and a living faith in the progress of humanity, which is the ultimate accomplishment of the divine law of justice on the earth. There was not only a sentiment of self-love in the just impatience of Byron to acquire the rights of his own inheritance; he had also the more noble love of humanity, which he showed afterwards when he employed his powerful pen and word in favour of the Irish Catholics, and thus scattering the seeds of those free institutions destined to spring up in our time—a prophet, like all great intelligences, of a new social system.

But Lord Carlisle responded to all these lofty aspirations with culpable indifference. Indeed, he manifested the most lively desire to thwart the noble ambition of his nephew. He mislaid the necessary legal documents in order to retard his official reception. He received with contempt the dedication of some poems, which, though the works of a youth, were destined to glorify his name, while his own writings, those of his old age, were already forgotten. And at length he refused to present, in the Assembly of Peers, the genius who bore concealed in his brain a heaven of immortal poetry. Lord Byron entered the Upper House accompanied by a distant relative, with whom he was barely acquainted. The House of Peers devotes itself to its ordinary business with that mathematical regularity common to English habits. No one in that aristocratic assembly divined that the young nobleman come to fill one of its senatorial chairs would be in the future the interpreter of the thought of his age—the poet destined to chant its doubts and its sorrows. Perhaps Lord Byron, from the depths of the degradation into which he had fallen, and notwithstanding the disenchantment which cruel criticism had engendered in his heart, foresaw, with the consciousness of his own talents, and with the natural acuteness of genius, the crown of laurels concealed under the wreath of thorns, and the transfiguration reserved by the future to his merit. Doubtless a mysterious atmosphere surrounded the youth, and a circlet of future glory sparkled on his brow. He was one of those symbolic men chosen among many to personify and represent an age. Like our epoch, he was destined to crawl with his body on the earth as a reptile, and his soul to soar like a luminary of heaven towards infinity; to search after sensual pleasures, and to find enjoyment only in intellectual contemplations; to ridicule creeds, and to die for the faith; to appear a degraded epicurean, and to merit a name among heroes by his life, and among martyrs by his death! His remarkable face, the beauty of his Grecian head, his spacious forehead, his arched eyebrows, the depth of his eyes, which in repose assumed the pure blue of the heavens, but which any emotion deepened to black, like an ocean of changing thoughts; the perfect line of his lips, sculptured as if to vibrate eternal harmony; his aquiline nose; his beard, divided with incomparable grace; his Olympic gestures, his majestic attitudes; his stateliness, tempered by softness; the genius flashing from his features; his pale and delicate complexion, resembling the colour of antique marble gilded by the suns of centuries; all his being, all his person, declared that, in chiselling that perfect vase, the Creator did not design that it should remain empty, but be filled with immortal fragrance.

His entrance into the Upper House was cold and formal. The session was commonplace, and the assemblage small. The Chancellor administered the oath, and declared the admission in the unimpressive manner in which all formularies are delivered.

I never beheld the old House of Peers, but I have seen the new Houses of Parliament, and I declare that the sight of them awakened in my heart the most profound emotion, like that I experienced at seeing the Cathedral of Toledo, the Colosseum of Rome, or the Cemetery of Pisa. Though there is but little originality in the architecture and an excess of ornamentation; the lofty Gothic walls, the formidable towers, the vastness of the proportions, the sombre colour deepened by volumes of smoke from the different manufactories and the exhalations from the river; the gilded angles of the high cupolas, looking like dark cypresses lighted up by the mysterious rays of a deeply veiled sun—all this leaves in the mind an undefinable image of grandeur like the sublime expression of the sovereignty of a people become great by the consent of ages. The paintings and sculptures are alone remarkable from their imperfections, yet the high pinnacles and the broad lines fill the mind with an idea of greatness. But, however, what one admires most is not that which meets the eye, but all which is done and thought under those vaulted roofs—the strength of English institutions, the extent of English liberty, the progress which nothing interrupts, the prestige of a race that has known how to protect its rights from the universal serfdom into which all others fell in the sixteenth century, when absolute despotism prevailed.

In that immense palace I thought of the great injury done to the country by the persons whose bitterness and envy drove Byron from those benches, filling his soul with inextinguishable hatred. Perhaps elevated social ideas and progressive political reforms would have saved him from the abyss into which he fell, and have nourished his infinite desire to love. Perhaps the passion for liberty would have filled his soul more positively than the worship of the ideal. Perhaps to the crown of the poet the glories of eloquence would have been united. Liberty is not the Bacchante which the world's reactionaries imagine, but the faithful spouse of austere virtue and of chaste fecundity. We can suffer for her, fight for her, die for her, convinced that future ages will gather the fruits of our sacrifices. But the enemies of Byron forced him not only to leave the House, but the country. In his rage unnumbered curses burst from his tortured heart. England flung him from her soil, iguorant that in the future he would be one of the first stars in her literary firmament.

That departure of Lord Byron was not a voyage, but a banishment. He himself tells us that he went forth from England sad as Adam from Paradise. When your country believes you to be incompatible with her repose, her institutions, or her religion, there is no choice left but to abandon her, though in so doing you forsake the half of your existence. Everywhere you can breathe air, but not the air which heard the sighs of your first love. All nations may shelter you under their roof-trees, but none can offer you the home where you received the benediction of your mother. Heaven is great and extended over all, but not the Heaven under which you dreamed of felicity, where your hopes withered in the blossom, and you were happy with smiling illusions. Any part of the earth may conceal your body, but, alas! your bones will be more isolated in a foreign grave which contains not the remains of your fathers. To die in a strange land is the most cruel of punishments. Not in vain are we born in our motherland. We have from her soil an essence like that which the earth collects from the root of the tree, and its heaven blesses us with an immortal kiss. Our hearts are moulded of her clay, our ideas mingle with the words which our country has put upon our lips. Exile is a mortal malady of the heart. We anxiously desire to live amongst people with whom we have a community of origin, of blood, of life, and of language. *That* constitutes the being of our country, the happiness of our own existence. And after having beheld the great nations of the world, the most celebrated cities, the most sublime monuments; after having discoursed with the most illustrious persons, after having been present at the session of the Parliaments of Paris and of London, at High Mass at St Peter's in Rome, at a sunset in the Bay of Naples, at a serenade on the Grand Canal of Venice; after having climbed to Alpine peaks among their eternal snows, and heard the roaring of cascades falling in the valleys, and seen the eagles mount among the heights, we turn our eyes sadly to the distant land which was our birthplace, and feel that our utmost ambition is to be the last of her children, the most obscure of her citizens, and to possess a home among our friends and families to-day, and to-morrow a forgotten sepulchre in the earth of our fathers!

Love, love alone, could have created for Lord Byron a new world of hope and of happiness. But the truest affection of his life, the first really serious love of his heart, did not meet with the response which would probably have made his eternal felicity. To love, and not to be loved! Who can conceive greater torment? The lonely heart can only bring forth serpents like the desert. No one to care for our life, no one interested in our destiny! The brightest conceptions fall by their own weight into the abyss of the soul, when there is no one to whom we can communicate them, wounding and destroying it. You come forth from your house and no one detains you, and return with none to regard you. Your health is yours only, and you expose it to the greatest perils. You play it as a trump card, and as death can strike but one solitary heart, you regard it with indifference. There are none to partake your joys and sorrows. The divided soul may enlarge itself to infinity, but alone it dries up and withers like green fruits fallen from the tree. When the powerful emotions of a manly heart, when the roughnesses of a mind which has deeply suffered, have not the smile of a beloved wife to temper them, they assume the aspect of savageness, like a field abandoned by the husbandman. For the solitary soul, after a tempest, there is no calm; after the night, there is no morning; after doubt, no faith ; after sorrow, no consolation. A life without love is a heaven without stars !

Miss Chaworth forsook Lord Byron, and by so doing probably cut the wings by which he would have mounted to the skies, and left him the prey of his own passions, and to the solitude of his own thoughts, among the whirlwinds of the universe. Before his departure the poet desired to see her. He was, in fact, brave enough to look once more upon the woman who had forsaken her first lover, and who was happy with another. Trampling upon his own heart, he entered the house which he had fondly hoped would have been the temple of felicity for himself.

The fair head bent in salutation. The looks of the lovers—for ever separated—met in those supreme adieux. Byron told her his sole desire was the happiness of his beloved, and that he left England content in her welfare ; that though in deep affliction, before all and above all, he felt for her an infinite tenderness ; that he felt even capable of loving her husband because he loved her also. When he beheld the little son of Mary Chaworth, then scarcely two years old, when he recognised in the infant's face some of the features of his father, his jealous heart beat almost to bursting. But on observing that the child had the eyes of his mother, he pressed him to his heart, and almost suffocated him with kisses. At last he departed. We shall see him again on his travels, his mind clear as a ray of light, his heart surcharged with sorrow.

PART THE THIRD.

TO leave England, to quit that ceremonious society, in which the restless genius of the poet could scarcely move or breathe, was an absolute necessity of his mental life. He burst the bars of his prison, and plunged into the sweets of liberty. Passing from British fogs, he bathed in our extended horizon, in our brilliant light, under our azure heavens. If the children of the South cannot contemplate a sunset, when the clouds are tinged with purple, and the outline of the mountains is clear before them ; when the bright waters are beautiful with changing shades—if they who are accustomed to this glorious sight cannot look upon it without being enchanted by this festival of harmonies and of colours, what must these be to the native of the North, who sees always his gigantic trees and his pale sun through the veil of his nebulous atmosphere !

For the moment Lord Byron experienced a delight heretofore unknown ; his morbid ideas, his continual melancholy, his doubts, and his despair, fell into the bosom of the blue waters, as if the amorous kisses of the sea-breeze penetrated into his soul. Indeed, nothing invigorates and comforts us so much as the grand spectacles of Nature—the wind, caught by the swelling canvas ; the foamy waves, rent and furrowed by the conquering keel ; a depth beneath our feet, and an infinite height above our heads ; life on all sides, intoxicating us with its voluptuousness ; the light dazzling and increasing in the transparent waters ; the saline aroma of marine vegetation mingling with our blood ; the vigour of the will manifested by the struggle with the elements ; and the human dignity realized at each moment by the victory.

We find by the correspondence of Lord Byron that his soul grew younger on the ocean, that his life became greater with the infinite life of the universe.   In fact, whatever may be our ideas of Nature, we may consider her as a veil which conceals the Creator, or, after the manner of the Mystics and Pantheists, as the embodiment of universal life. When we give ourselves up to the enjoyment of her beauty and grandeur ; when we breathe the vivifying air which circulates around her bosom, or contemplate the glories of the starry heavens, which seem to look upon us lovingly ; when we repose in her meadows, enamelled with the flowers of April, and gay with butterflies of brilliant hues, and hear the chorus of her myriads of birds, and the sweet orchestra of her mysterious murmurs, and cast our eyes on the far distant horizon — suddenly we become converted into poets, and though unable to express our ideas in eloquent and glowing language, we feel the tremblings of inspiration thrill through our agitated nerves like the chords of a harp, at the same time that the current of universal life centuples the vigour of our own frail existence.

Few poets have sympathized with Nature like Lord Byron. True, he loved to disturb her serenity with the wail of private sorrows, but he showed how her sap penetrated his imagination, and caused it to bring forth blossoms, as the spring juices swell the buds of the dry almond-tree. He has most admirably described his arrival in western countries, after passing the stormy Bay of Biscay, the enchanting shores of the old Lusitania, the mouth of the Tagus, the mountains with their lofty peaks half veiled in clouds, the golden fruits hidden under the broad emerald leaves, and filling the air with aroma; Lisbon beholding herself in the mirror of her bright waters, and the blooming groves of Cintra, through whose narrow streets is seen a monastery inhabited by gloomy penitents, or the crosses which mark the scenes of horrible assassinations; but above all, the granite rocks with their dentated summits, seeming, in the quick changes from light to darkness, to be moved by the wind; profound valleys, where the northern vegetation mourns the sun's absence; the declivities covered with orange-trees; the heights crowned with white honeysuckle; the roar of its thousand streams breaking into cascades, and the distant view of the great ocean reflecting the light on her azure bosom.

Lord Byron crossed the Guadiana. On entering our country, the shade of Spain in her days of chivalry rose before him. The heroic nation seemed to him wounded by all conquerors because of her beauty, and dragging them at the heels of her war-horse. In the immense Spanish plains, in the clouds of dust tossed about by the wind, his imagination beheld the bitter struggle between the Moors and the Christians, who have mingled their blood in the furrows of our mother-land. And when the night appears and the stars shine in the pure heavens, one seems to hear around the music of the guitar, the romances of ancient heroism, the songs of eternal love. I have gone over the loveliest plains of Europe, and neither on the shores of the Rhine, amidst the soft dreams of Germanic poetry, nor in the Gulf of Naples, where the sirens raise their marble brows crowned with Greek epigrams, have I felt the touching sadness of poetry, such as I have experienced in the nights of Andalusia, when, on the warm earth, under the changing light of the stars, beneath the vine or the palm tree, the gitana with her black eyes and bronzed complexion, flinging on her shoulders her ebon tresses, whose weight obliges her to raise her head, and extending her arms to the heavens as if about to fly from the earth, dances as if in delirium to the sound of the guitar's sorrowful com-plaint, and of the song of love, sad as an elegy, sustained in long cadences like a series of uninterrupted wailings.

Lord Byron arrived in Spain during the War of Independence. Her rural soil, her rude stubble, was on fire. On each of her hills a fortress had been erected. Everywhere cannons opened their deadly mouths. Every Spaniard arose, his blood-coloured cockade in his hat, and his arms under his mantle. Saragossa writhed on the rack of torment, terrifying the world by her contempt of death. She seemed an entire city immolating herself like Cato—one woman dried her tears, and amidst mountains of smoking ruins and heaps of mouldering corpses, applied with her own hands the match to the cannon which defended the martyr city, converted into a vast cemetery. This sublime delirium of Spain in defence of her independence has been eloquently described by the poet, who, laying aside his usual flippancy and his ironical scepticism, rises to the heights of epic poetry, the spirit of which his absorbing genius had caught from the ancient Romancists.

But yet he observed our customs somewhat too lightly. The sight of Seville should have inspired him with something better than the insipid story of the two lodging-house keepers with whom he lived but four days. Coming more especially from England, how much there is to admire in the tower from whence Arabian sages studied the science of astronomy ; the hospital erected by penitence, and containing the paintings of the Water flowing from the Rock, and the Multiplication of Loaves, which may be called pictures of life; a id with these some others so terrifying, that they may be called pictures of death; the Gothic Cathedral, severe as the Middle Ages, and already illuminated by the dawn of the Renaissance, as if the shadows of an epoch were in its base, and the daybreak of another epoch in its oriels; the silent palace chiselled like a jewel, and adorned with all the colours of the East; the *patios*, with their vases of flowers refreshed by murmuring fountains, whose crystal showers sprinkle the marble pavements; where repose those lovely women with bronze complexions and lustrous eyes, whose ebon depths speak of love and tenderness, and who so forcibly remind us of the virgins of Murillo.

Cadiz inspired him with some exquisite verses. But why did not Lord Byron—who showed himself so keenly sensible of the valour of Spaniards—why did he not also appreciate the virtue of Spanish women? The virtues of men are easily discovered, for they shine in the field or in the senate. Along the walls of Cadiz you may still see the broken bombs of Napoleon. But the virtues of women are hidden in the home, in the sanctuary of the family; one must seek them, as pearls in their shells, in the depths of the ocean. A traveller passes some days in a foreign town: he sees all things superficially, finds vice and vicious pleasures easy of attainment, and generalizes his emotions. Thus I explain the injustice of Byron, and the hard words in which he so lightly mentions the women of Cadiz. But doubtless, had he entered into those homes, and beheld the treasures of tenderness, the devotion of passionate affection, joined to the strictest fidelity, his ideas would have been altogether different. Nowhere else are families so loving and so united in spirit; nowhere else is a whole life so faithfully consecrated to one only attachment. I have seen many attractive women, born to enchant society, languish in retirement, devoting their years to the memory of the absent ones gone to die upon inhospitable shores. I have beheld them, widows of a first unhappy love, remain faithful to that only love, to that virgin affection, until death, and die hoping to find their beloved in happier regions. I have seen them from their earliest growth keep up their friendships for ten or fifteen years with the chosen of their heart, and in all these fifteen years not one kiss has soiled the purity of their lips, not one unchaste thought the modesty of their souls. I have beheld young and beautiful mothers die to the world the day they became widows, converting their houses into cloisters, and holding no other relations with society than those necessary for the education of their children. Passion takes among us the infinite intensity of the ardent climate, but, like all else that is infinite, it goes beyond the limited regions of matter, too frail and too narrow to contain it, and plunges into the boundless regions of thought, where it is clothed with an almost divine purity, and acquires an almost celestial existence. Byron should not have been contented to behold the fire stolen from heaven by the black eyes of our Andalusian ladies, the passion which flashes from under their silken lashes, the long tresses of rich hair which twine over their shoulders like serpents; among so much beauty he should have dis-covered the delicacy and the loveliness of the soul.

He soon quitted our country. As a poet, he desired to visit the land of artistic forms, the land of perfect expression. There is no country in the world that has so completely carried out and embodied the beauty of ideas as Greece. Scarcely a thought can pass through her mind than she clothes it with an immortal outline, which is the delineation of perfect beauty. A few strokes sufficed her painters to trace in the marble those bas-reliefs whose simplicity is confounded almost with the native simplicity of ideas, and whose beauty is the calm perfection of eternal serenity. The Greek ideas are like the most natural melodies of the creation, like the murmur of the rivulets, like the song of the nightingale. Her statues are the most beautiful realization of the plastic art. It seems not as if the marble had obeyed the hammer, which sepa-rated it from the mountains, or that the chisel had clothed it with form, but as if it had been formed by the will and the imagination. The statue, so to speak, has risen from the stone at the invocation of the artist, with the same exactness with which Adam arose from the clay at the command of the Creator. An immortal soul seems to lay enshrined in those divine features, and to shine upon that ample forehead. The Greeks, being masters of a language above all others remarkable for flexibility and richness, their souls became the channels of ideas in those glowing words, as an instrument of music conveys harmonious notes. They can never forget their great past, while they read in the original the verses in which Thetis consoles her son, the description of the valley of Colonna in the Œdipus of Sophocles, of the fear-inspiring furies in the Orestes of Æschylus, and the immortal periods of the Timeo of Plato. It must be acknowledged that humanity has been able to do nothing better than to copy and re-copy these eternal models, as a young student of painting copies the picture set before him, borrowing its tints and touches, perhaps at times putting some superiority in the expression, or in one of the features, but never attaining to its perfection. All artists, whether classical or romance writers ; poets, painters, sculptors, or architects ; those who cultivate the art of speaking in the senate or in the professorial chair, have to seek in Greece the beauty of form. Byron did not fail in this. The country of the arts seemed to him like an empty skull which once bore the weight of a living soul, a soul almost capable of grasping the infinite, but which in decay can scarce afford a habitation for an insect. The perfidy of man seized even the ruins of the Parthenon, and conveyed them to the British Museum. With sacrilegious hands they outraged a corpse to despoil it of its riches. I have seen in the Museum of London the broken marbles of the Parthenon, animated by the chisel of Ictinus, of Callicrates, and of Phidias; I have beheld them with my eyes, and I could have pressed them to my lips, as the pious pilgrim kisses the sacred soil of Jerusalem. I have seen the theories, the processions, the defiles of gods and of heroes; the Grecian virgins offering the presents of Attica; the demigods, conquerors of the Centaurs; the victims destined for the sacrifice, unclad youthful warriors mounted on their barebacked horses, each perfect in serene and immortal beauty; but in lonely sadness, far from the hills where grew the olives of Minerva, and from the streams bordered by the bays of Apollo—surrounded by an atmosphere dense and heavy from smoke and the exhalations of the Thames, instead of the pure zephyrs among whose caresses they sprung into being, the perfumed breezes of Mount Hymettus, and the harmonies of the Ægean Sea; in a foreign land, they are for ever strangers—they, the genii of the South, the representatives of art and of light, in the shadows and sadness of a northern clime, more unhappy among the mists of Albion than Eurydice in the darkness of Inferno!

Never has the genius of man inspired pages more beautiful than those in which Lord Byron describes his travels in Greece. The poem is an elegy in which we

know not which is the most admirable, the perfect
composition, the grandeur of ideas, or the bitter melancholy.   The plastic gracefulness of the Greeks is
there united to the profound sadness of the Christians.
When I read them I seem to behold again the lovely
statue of " Night," by Michael Angelo, extended over
the sepulchre of Florence, that powerful Grecian deity,
chaste as the Venus of Milo, but sad as a Dolorosa
of Rivera.   The vessel of the poet is coasting among
the Greek promontories, and his spirit invokes the
voices of the ruins, the lamentations of the shores de-
spoiled of their deities.   Never, since Plutarch wrote
the lament heard by Thamo near the cave of Messina,
when Natural Religion expired—never have there
been lines so touching.   Tears gush from them, burning tears, fit to call forth the gods of antiquity from
the cold ashes of their ruined altars.   From his vessel
Byron saw the shadow of the rock overhanging the
sea of Leucades, where Sappho appeased in the waters
the infinite desires of her heart.   From thence he
also beheld the little bay in which the practical genius
of the West, personified by Augustus, overcame the
more exalted genius of the East represented by that
powerful but luxurious Marc Antony, he who
sacrificed his love for Rome to his devotion to
Cleopatra, the maga, poetess, enchantress, capable
of reviving with her soft embraces and voluptuous
dances the Oriental theogony even in the Grecian
temples, and twining herself, like a serpent of Asia,

around the Eternal City, suffocating it to avenge the slavery of her fathers and the destruction of her gods.

An astonishing flexibility is the distinctive characteristic of the poet. In him are united the ancient classics, modern romances, and the glowing imagery of the East; and to dreamy, and vague idealism he joins a more crude and severe realism. He is the embodiment of his caustic epoch. He is an instrument which every breeze may soothe or irritate; sometimes he is lulled by the celestial breath of morning, filled with aroma and with harmony; and sometimes maddened by the roar of the hurricane, laden with dust and ashes. The ocean does not reflect the changes of the heavens more faithfully than his conscience repeats the changes of ideas; it does not picture the varying clouds more truly than the soul of the poet expresses the thoughts of his epoch. In this feeling, being, as he is, a subjective poet, he is never unmindful of his personality, dragging the chain of his individual sorrows on the earth, sensitive as must be a faithful poet of this uncertain age, which from its commencement has vacillated between faith and reason, between right and tradition, between liberty and despotism. Action and reaction never struggle with more force, and never preserve a greater equilibrium, than that which proceeds from this mutual paralysation. In this sense Lord Byron is the poetic age. Different ideas combat powerfully in his conscience, and he clothes all his characters with something from his own soul.

After passing by the classic shores of Attica, evoking in verses of perfect purity the guardian spirit of the ruins, he went to Albania, and felt strongly attracted by a spectacle much opposed to Hellenic severity; by the Oriental customs, the hyperbole, the sensual habits, and the voluptuous feasts of Asia. His eyes were offended by the mountaineers of Albania, with their great leather boots embroidered with silks; the full white garments; the coloured belt, with its weapons of Damascus steel brilliant with jewels; the jacket and vest of fine scarlet cloth, bordered with gold; upon this man the large tassel falling from the Greek cap, and with that the great firelock inlaid with ivory; the complexion bronzed by the ardent sun, eyes black and brilliant, the features perfect, the stature tall, and the form flexible; agile as the deer of their mountains, emanations from the first races of humanity, bearing still upon their brows the august marks of their pristine greatness.

The Governor of those regions received him as Turkish officials know how to welcome the English aristocracy. The hospitality of Ali was a continual enchantment for Lord Byron. In a white marble pavilion, from the centre of which rose a murmuring fountain; reclining on soft cushions of richest silk, on one side an amber dish of perfume, and coffee on the other; before each a large pipe, the golden light beaming through the lattice, and half revealing the luxurious vegetation of the East, the palm mingling with the cypress—in such a scene Lord Byron and Ali conversed, surrounded by Albanians in their picturesque costume, by Macedonians in their red mantles, graceful and athletic Greeks with their sculptured features, negroes brought at great cost from Nubia; and without, on horses fleet as the wind, caracole troopers of different Asiatic races, preceded by rude music and light·tambours; while from the highest minaret the solitary mollah announces the hour of prayer, as a reminder that ideas of religion and of the Deity surround, like a moral atmosphere, all the grandeur of the East.

But Athens was the true home of the poet. There, flying from the gloomy shadows of the North, he acknowledged his country. Long ages, and the unthinking wrath of men, have passed over the temples, the statues, and the columns; yet still the azure sky shows the delicate outlines of the mountains, the groves of olives, of laurels, and of the shady mastic trees, as in the days when the gods chose these shores for their abode; still the sweet thyme of Hymettus distils the delicious honey on which fed the poets, whose lips vibrated with harmonious canticles; still the bees which Plato admired whirr their bright wings in the fragrant air, and construct in the trunks of trees the honeycombs from which flow streams of liquid gold upon altars crowned with flowers; still the warm rays of Apollo gild with their immortal light the marbles from which come forth statues of eternal beauty; and the voices of sylvan fauns mingle with the sighs of sirens which issue from the waves; because, if gods and heroes have departed, if art has expired, if glory and liberty have passed away— Nature still exists and is fruitful. This religious sentiment towards the universe is another of the most beautiful characteristics of Lord Byron's poetry. It is easy to perceive that it is not a conventional feeling imposed by an æsthetic law, like the sentiment of Goethe, but an emotion born spontaneously, and that rushes like a torrent from his soul, replete with universal life.

While in exile he did not fail to meet with adventures. The first happened during his stay at beautiful Florence, where he twice escaped the persecutions of Napoleon. Afterwards, in Athens, he became deeply enamoured of three lovely young Greek girls, who refused to accept the offer of his too universal and expansive affections. However, he contracted a friendship with one of the least understood and most eccentric persons of the age—Lady Hester Stanhope. The soul of the poet was able to comprehend that of the English lady. If her age and her well-known homeliness opposed obstacles to love, the exaltation of her character, and the poetic tendency of her disposition, united them in the strictest relations of friendship. Lady Hester had also fled from the fogs of England in search of Eastern light and beauty. And on leaving the country she had condemned its conventional society, quitting it for the companionship of the clouds, of the eagles, of tempests, of the winds, of all that comes or goes from the Infinite in mysterious airy circles. On entering those Asiatic regions, she had laid aside her Protestant creed as the serpent casts his skin. Her Bible was the universe, her temple the primeval forest, which still exhales the breath of the deluge; her altar, the mountains of Lebanon, whence the Hebrew prophets cut their gigantic harps; her habitation the caverns; her companions the huge cedars, whose deep roots absorb the moisture of the earth, and whose tops mount towards the lightning; her Deity, the unimaginable Infinite; her profession, prophecy as in the times of the Sibyls; her means of divination, magnetism; her mode of expression, a nervous style, replete with flowery images like the Oriental; her only motive, a certain restless poetry, incapable of expression, which, being unable to embody itself in great works, excited her to marvellous actions and a wandering life; but the leading characteristic was a real, although a sublime, mental derangement. If I mistake not, Lamartine also met that extraordinary woman during the happy period of his Eastern travels. It was the supreme moment of his life, and the supreme crisis of his genius. The Royalist left behind her in Europe her aristocratic convictions—the Catholic his faith, an unsettled aspiration for the happiness of the human race swelled his heart; other desires, not less waver-

ing, led him to a sentimental pantheism. As there
are birds of the dawn, so there are intelligences which
do not reach the full light of day. They are like
angels lost between heaven and earth; their heads
in sunlight, and their feet in shadow, dwelling
strangely between brightness and darkness. Thus
Lamartine wandered, then handsome and young, a
celebrated poet, with his "Meditations" in his hand,
as the testament of his early years, his heart and
mind already fixed on more extended regions. Lady
Hester Stanhope declared to him that the destinies
of his country would one day be in his hands. This
gifted and eccentric woman would have passed for a
miracle of prevision and prophetic power, if her death
had not disclosed her insanity. M. Lescure, who has
written a beautiful and instructive biography of Lord
Byron, promises to study the life of this spiritual
sister of the poet, who, like Lord Byron, left England
cursing its society; like Byron, gave herself up to
ideas mingled of faith and of doubt; like Byron,
united to an expansive temperament a profound
melancholy; like Byron, sought in the sun of Oriental
countries warmth for her chilled heart; and, like
Byron, died on the bosom of Nature!

But friendships of this kind were not the only ones
contracted by the poet; he had also adventures
capable of exalting his heart and his imagination,
both of which overflowed with his surpassing genius.
It is impossible to read the poem entitled " The

Giaour," without feeling the sublime tragic terror expressed by its daring images, thrilling your nerves with its electric current.   Leila was one of the loveliest women of Hassan's harem.   The flower of the pomegranate had dyed her cheeks, the black and transparent lava of Etna, with its brilliant flame, had made the crystal of her eyes.   Enveloped in her robes of white gauze, she shone like a star among clouds.   But she wore a mantle still more beautiful, the covering of her raven tresses, which descended to her feet, white as unstained snow when it falls from the cloud upon the peaks of the mountains.   A Venetian saw and loved her.   His love was requited, and for a short period these two, whose souls an infinite affection had united, were happy.   Hassan suspected her.   On the delicious shores of Greece, in one of those little creeks from whose borders arise mountains enamelled by the rosy light of the southern sun, there occurred a terrible event.   A boat appeared bearing a sack.   Within the sack there was a human body.   The sack and the body were cast into the deepest water.   But when Hassan returned from accomplishing his vengeance, a man, more relentless than the tigers of the desert, stopped him, fought with him and his followers, almost tearing off the hand which held his scimitar, and then left him writhing in agony till he expired on the dust of the wayside.   And the pitiless one goes to a Christian convent, begs admission in exchange for riches,

without making any vow, or observing any ceremonies, but looking continually to the distant sea,
and uttering only a few half-broken words, in which
are expressed love and death—like a spirit of darkness accomplishing a penance. At last he died,
demanding but forgetfulness of his name and a
wooden cross for his monument. I was wrong, he
also begged—if it be true that those thus drowned in
the sea leave it to ask of the earth a more tranquil
grave—that the unhappy Leila should lay her cold
fingers on the forehead of her lover, press them on his
burning heart, and, placing herself by his side, should
sleep thus, never to be separated.

    *   *   *   *   *

But the whole of this poem must be read to be
understood and appreciated. It seems to be a translation from the Arabic, from its richness of conception,
and from the boldness of its images. The final elegy
alone resembles the psychological literature of the
North, and the Norman temperament of the author.
This beautiful legend was inspired by some of his
own adventures. That same Ali, who so hospitably
received Lord Byron in his palace, had caused twelve
Turkish women accused of infidelity to be sewn up in
sacks, and to be thrown into the sea. Not one of
them uttered a complaint. They all accepted death
with resignation and in profound silence; beautiful
toys of destiny, broken like glass against the rocks!
Such occurrences were frequent.

A Neapolitan nobleman, passing through Janina, fell deeply in love with a Turkish girl of sixteen years. This attachment was suspected by the police, who watched the lovers and found them together. The police stoned the girl to death, and banished the Italian to another town, isolated on account of the plague, where he died, not of the pestilence, but of sorrow.

In a similar scene Lord Byron had been an actor, and perhaps the extraordinary warmth of expression in " The Giaour" is due to this circumstance, for he frequently describes his personal emotions. Moore and Medwin relate, that when in Athens the great poet became enamoured of a lovely young Turkish girl. The seclusion in which Turkish women live; the melancholy retirement to which they are compelled by their countrymen ; the necessity of sharing any affection they may receive with several others ; their own ardent nature, exalted by the visions of solitude, and the dreams and imaginings which come to them from the outer world through gauzes and gratings—all these develop in them a wonderful aptitude to sacrifice themselves to one of those amours prohibited by their laws—a love the most intense when most perilous, and of which the attractions increase with the continual threats of death ; these being but the nourishment of a fatal passion, which in its transports and delirium makes them court and enjoy danger, thus joyfully showing all the treasures of a tenderness capable from its intensity of changing the supreme agony into a supreme voluptuousness, and of making the last sigh of life a breath of eternal love.

Byron, from his personal accomplishments, must have inspired the most exalted passions. Of these there is some record in the description of Haydée, never sufficiently admired, and of those meetings by the light of the stars, and the music of the waves. Byron and his beloved frequently saw each other. But their intercourse was interrupted by the Turkish Ramazan, the regulations of which are extremely strict with regard to love affairs. The poet did not feel this obligation, and made some efforts to see the lady. These were unfortunately discovered, notwithstanding the greatest precautions. One evening he rode on horseback through the Piræus, followed by his strong escort of Albanians. In the middle of the square he saw a group of Government agents dragging along a large sack. A stifled groan, a bitter sob, floated on the air. The blood rushed to the youth's temples, and a terrible presentiment shot through his heart. With the quick divination of genius he fancied he saw struggling in the waters, in the death agony, the lovely woman so dear to his enamoured heart. And he was right. His distinguished appearance, his imperious gestures, the richness of his apparel, his numerous followers, the influence of the English name over the Turkish officials, stayed the execution of that fearful crime when about to be perpetrated by Mahometan justice, implacable as destiny.

The sack was opened, and Lord Byron beheld the young girl, pale as a corpse, whom he had loved more than life. There, in the presence of the people, he tore her from her murderers, placed his own bosom as a shield, and declared they should be united in death. The official of the Athenian Government was moved either by compassion or terror. He deferred the execution, and this act of clemency was confirmed by the Turkish Governor of Athens. But solely on the condition that the lovers should remain apart. Banished to Thebes, the unhappy beauty died, if not in the depths of the sea, in a sorrowful seclusion, fading and withering like a flower deprived of its sap. Medwin and Moore, who relate this anecdote, particularly mention her fate. Moore also speaks of the account given by the Marquis of Sligo. But, according to Hobhouse, Byron saved a Turkish woman from death, not because he loved her himself, but because she was beloved by one of his travelling companions or servants. At all events, whether as protector, actor, or witness, these Oriental adventures touched the recesses of his soul, filling him with all that sublime horror expressed in one of his most beautiful poems.

The sojourn of Byron in Constantinople did not inspire the thrilling verses called forth by his stay in Greece. Touched by an English enthusiasm, strong in his anti-Britannic temperament, he places St. Paul's Cathedral above Santa Sophia in Constantinople. His visit to the Dardanelles was remarkable for an event worth relating.

The poet was an experienced swimmer. He had inherited a love for this exercise from his predecessors, for his ancestors were expert mariners. His skill was so great in this accomplishment, that in Venice he was called "the English fish." Moreover, as his chief characteristic was an intense admiration for nature, and his spirit was profoundly pantheistic, when he undressed to plunge into the water he fancied he had returned to the innocent estate of the primitive Eden, free from any defence against the propitious and beneficent elements, immersing himself in the principle of universal life, and absorbing it through all his pores, his heart dilating to an infinity like that of the ocean itself.

The way in which Ovid has illustrated these celebrated scenes is well known. On one side are the shores of Asia, on the other those of Europe. Since the beginning of time two worlds behold each other face to face, draw near as if to embrace, yet scarcely ever arrive at a mutual understanding. One is the world of the Infinite, of religion, of despotism, of caste, of fatality; the other is the world of the finite, of philosophy, of democracy, of liberty. And on these two coasts there were in former times two loving hearts—those of Hero and Leander. The father of Hero, to preserve her from this fatal passion, had confined her in a strong tower erected on one of the banks of the Bosphorus, while Leander was consumed with love on the opposite shore. But love can conquer impossibilities. This passion, which removes all impediments, could easily overcome the abyss between Europe and Asia. When night hung over the Bosphorus, when the navigation of the channel was suspended, when the two continents slumbered, Hero placed a light in the highest part of her tower, and Leander swam, having for a guide that star illumined by love. A thousand times the darkness betrayed him, and the light alarmed him. Often he arrived rigid with cold, exhausted, ready to expire. But a look from Hero, a sigh from her lips, reanimated him. Then there came a fatal night. The traitor sea calmed and slept; Hero's light shone brilliantly through the darkness. Leander swam, expecting a loving word for his reward. When near the shore, the hurricane was unloosed, the waves boiled, the lightning cast its dreadful rays over the spectacle of Nature in torments, over that fury of wild waters. Hero knew that Leander was in peril, and flung herself from her tower into the foaming water. The next day two corpses floated together in the Bosphorus, their nuptial couch, resting in the arms of death.

Lord Byron was anxious to prove if the expedition of Leander was possible. It is scarcely a mile from one coast to the other, but the currents are extremely strong. At first he was unable to conquer the resistance of the water, but the second time he was successful. He was a poet in his imagination, a poet in his genius, a poet in his life; the last and most sublime representative of the artistic ages, replaced by our period of prose and industry.

From all these exciting expeditions Byron drew inspiration for two cantos of " Childe Harold" and "The Giaour." The same uncertainties which prevailed respecting his opinions were common regarding his writings. A bad judge of himself, he preferred the diffuse Commentary of Horace to the melancholy pages of the Odyssey, in which he beheld the human mind afflicted by doubts, bending under the weight of the rich inheritance of ideas, traversing the tombs of the departed, and feeling in those heaps of dry bones the warmth of life. His desires were never satiated. Overflowing the too narrow limits known to our organism at its unfolding, he rushed uneasily in search of new emotions, without examining either their nature or their origin, seeking only to be profoundly touched. Byron might have said, transforming the utterance of Descartes, "I feel, therefore I exist." He did not study ideas, the universe, society, shut up in his chamber, with the cold analysis of Goethe, aided by the experience of other men of genius, and by the labours of former ages—no; he arrived at the knowledge of society by his own passions; of the conception of the universe by his own travels; of comprehension of ideas by his own beliefs; he gave utterance to his sentiments, and became acquainted with Art, not by the inspirations of fancy, but by the actions of his own life. To see, to experience, to suffer or to enjoy, to struggle, to live rather than to think—these were the characteristics of Lord Byron. His belief was in action. He considered poetry, not as a dream hidden in the depths of the soul, but as a bas-relief graven on the bosom of nature. The earth, society, the heavens reflect themselves in the course of this tempestuous life, taking their own hues. An individualist, like the rest of his race, filled with the spleen created by Northern mists, an aristocrat by education and opinions, the necessity of sympathy brought him to the heart of humanity, to the worship of generous and just ideas, as the means of expressing his sentiments and of enjoying them afresh—brought him to convey them in the most sublime language of poetry. Certainly there are observing men, who, like the bird of Juno, have a retina of extraordinary power in every pore. Byron might have said that in every pore he had a beating heart. His songs are the vibration of his nerves, and his ideas are as sensitive as his verses. The human body is like a great tree, which, after its roots, trunk, and branches, terminates towards the heavens with a spherical blossom—the most beautiful of all flowers—called, from its form, the head; from its contents, the cerebrum. Well, the life of Byron ended in the heart. I believe he bore it in his head, and that there was the pendulum, the needle, and the machine, which moved, which announced, which expressed his sentiments.

The most lofty mountains bear traces of the first fire in which the earth burned. See how the granite, notwithstanding its coldness to the touch, appears yet to burn by the sparkling of the quartz—by the black particles resembling powdered coal. And surely as the planet bears marks of the primitive fire, the age bears, for those who comprehend it, traces of the griefs of Byron. His heart, like a sponge pressed upon our brows, has poured forth the flood of its feelings, its aspirations. It has infected us with his sentiments, and baptized us with his blood. There is no child of this age, no one who carefully examines his inmost feelings, who does not perceive in the depths of his conscience some drops of the gall of unbelief, or find in his overburdened heart some unuttered cry of despair. There is, then, no one with whose being some song of Byron is not woven; as in the thirteenth century there were none whose lives were without a fragment of the Inferno of Dante—a scar not the less real if concealed.

Our sorrow arises from the disproportion of the ideal in our own souls with our powers and the time we have to realize it. To do so, an immortal life would be required, like the lifetime of humanity. It would necessitate a universe like the *via lactea*, where there are worlds within worlds, infinite planetary systems, moving in an infusion of *materia cosmica*. And our life is but a span. We are undeveloped insects, hidden in a poor atom of dust! This is the secret of our sorrow, though often concealed from us ; and the greatness of Byron consisted in this—he knew how to complain.

Let us conclude in a few words this period of his life, which comprises his return to London. Desirous of becoming better acquainted with countries and with epochs, and consequently with life, he greatly desired to visit Egypt, wishing to lose himself in that immense necropolis, where the solemn voice of death is always audible, cheered by the smiling hope of immortality. But this intention, which would have extended the horizon of his imagination, could not be carried out for want of money. To the wings or to the feet of genius these morsels of metal are attached, as a perpetual reminder of its cradle of clay and its sepulchre of dust. In vain he wrote to his mother and to his lawyer, begging them to send him supplies. Neither of them could satisfy his necessities. The poet then proposed the sale of Rochdale, in order to obtain a sufficient sum to continue his researches through the great countries of antiquity. The only estate of which he resolved not to deprive himself was Newstead, for there he had deeply suffered. Sorrow is a strange guest. We fly from it, and yet we love it. We have a sort of worship for those Calvaries on which we have been sacrificed. And at the close of life we love even our crown of thorns, the wounds which knowledge has opened in our bosoms, and those which sentiment has pierced in our hearts.

The private affairs of Byron were so embarrassed, that it was not only impossible to him to travel in Egypt, but extremely difficult to continue his sojourn in Greece. A series of loans, contracted to support the first follies of his boyhood, had fallen like a whirlwind upon the remnant of his property. To these succeeded lawsuits, which deepened still more the abyss of his ruin. A lawyer put up for sale the house which Byron so much wished to keep, as the cradle of his thoughts, the nest of his first love, the pantheon of his illusions.

At last he left Greece to return to England. All he brought home from this expedition were some pieces of marble, some Greek skulls found in ancient sepulchres, three servants, two tortoises, and a phial containing juice of the plant which poisoned Socrates. But in reality the western world received something extraordinary from these travels—the poet himself, grown greater by the sight of the monuments of antiquity, from plunging into the life of nature, from the experience of undying sentiments, by the infinite aspiration after great ideas, by the sorrow which is like an unquenchable thirst, like an unsatisfied hunger— a sorrow not the less felt because it is ideal—a sympathy for human suffering, a grief which words cannot utter, but which is as true and incomprehensible as the mystery of death, as the magnetism of inspiration, as the electricity of sentiment, but a trouble without which there never has existed, and never can exist, a true genius. Life is a struggle. Glory is the result of this continual labour and warfare. Genius is like the fire of slow martyrdom. It scorches the flesh, boils the blood, in the furnace of affliction. The heart writhes in the pain caused by the immense disproportion which it finds between the ideal and the real. Everything of yesterday appears lifeless, faded, and melancholy. Everything belonging to the morrow pleases while it is merely pictured on the mind, but disenchants when brought visibly before us. But the sorrow which sympathizes with all troubles, the aspirations which desire benefits for all humanity, the necessity of consoling, of aiding, of encouraging, forces genius to activity. And this necessity of its nature sometimes causes it to produce works of the first order of merit—works which confer immortality on their author. Then he is indeed a genius, and has become a symbol of the age which gave him birth!

And how truly we should welcome the works of those extraordinary persons who have allowed us to enjoy the benefit of their greatness! They have opened before us an enchanted world bathed in the glowing hues of that uncreated light which is called thought. So on leaving the noise and dust of cities, and wandering among groves at the foot of mountains, on the banks of rivers, we say, "I am a man;" if brought into communication with the Infinite by means of a work of art, we say, "I am humanity." Beauty is the moon which lights with melancholy splendour the darkness of the soul. Poetry elevates us, as if with wings, from the busy world of industry we inhabit, to the boundless heaven of the ideal. Blessed be all poets ! Blessed be beauty, inspiration, the arts, the angels which beckon us to the end of our career—the Infinity of the Creator !

FROM his return home till the time of his marriage may be called the golden age of Lord Byron. The first cantos of "Childe Harold," so highly poetical, raised him to the summit of the English Parnassus. He suddenly became the most celebrated poet of his country, and one of the most distinguished men of his age. Those who had so severely criticised him, now exalted him. Society, which had formerly despised him, placed him at its head. Ladies contended for a smile from his lips; editors disputed for a verse from his pen. The most aristocratic saloons were opened to him; there he was surrounded by a court of admirers, and drank deeply the incense of adulation. He was nominated an honorary member of the best clubs in London. The Prince Regent invited him to his banquets, and in the presence of all the English aristocracy pressed the hands which held the immortal lyre. The House of Lords, which had treated him as an obscure youth, gloried in his greatness. And even orthodox Protestant writers, according to Macaulay, were not so strongly irritated with the sublime genius

that undermined the foundations of Christian principles, being dazzled by the splendour of its rays.
Byron, whose chief characteristic was sensitiveness,
drank copious draughts from the golden cup. Disgusted with the world and his passions, he fancied he
could exist in a cloud, like the gods of antiquity, hearing a perpetual hymn in praise of his genius. Flat-
tery, applause, glory, sound sweetly in the ear. At
first the inexperienced heart believes such demonstra-
tions of enthusiasm to be eternal, that the flowers of
victory will not wither. It forgets that there is in
the depths of society, as in the bosom of nature, the
sting of pain to give life an impulse, to spur and to
wound it. It ignores that those souls which have the
most genius contain also most evil and misfortune.
Nature, after having endowed her chosen children with
the grand qualities which lead to glory, obliges them
to merit these gifts by their labours and their struggles. Thus there is always an abyss in the depths of
all genius. A crown of stars cannot be placed upon
the brow, unless there is at the same time a crown of
thorns around the heart. One cannot enter the temple
to inscribe an immortal name, but at the cost of
writing it in the blood of one's veins. Once in an
age a genius appears, labours, struggles, falls, again
and again, dies forgotten in the path to glory, and posterity alone acknowledges his merit, and avenges the
injustice of his epoch. What more? In these posthumous judgments, which are thought to be definitive

and implacable, there are great alternatives and great eclipses. Shakspeare, the most beloved and admired poet of our age, passed through other ages for a barbarian. There was no academical poet, of those who have combed out phrases, almost converting syntax and prosody into the art of the hairdresser, there was no one who did not condemn the taste of the great poet, and who did not believe him only fit to divert the vulgar with his horrors and monstrosities. And yet, without doubt, Shakspeare is now the great glory of England.

Life is full of complications, and for the same reason of insuperable difficulties. And as there are great contrasts in nature, there are also in society opposed forces. By the side of the prophet who announces the future, arises the magistrate who believes his mission is to be the conservation of the present system, and who, as a result of this conviction, persecutes the prophet. In the vicinity of every new thinker there exists an association which believes itself infallible. Beside each reformer is placed the eternal cup of hemlock. It appears that seeds cannot fall upon the earth unless the vase which contains them is broken. Every old prejudice feels itself wounded by a new idea, and hates it accordingly. Every privilege oppresses and calumniates every right which contradicts it. Society is movement; but those who move it fall under the weight of its crushing wheel. Society is renovation; but those who renew it are slain by its old errors. We cannot aspire to be blessed by posterity without being cursed by our contemporaries. Savage beasts do not disappear from a country without having been long and patiently chased. How many bright intelligences fall, how many fail, how many die and depart like shadows in the struggle which is necessary to rid the earth of monsters! The greater number of people believe you are tearing their souls from God if you endeavour to uproot one of the prejudices or errors under whose shadows their fathers lived for ages!

And you, poetic souls, you who come from purer regions crowned with flowers, beating your white wings, clothed with ether; with an immortal song upon your lips and a lyre in your hands, like the first angels who gazed upon chaos at the birth of the universe; you, who bear imagination like a star upon your brows, and who live awe-struck and ecstatic in the contemplation of a world of ideas, which to us weak mortals whose vision cannot penetrate it appears a world of shadows; you cannot enter this sphere of realities without falling into an abyss, without tearing your wings, and wounding your feet with thorns; you cannot descend from the fire in which you have been moulded to the coldness of our shades, unless the dew of your tears is frozen in their fall, and the transparent vase of your hearts is broken by the hailstones.

Without doubt, the sorrow of sorrows consists in the existing disproportion between the ideas of goodness, of beauty, and of justice, and the realities of the world. The only means of lightening this sorrow, is to labour for the modification of the reality; to chisel and shape the world, as it were, as the sculptor chisels a statue till it approaches his conception, and to live and die in the assured belief that this work will never be interrupted, but that it will be continued by other hands.

Every poet feels that which is called in common language home sickness—the sorrow of exile, the longing after things higher and holier. Every great poet is like an exiled angel. Byron felt, more than any other, this immense, this infinite regret. That which is in Virgil, in Petrarch, in Bellini, in Raphael, a gentle melancholy, sweet and unruffled as moonlight, is in Calderon, in Cervantes, in Shakspeare, in Michael Angelo, in Dante, and in Byron an abandonment of grief, which borders on despair, like the roaring of a hurricane above the foam of the ocean. Many men of genius console themselves by unfolding their souls in their works and writings. Michael Angelo secluded himself for many years, and peopled the vaulted roof of the Sistine Chapel with prophets, with sibyls, and with sublime Titans. Each of these figures cost him the most profound emotion. All of them are the produce of his soul's agony. Their positions show them to be beyond the limits conceded to ordinary works of art. I feel sure that the nervous excitement of the great artist was soothed and comforted in the midst of these masterpieces—his immortal works. But

Byron sought for his consolation in real life, in the world, in the same cup from whence flowed his trouble. And none of the women he met responded to his cherished ideas.

The Countess Guiccioli approached in some degree the women of his imagination. None of his friends loved him with the sentiment of exaltation which in Byron himself amounted even to hero-worship. His orgies never satisfied the fever of ideal pleasure which existed in the chaos of his mind. None of his travels allayed his thirst for knowledge, or slaked his desire to travel on to Infinity. Among the waves of the ocean and the stars of heaven, across the coast of Spain, embrowned by the rays of our splendid sun ; in the shadows of the Giralda, and beside the laurels of the Alcazar of Seville ; on the summit of Mount Vesuvius ; upon the coasts of the Adriatic Islands, and those of the Grecian Archipelago ; by the shores of the Bosphorus, and on the ruins of ancient Rome ; in the silent nights of Athens, when the silvery moonlight bathes with her melancholy splendour the marbles of antiquity, those ivy-twined columns, above which wave the palm-trees, stirred by the breezes of the Ægean Sea—in all those great theatres of art and of history, everywhere in the world, he always found the disgust which he bore in his own soul. The sea falls like a drop of gall, and the earth like an atom of powder, into the unfathomable abyss of desire. Hence human life—this life full of infinite aspirations—is not like the circle which a child produces by throwing a stone into a calm lake, but resembles the infinite system of worlds, which the Almighty called forth in the immensity of space by his creative fiat. Human life is infinite. From the moment in which we become convinced of this truth we compare the deeds which are within our limited reach, and are possible, with the desires and aspirations in our own minds, which are impossible for us to realize; thoughts which flash from time to time like mystic flames in the eternity of the future, which stretches to the bosom of the Deity.

Lord Byron had painful struggles with his present life. On the 14th of June, 1811, he returned to London, much invigorated by his travels. Shortly after he found in Mr. Murray a publisher, who has united his own name with that of the poet. At this period life seemed to smile upon him. But, as if an evil genius pursued him, almost all the friends for whom he felt sincere affection died, following each other in quick succession. Life is full of strange mysteries. Each cradle is placed upon a heap of tombs. Our very existence is the consequence of a long series of skeletons lost in the depths of the earth, like the roots of a tree. To trace back our genealogy is to count a pile of bones. And doubtless there is a time in our lives in which innocence is the atmosphere of the soul, and the world is then a paradise. We seem to have so much time before us that the sensible horizon of our individual existence is almost confounded with the vastness of eternity. Not only do we ignore the probability of our own death, but we endow those we love with immortality ; though the devouring monster is ever present, striking down and rending asunder, suspended over us, like a spider among flies. We think death is impossible. But one day, in the spring-tide of our life, the blossom of our youth, we are overwhelmed by the death of some beloved companion ; the mother from whose sacred breast we received the stream of life, the friend with whom we shared our joys and sorrows. This first sad experience wounds us to the soul, and goes to the depths of our hearts.

In the presence of a corpse we are surprised at the facility with which human beings die. And that which is the most strange to us is the continuation of our own life, after the extinction of that life without which we thought it impossible for us to exist! But though we do not die instantly in those first hours of supreme sorrow, we begin to die. With the first beloved dead we give a portion of our hearts into the jaws of death. Afterwards, one by one, beings who are dear to us fall into the earth already moistened with our tears, like dry leaves in the autumn. And not only do we bury our affections, our friends, our mothers, our beloved, but we also lay in the grave our hopes and our illusions. And when death comes to us, we are like withered and leafless trees, on which love sometimes places a nest as a promise of the continuation of life through future generations.

The first blow which Lord Byron received was caused by the death of his mother. Though not sufficiently careful as to the education of her son, often too violent in temper, *she was his mother!* For a long time the proud lady was aware of her approaching death, but grieved at the prospect of departure without seeing her son. How unfortunate are those who have not received the last look of their dying mother, that pale and sad ray of the sun as he sets in the west, often full of the counsels of virtue and promises of immortality! If, in the moment of committing an evil action or of cherishing a wicked thought, we remembered the holy look which asked of us an imitation of a mother's virtues and of her love, and expressed a hope of an untroubled future, if we remembered this treasure of the soul, we should hold it pure and unsullied.

To understand the worth of virtue, we must see a virtuous mother die in divine serenity. To believe in immortality, we must contemplate death. The death of Lord Byron's mother was violent as her own character. She was already suffering, when a cabinet-maker presented her a very long account for alterations made in her house. She fell into a passion, which ended in a fit of apoplexy, and killed her like a thunderbolt. The mother and son did not meet in this last hour. When the latter arrived, he sank

down motionless at the head of her coffin. A bitter
sob burst from his heart, soon repressed by his indomitable will. The young poet followed the custom
of southern peoples, who do not usually accompany
the bodies of their friends to the grave, like the French
and English. When the body had been brought from
the house, he invited one of his servants to hold with
him a wager and boxing match, so common at that
time in England. He endeavoured by these bodily
exercises to chase the gloomy thoughts which oppressed
him ; but soon, overcome by mental exhaustion, and
unable to sustain his feigned serenity, he shut himself up in his chamber, and gave way to a burst of
tears.

The links of life's chain break easily. The three
most beloved friends of his childhood died shortly
afterwards. The one for whom Byron mourned the
most was Edleston, a chorister of Cambridge, a youth
of almost angelic voice and beauty, of whom, from his
earliest years, it was predicted he would be in the world
but a passing apparition, like a flower or a butterfly.

The grief of the poet was so violent that he made his
will, thinking he could not possibly outlive the rude
attacks of destiny. This testament, written by his own
hand, was short and tragic. He divided his fortune
among his legitimate heirs. He laid upon them a solemn
obligation to give him a modest and private funeral in
the garden at Newstead, but without in any way dis-
turbing the body of his dog, which was buried there.

His nerves seemed to snap like the chords of a harp when strained unduly. He passed his days in a languor which resembled death, and his nights in a state of excitement bordering on insanity. His desolated hearth was no refuge, he had no comfort in friendship —his friends had departed: no relief in his own imagination, which was more sad than a sepulchre. The woman he had loved was wedded to another. Her son, which should have belonged to him, tortured him with his caresses, and recalled the happier lot of his rival. The heavens seemed to frown upon him, the earth on which he walked was a desert, his thoughts were a tempest, his heart a bleeding wound. Then, desperate from sorrow, and demanding, like Job, the cause of so many incomprehensible evils, he resolved to give himself to the world and its vices, and he entered anew into society with curses on his lips, but with tenderness in his heart.

The years 1812, 1813, and 1814 were the three years of Lord Byron's greatest fame. Undoubtedly this was the most dramatic portion of his existence, and also the most unknown. The memoirs, which the poet wrote in a style superior even to his verses, if we can judge by some remaining fragments, those sketches which would have been one of the most faithful historic testimonies of the times, have disappeared through the prudery of the English aristocracy, who were there painted nude, according to the method of great artists. Once Lord Byron was on the point of fighting a duel with Moore, the Irish poet, but the affair ended in a banquet, and in a lasting friendship between the two. This friendship was so real in the heart of Byron, that he gave up his memoirs to Moore. But Moore, who was crafty and cold-hearted, incapable of telling a truth, and desirous to frequent high society, becoming the possessor of tragic and comic descriptions of ladies of rank, and thinking it unwise to reveal their secrets, broke the mirror in which posterity could have seen the face of the great poet and of his epoch. Consequently, we are without the key to many events which occurred at this period, to which reference is often made, but of which comparatively little is known.

In 1812 Lord Byron went to live in No. 8, St. James's Street—a central part of London. He was then in the zenith of his fame, in all the pride of youth and manly beauty, in the fulness of his mental vigour, in which his lips scattered oracles, his imperious glances magnetized those before him. The man bore candour stamped upon his features. His eyes of a rare brilliancy and of an undefinable colour, seemed to possess an immortal brightness. Whatever the sculptor has chiselled in order to express genius, either before or after his time, appeared in Byron, from the Apollo Belvedere to the bust of Napoleon by Canova. I well remember the day in which I first saw that bust on one of the tables of the wonderful Palazzo Pitti in Florence. The bust is not a portrait, but an apotheosis. The sculptor saw the Napoleon of Manzoni with genius, glory, heroism, immortality, inspiration on his brow, the world at his feet, two ages striving beside him, and crowning his temples with lightning. The sculptors of the heroic times of the Roman Empire thus represented the Cæsars, when they desired to elevate them to the altars of immortality. That is the head of a god, one says on looking at the bust. At first sight I thought, from its likeness, it was the head of Byron. Perhaps it would be impossible to paint or model genius, without copying the features of that truly Apollo-like physiognomy over which inspiration has flung sublimity.

The sap of youthful genius burst forth in writings and discourses. Lord Byron entered the House of Peers once more, and delivered three speeches. In all of them he advocated that supremely righteous cause—the cause of the oppressed. Never can human language—that gift of gifts—be so gloriously employed, as when consecrated to the cause of justice. There is no music in nature to be compared to that of speech, each of whose phases is an idea, and each of whose ideas may be the seed of a new world. To sully it with a sophism is an error, to degrade it by adulation is a crime. Eloquence is the angel's trumpet which calls down the judgment of God upon tyrants, and unfolds the infinite joys of a new existence.

Lord Byron possessed all the faculties essential to an orator—sensibility, imagination, ideas, a flexible voice which responded to the various tones of thought, a flow of words, clear notions of justice. He failed only in stability of purpose. His uneasy genius lifted him to other heights of art, in which his too highly-developed individuality could expand itself in all directions without obstacle. To ascend was for him a necessity. His aspiring soul felt itself too near the earth in the senate, but in poetry it unrolled itself to the full. And the three discourses which remain to us, without being extraordinary, make us lament that his evil fortune drove him from London, and consequently from the British Parliament, before he had time to give greater play to his talents. His first speech was made against a cruel law which it had been proposed to enact against operatives, who, harassed by want, destroyed the new machines which kept them out of employment. His second speech was in support of Catholic Emancipation, Catholics being then persecuted by Protestant intolerance. The third was to complain to Parliament on behalf of a Major Cartwright, chief of the league for parliamentary reform, molested by the police on account of his demands—a yearly Parliament and a vote for all male citizens. So that in all the questions which so long troubled England, in the problem of labour, in the emancipation of the Catholics (the termination of which was due to the firmness of Gladstone), and in electoral reform, Byron has left traces of his intelligence, as a constant defender of the cause of liberty.

The world drew him into its vortex, and tempted him with its passions. Society had an extraordinary admiration for his poetry, but its seductive pleasures besieged him so continually as scarce to leave him time to write a new poem. Society resembles those people who, when admiring the beauty of a rose, or enjoying its odour, tear it from the stalk. It is not aware that all great vocations necessitate a continual and almost exclusive culture. The conclusion of " Childe Harold" made an extraordinary sensation. England felt his sadness in that sublime lament, his adventurous genius in that Odyssey of the West to the East of Europe, his national pride in those cantos consecrated to the war under Napoleon, and the eyes of the country were turned on that gigantic soul, which, notwithstanding its instability, ever remembered great sacrifices, and felt a loving sympathy for the heroic deeds of history. Around him arose a tempest of enthusiasm. The people of England all but suffocated their idol. Lord Byron could scarcely breathe under that abundant rain of flowers. There was no society, no saloon, that did not desire his presence ; no celebrated man nor woman who did not seek his friendship. Even those he had so severely criticised in his satires not only freely forgave them, but were proud of the wounds made by the lance of the youthful god of poetry.

The year 1813 was one continued triumph. In it he saw arise, as in a dream, the temple of his glory, and beheld the first of nations at his feet, offering him with transport the crown of genius!

And to all this he felt antipathy. Glory was bitterness to him, enthusiasm vanity, the passions called forth among these laurel pathways were venomous. His soul was devoured by this disgust of reality, against which he had but one refuge—the ideal. And being naturally practical and loyal, he struck the earth with his feet, looking for the flowing of its joys. The supreme joy for really great souls is the ecstatic contemplation of one particular idea, and their labour is a daily effort to realize the idea. But in the changeful mind of Byron ideas were vacillating flames, which were kindled or extinguished by his stormy passions. The scepticism which belonged to his character continually overturned his resolutions. He had no desire to cultivate that serene and equal happiness which constitutes the real charm of life. For friendship it was too late; and besides, all the friends of his childhood had departed. For marriage it was rather too early; and then no woman attracted him to the point of giving her his life. "Alas!" he exclaimed, "we cannot live with women any more than we can live without them." Doubt was the serpent he bore entwined about his heart, and which mingled poison with all his pleasures. To chase away this chronic malady he imagined a woman of superhuman beauty and goodness, in whose

society his weary soul could find repose. But these
aspirations were deceitful, and falsehood disgusted
him. After disenchantment, he returned to life's
reality, and went to the house of a married friend,
happy in wife and children, to see if he could learn,
as in a practical school, domestic happiness. He knew
not the charm that may be found in common characters, when he fancied he could learn practical lessons
of domestic felicity. Where among the world's pathways could he encounter the angel of his dreams?
In what society could he find rest from the stormy
passions which oppressed him? What could remove
the dark cloud which covered him? What safeguard
against the lightning of these sudden inspirations
which flashed through his brain, exhausting his nerves,
and making them tremble in mortal agony? What
specific against genius, that epilepsy of the soul?
On what shore unload this weary weight of human
greatness? Byron's malady was immortal. If he
has not found in another and happier world the infinity, the eternal beauty, for which here he longed
so vainly, his soul still suffers the inexhaustible thirst
which consumed it, and that was at once his glory and
his torment.

Requited affection can alone make the happiness of
a poet. Love balances the faculties, calms the passions, administers the opium of forgetfulness against
adversity, and is an ecstacy which reduces life to one
point—the object beloved—in whom centres the uni-

verse. Scepticism no longer torments us ; we have a belief. Human ingratitude avails nothing, for we have one friendship. Life's reality no more affrights us ; it is changed into paradise in the presence of her whom we love. Death loses all his terrors if she but share our grave. Two souls have become united, and *one* heaven is created.

Such was the happiness which Byron sought. But he failed to find it, perhaps because love was like an electric shock to his ardent nature, and not a mild and lasting splendour. He had some passing attachments. He had a friendship with Madame de Staël, an affection less of the heart than of the mind, produced by the greatness of two souls which approached without understanding each other, and that enjoyed each other's society without love.

But two women left ineffaceable traces in his memory. Two passions governed his destiny ; one unlawful, the other legitimate ; both were unfortunate, and the causes of all his other misfortunes. Lady Caroline Lamb was his first evil genius. A daughter of one of the principal families in England, of literary tastes, nervous temperament, and exalted imagination ; a course of romantic reading and a poetic enthusiasm had excited her passions, and given her an intense desire for adventure. An error of this nature is a poisoned stream, which overflows the boundary line between the world of poetry and the world of reality. This lady was a heroine of romance. The husband her parents had given her was unable to subdue these exaltations of a rash fancy, which resembled flaming skyrockets in the midst of the prosaic realities of life. Nevertheless, the marriage was at first happy. This arose partly from mutual attachment, and partly because nothing had occurred to kindle the imagination of Caroline; certainly her days passed in the tranquillity of domestic content. The young lady read her writings to an intelligent company assembled in her spacious library; and these occupations filled up her existence, and the applause she received from her audience satisfied her ambition, so that at this time there was no happier marriage in London.

But one evening Caroline and Lord Byron met at the house of Lady Jersey. The romantic young woman was deeply struck by the poet. She, who had so often described love in her poems, had never felt its fever till that unhappy moment. The fanciful creations of her novels condensed into a passion which invaded her whole soul and existence. The powerful magnetism which the extraordinary genius of the man possessed like a talisman, invincibly attracted her. The wings of her soul were bound to the heart of Byron. And from that hour there remained for her no more art or poetry; no world, no heaven, no ideas, no life; nothing but love! He had not enticed, but he had fascinated her. Without pausing or reflecting, she drew towards that guilty passion in whose intricate mazes she was to leave happiness, life, and honour. The world offered her numerous attractions, wealth laid its treasures at her feet, society respected her, literature gave her its honey and not its aloes; marriage its holy serenity; three lovely children the affection which should delight the heart of a mother; and she forgot all for her insane passion. She saw nothing, remembered nothing, sustained no battle with her own conscience, thought not of remorse; honour and modesty fled, scorched by the lightning blast fallen from a tranquil heaven. Caroline believed that evening that from all eternity she and Byron had been predestined for each other, and that it was as natural for her to give him her heart as for an inert body to be drawn to its centre of gravity.

Fatalism always tries to excuse the will before the conscience. But not content with betraying her feelings to her lover, she betrayed them to the world. It was a suicide of honour, of which we have no similar record. The name of her husband and the name of her family, the love of her children, the purest instincts of her nature, were all flung into the flames of that ruinous and devouring passion which, alike forgetful of reason and religion, mocked at the voice of conscience in its madness, and feared not the remorse of the future.

For some time Byron naturally responded to so much devotion, and was unable to extricate himself from the web woven around him. But he soon became indifferent, and unable to return so much affection. His passion—if he ever felt it—soon perished, consumed in the flame, like the delicate wings of a butterfly. It is difficult to balance the temperature of two hearts when one of them burns with an inexhaustible flame. The less loving melts like ice before the devotion it can neither comprehend nor return, and the eternal punishment of a continually changing fancy is, that no woman can long trust the man who follows all women. No pure passion can find shelter in a heart capable of admitting grosser sentiments. And Lord Byron was at that period of his life too much possessed by the spirit of adventure to be willing to give himself up to the worship of one woman, even though she loved him to excess.

Caroline thought that having sacrificed family, husband, children, and name at the feet of her idol, she would gain from his feelings of justice that which she scarcely hoped from his affection. Society was shocked and indignant. The English nobility might have forgiven the wrong, but they could never pardon the scandal.* The affair for a time attracted Lord Byron. Caroline disguised herself as a valet, and went to his house, saying she was the bearer of a letter. But in this strange attire Byron immediately recognised her.

---

* Señor Castelar is evidently not aware that Lady Caroline Lamb was considered of unsound mind, and that during the latter part of her life she was never suffered to be without an attendant, who was in reality a keeper.

She was sadly deceived in thinking she could fix his wandering fancy. For a person of his distinct individuality, impatient of any yoke, and soon weary of pleasure, the intense devotion which she lavished upon him became like a chain which tortured and oppressed him. She could not fix that fickle nature which changed as the shadows upon a lake, those desires which were the sport of each passing wind. She overwhelmed him with letters, even making appointments at her own house when her husband was in London. On these occasions, though always in danger of discovery, she wept, reproached, and expostulated. During one of these scenes her husband knocked at the door. Alarmed beyond measure, the eccentricity natural to Byron's character suggested an expedient, which proved successful. He drew a dagger, and brandished it in his right hand, while in the left he snatched up a jewel-case and rushed out, in danger of being taken by the police, and appearing in a court of justice as a burglar. But in the confusion of this tragi-comedy he left the lady in a nervous attack, flinging herself against the furniture, while a letter with his name and address fell from his pocket.

This state of things could not continue. Lord Byron would have gone through the greatest dangers for a woman he loved, but not for one to whom he was indifferent. When weary of pleasure, he took refuge in morality. He wrote angry letters, reminding Caroline of her duties of wife and mother. He spoke of the perils they both ran through her imprudence, and the necessity of speedily putting an end to so unpleasant a situation. Caroline believed herself the mistress of his heart, and defended her property with the ardour natural to her character. She pursued him everywhere, though acquainted with his infidelity. On one occasion he received a lady in his house. She had scarcely entered when a postilion appeared at the door, who, rapidly removing the disguise, showed herself to be Caroline. Byron describes this event in the story of Faublas.

Such a state of affairs was necessarily wretched. Both suffered in the struggle, he to disentangle himself from so fatal a passion, she to retain him in her power. Caroline spared no arts or efforts to secure the affections, or at least the sympathy, of the man to whom she had so weakly sacrificed her reputation. One evening she was asked to dance in one of the most brilliant assemblies of London. Blushing deeply, she turned timidly to ask the permission of the poet. She must have remembered the lament in which, in one of his earlier verses, he complained of the profane arms which encircled in the gay waltz the waist of his Mary. But Byron answered rudely, that it was useless to ask permission of one who had neither the right nor the desire to exercise any influence over her. Then Caroline flew into a passion of tears, utterly forgetful of the numerous company which surrounded them. The ill-natured world was much amused at the absurd position of the great poet, pursued by so insane a passion. Meanwhile, many adventurers approached the forsaken and disdained lady, offering her love and vengeance. To one of them Caroline said she did not love him, but she promised him her gratitude and friendship if he would kill Lord Byron in a duel.

In all this he saw but the exaltation of a disordered fancy; but it was really the expression of a devoted affection. These follies were proofs of love, proofs of jealousy, proofs that her love bordered on madness. One day, her agitation being insupportable, she resolved to return to the house of the poet, to throw herself at his feet, to bathe his hands in her tears, to ask from him love or death, which she feared less if coming from him than the prolonged martyrdom she was suffering. She entered his house, the spot which she would have been content to make her universe, provided she could have kept him by her side. There was no one there. Caroline felt a sad pleasure in looking over the saloon, and examined the furniture with the minuteness with which passionate souls dwell on every object that feeds their sorrow. She reclined on the cushions where Byron had reposed. She threw herself into his accustomed chair. She saw upon a table the favourite book of her former lover. Touched by her fond recollections, intoxicated by the aroma which exhaled from those beloved pages, she took a pencil, kissed it, moistened it with her tears, and traced upon the book this supplication of her broken heart, " *Remember me!* "

Byron was not moved even by this touching appeal, which he considered a threat. He angrily took his pen and wrote these words, which he sent her under an envelope : " Remember you ! remember you ! Until the waters of Lethe have flowed over the burning torrent of your existence, shame and remorse will cry in your ears, and pursue you with the delirium of fever. Remember you ! Do not doubt it, I will remember ! And your husband will also remember you. Neither of us can ever forget you. To him you have been an unfaithful wife, and to me, a devil."

These were cruel and terrible words. Caroline felt deeply wounded, and swore to be avenged. Her love changed into hatred. Not being able to use a sword, she took up her pen. Filling her ink-bottle with venom, she poured it on the name of Byron. She revealed her own shame to the world. She poured out her guilty heart to society, as Agrippina bared her breast when the emissaries of her son were sent to murder her. Society fled from her in disgust, fled in order to avoid the poison which had taken possession of her soul. She called her book of vengeance " Glenarvon," and in it she described Lord Byron as the Genius of Evil, with all the seduction and treachery of the serpent which deceived the first woman. But in her case Byron was not the seducer; he was the seduced.

Caroline was guilty, but she dearly suffered for her offence. Grown old in her youth, miserable in her splendid home; despised by the society in which she had been admired; buried alive with a husband who was her judge, and with children who were her punishment; wretched in the possession of her useless riches, degraded even by her own literary works, in which she more and more proclaimed her own dishonour; in affliction, but without the solace of sympathy; for life a fever, for consolation the recollection of past happiness, which was her present torment; for the future, the contempt of the world and the stings of conscience; for her only hope, death and forgetfulness; a moral evil, followed by a physical infirmity; these emotions plunged her in a deplorable languor and debility, from which she never wholly recovered.

One day the great poet, whom she had described as a criminal, died in Greece the death of a hero. By his last desire his ashes were placed in the ungrateful country which had not sufficiently honoured his genius while living. Caroline happened to be at her window, enjoying the sunshine. The same light which beamed upon her gilded the coffin of him who once loved its brightness. In fact, at that moment there passed along the road, before the door and the window where Caroline was standing—going to the eternal repose—the bones of Byron: those bones which, when animated with life, had brought so much trouble to the solitary mourner. The coffin was borne in a hearse, covered with a funeral pall; a dog followed the hearse, howling piteously. Caroline uttered a heart-rending cry, and fell to the ground insensible. Her friends raised her, and placed her in bed, from which she never arose. From that bed she passed to the grave.

The genius and the beauty of Byron were fatal gifts for himself. These endowments, which would have been for other men a continual source of happiness, were for him but the cause of constant sorrow. He compared himself to his grandfather, who, being a great traveller, never embarked without seeing the elements unchained, and being exposed to the fury of a tempest. So Byron never gained a heart without afflicting it and himself. All the sweetness of his rich fancy turned to bitterness at the presence of reality. Aloes were mingled in his cup, and there was a sort of fatality in his life, so that his affections seemed less to comfort than to wither their object. He was like one of those Greek heroes—youthful, resplendent, as skilful with the sword as with the lyre—beloved by a beautiful woman, conqueror alike in sports as in battles; and yet condemned from the cradle by a cruel destiny to the infernal deities. Against this tragic fatality of his existence there was but one remedy; to renounce a life of adventure, and to enter into the conditions of domestic life, to make for himself a home sheltered from the tempest of passion, to unite himself to a woman whom he should love tenderly and tranquilly, with that serene, calm affection under whose wings alone marriage can be happy.

Without doubt, this idea of marriage was one which, had it been successfully carried out, would have saved Lord Byron. He arrived at it from a thoughtful study of his past life, and from the imperious promptings of his conscience. At last he found the woman to whom he was to resign his destiny. The only daughter of a distinguished family, educated with Puritanic strictness, learned in metaphysics and in mathematics, cold in temperament, proud of her aristocratic name and of her lofty virtues, encompassed by English customs and the social laws of her time, as in her centre of gravity, capable of exalting the etiquette of society to a dogma as imperious and inscrutable as that of the Koran—she was at the same time incapable of comprehending Byron, or of calming his excitable nature caressingly, for to do so would have disturbed her implacable serenity, and she refused to enter even for a moment into the whirlwinds of genius.

Her name was Miss Milbanke; young and pureminded, she had dared to protest against the irregular and stormy passions which inspired " Childe Harold," in verses which passed from hand to hand, and which excited Lord Byron's fatal curiosity. A lark from her humble nest boldly defied the lordly eagle, which held the clouds in his talons, the lightning, like dry straws under his wings, infinite space like a crown upon his head, and the sun in his retina. The poet wished to become acquainted with this bird of ill omen, which scattered mistrust into the hearts of his numerous admirers. He heard she was expected at one of Lady Strafford's receptions, and he went there to see her. At the entrance of the house he stumbled, and was near falling. A Roman, under such circumstances, would have returned home. He went in and saw the young lady very simply attired, seated on a sofa, with a candid and modest countenance. Her features, though somewhat irregular, were delicate; her figure was graceful and flexible, her manner soft and unpretending; affording a contrast to the artificial manners of English society at that period.

Lord Byron possessed that greatest quality of genius—frankness. Miss Milbanke had the peculiarity often seen in the feeble—craftiness. The poet went nearly as far as a declaration. The lady nearly to one of those negatives which excite the passions by not depriving them of hope, and which gave the semblance of love to his attentions, and to her refined coquetry a certain victory. A year passed away thus, in doubt and vacillation between the unconquerable aspirations of his nature, which led him to take part in the world's battles, and the stern counsels of his conscience, which beckoned him to the tranquillity of the fireside. It is impossible to say how much this sublime satyr wished to experience all sensations; to swallow life at one draught; to twine himself like a gigantic serpent around the trunk of the tree of the universe, from the roots to the topmost branches; to exhaust mind and spirit; to pass at one bound to the highest step of the infinite ladder of humanity; to lose himself in eternity; to plunge himself in the unfathomable ocean. And yet he shrunk terrified from reality, would weep like a child, was contented to have no other friend than a dog; for all his happiness the small heart of an ordinary woman, and with his brilliant imagination, with his conscience, his feelings, his aspirations, he was the sport of destiny. But he could not thus crush his heart and brain with impunity, without wounding them, and staining them and himself with his own blood.

To Lord Byron may be justly applied these words of Emerson: "The story of Thor, who was condemned to drink from the horn of Asgard, to wrestle with an old woman, and to run with the swift-footed Lok, and the result was that he drank the ocean, wrestled with time, and ran with thought; this story represents those among us who are constrained to measure ourselves in the midst of apparent weakness, with the supreme energies of nature."

At last Lord Byron resolved to marry. His choice fell upon the young Puritan, whom the aristocratic and monarchical society of London counted among its idols. The simple and modest young girl he had first met at the house of Lady Strafford was to be his bride. Although heiress to a large fortune, at that time she was not rich; and this was, in his eyes, an attraction. Besides, she belonged to the circle distinguished for its aristocratic and Protestant principles, which was offended with his Jacobinism, and for this reason he wished to convert her. Because she was naturally of an imperious temper, Lord Byron determined to conquer her. Because she had written a sort of anti-Byron, he desired to demonstrate that the young Tory was like Frederick of Prussia, who wrote an anti-Machiavel and practised Machiavelianism. Fatal error! Instead of entering the married state with real views of life, he was like one walking in his sleep, in danger of stumbling and of falling into a bottomless abyss. It was in the month of September, 1814, that he wrote a letter asking the hand of Miss Milbanke. Just as he had finished it, one of his friends entered, who had before expressed himself opposed to the marriage ; he read the letter, and it appeared to him so beautifully written, that he could not bear to see such a perfect composition wasted, and without object. The letter was, therefore, sent to its destination ! Five days of great anxiety passed, and on the 20th of September the Muse of anti-Byronism promised her hand to the poet. Two letters were sent to him, one to his country seat, and the other to London. He became almost mad from excitement and enthusiasm. Already he believed her the mother of future Gracchi. His exalted fancy endowed her with all possible virtues. He was proud to be preferred before six other suitors. And in his triumph he only regretted that he did not better deserve so much happiness.

What a wonderful flexibility there was in his soul! In childhood he seemed a worn-out and useless being, from the excess of sentiment ; and in his maturity he was like a youth, who for the first time dreams of the joys of love. He paid without regret a wager of a hundred and fifty pounds, which he had laid that he would never marry. He gravely discussed the question of his wedding suit—as to whether he should wear a black coat or a blue one. The second of January, 1815, was the date fixed for the marriage. One day one of his gardeners saw him digging in the garden, wearing the ring which had united his parents in that unhappy marriage of which he was the issue. The poet kept it for his own wedding, which was still more unfortunate. He rose on his marriage morning in much depression of spirits. To pass the time, he sought, according to his custom, a refuge from trouble in the arms of Mother Nature, and took a long walk in one of those English woods, at this season leafless, cold, and melancholy as death. The day was harsh and unpleasant. Mists hung over the earth and upon his soul. Perhaps in those moments he thought that, like Plato, like Newton, like Michael Angelo, like Calderon, he belonged to the race of the great, solitary sons of earth, of those who, remaining single, are wedded only with the ideal, and from this spiritual union spring their children, that is to say—their immortal works; fruitful offspring, bringing forth generations of souls progressing with the times. Perhaps no one else could comprehend and feel this immense power of mind, after the bitterness of a life of pleasure, which had left him but the sad memories of passing friendships and of passions rapid as lightning.

Lord Byron's love was an ardour of the brain. How often he had met real enchantment, how often he had seen exquisite beauty, on those shores, that like a choir of sirens bathe in the blue waters of the Mediterranean; and true love in those interminable horizons of the south, where the play of light produces changes that appear reflections, and golden clouds resplendent in bright illusions! How often he felt happy in those nights, when the eyes of the women under their black eyelashes shone like the stars of heaven amongst the shadows! A voice from Heaven should then have warned him, that he was flinging himself into life's cold realities, and that the home he so fondly desired would become the winding-sheet of his heart. Some old memory must have brought before him the happy past—the time when on the hill crowned with huge trees he saw the heavens reflected in his Mary's eyes—she who was afterwards the wife of another but always the bride of his soul! . Perhaps these reflections taught him that happiness, when once lost is never regained, and that true love is never repeated in a lifetime. Sometimes in hasty confusion he would see the shades of other women, telling him that one woman was destined to avenge the wrongs of many others.

However, at the hour appointed he went to the church, and repeated his marriage vows before God. When he uttered the eternal YES, he trembled, and his limbs almost sunk under him. But he quickly suppressed all appearance of emotion under an air of stoical indifference. The one, however, really impassible was his bride. The only emotion evident in that ceremony, was the audible sobbing of Byron's mother-in-law. When the hour of departure arrived, the bridegroom was so absent, that, contrary to all English ceremonial on such occasions, he addressed his wife by her family name. Even at first he found her a sort of exacting mistress—as if the shadow of his mother-in-law had been prolonged till it entered his home, and filled his married life with bitterness.

After a month had expired, Lord Byron discovered that he did not love his wife, but that he still esteemed her. Doubtless he waited in hope, trusting that love would come with the birth of an heir. They removed to London, where a large expenditure was required to support the luxury which the pair conceived necessary to their position. These expenses greatly embarrassed him; he was already oppressed by debt, and he became still more hopelessly entangled. His creditors, who had rejoiced to see their debtor married to a wealthy heiress, became importunate when they were made aware that the marriage served but to increase his debts, instead of paying them. In the house of a young English lady of rank—rich and accustomed to luxuries and splendours, that in the other parts of Europe belong only to the throne —bailiffs entered with an order to seize even the nuptial bed. Moreover, the incompatibility of temper which existed between them from the first, soon became visible in this unpremeditated union, for such it was, notwithstanding the long preparation.

Lady Byron had little capacity to govern, and much to be governed. Her regular life and habits openly clashed with the irregularities of her husband. She was offended if he was not present at the solemn hour of *tea;* she was in despair because he did not eat after the English fashion; she kept the books and the library under lock and key; she could not endure his being awake while she slept, nor that he should sleep while she was waking. The light reflected from his eyes when possessed by inspiration terrified her like the glance of a tiger. The incoherent words which issued from his lips in the hours in which he composed his poems, filled her with the impression that he was insane. The different political opinions held by them as to the future of human society, widened the gulf between them. The contempt which Lord Byron expressed for British etiquette appeared to the education and to the temperament of his wife little short of sacrilege. His blunt sayings in the midst of such formality shocked and irritated her. She calculated all her words and actions, and he improvised his own; she was an advanced scholar in mathematics; he was a great master of poetry—and naturally the two could not harmonize. Her virtue, severe but cold, could not consent to the moral disorder, nor to the immoral actions described by the poet. She felt she had fallen from the unalterable serenity and dignity of her existence into chaos. Her terror went so far that she consulted lawyers and doctors, instructing them to put searching questions to her husband, in order to be enabled to confine him to a lunatic asylum, though he deserved an Olympus. Her natural reserve and his natural frankness were the occasion of continual jarring. Some of the later adventures of Byron, which passed like shadows across her horizon, drove her to desperation. At last, feeling herself about to become a mother, and cruelly choosing that moment of hope and love—that period in which life has some value and some definite purpose, in which the heart expands with an unknown and pure affection, in which a woman becomes the sanctuary of a new existence— she chose that time of transfiguration to contrive her criminal project of abandoning her husband!

She gave birth to a daughter, and was scarcely recovered when she expressed a wish to visit her parents. Lord Byron consented, and when she had arrived at her father's house she wrote him a letter, to say that her departure was a flight and not a visit, and that they were separated for ever before God and men.

It is not possible to express the indignation with which England regarded her illustrious son. History has no example of similar anger. All the reputations he had wounded, all the jealousies he had sown with his genius, all the old customs he had scorched and ridiculed with his satire, all the privileges he had combated with his eloquence—the Protestant clergy, the British aristocracy, private society, literary men, the Ministers, the Court, the people, so easily deceived; in fine, all English prejudices arose against Lord Byron like so many vipers. The doors of all classes of society were closed against him. The hands which had woven him crowns now recoiled from his touch, as if fearing to be burned with some poison. The street boys flung mud upon him. In the theatres he was hissed. The most obscene libels attributed to him most shameful vices. The daily papers represented him with horrible caricature. Fathers hid their daughters from his basilisk glances. Women, so jealous of the prerogatives of their sex, were dismayed on seeing such a monster. To the eyes of society he was a devil illuminated with genius, the better to show he had neither heart nor conscience. For these troubles there was but one remedy; after having lost his home, he lost his country; he fled, an exile without glory, a martyr without his crown, unhappy among the most miserable—a fallen angel, covered with the mire of London streets, flung upon his sculptured brow by a people intoxicated with hatred!

Poet! mighty poet! men know not the impossibility of having grand qualities, without having also great defects. They know not that all extraordinary virtue, all surpassing merit, is born of a disproportion between human faculties. They know not that the perfect sense of hearing has a relation with the imperfect sense of vision; and, at times, the perfection of imagination with the imperfection of conscience. They do not reflect that as the organs of animals are proportioned to their destiny in creation, so the faculties of giant minds are proportioned to their destiny in history. Demand of the Creator why the eagle sings not like the nightingale. Ask Him why the horse has not the strength of the bull. Let us not desire to discover too closely the physical fatalities which surround us, and which trouble us within and without our organism. Talent is in the soul, but it throws its influence on the body. All supernatural genius is an internal infirmity. The singing which enchants us, the melody which transports us to the world of dreams, has often been the consequence of an aneurism; the poem which inspires us with lofty ideas, great aspirations, has been written with bile; that wondrous work which leaves an indelible track in history, devours and destroys an organism; that discourse which awakens a generation to new ideas, is but a nervous crisis; that powerful intellect, able to weigh the stars, and to trace as on a map the limits of human reason, is for the body but weakness and sterility; and all genius is a mortal infirmity.

Believe not in the impassibility of great men like

Goethe and Rossini; believe not that with Olympian indifference they could pass from the torments of life to the heaven of immortality, as if in this world they were of marble, instead of being of the flesh which burns the bones, and of the blood which is mingled with fire. Genius is a divine infirmity; genius is a martyrdom. The poet seizes upon the light, the stars, the mountains, the seas, to convert them into ideas, into canticles. The poet dissolves the universe to mingle the colours for his pictures. But he cannot undertake this Titanic work without insuring his own destruction. He cannot go into the fire without being burned; he cannot mount to the extreme heights of the atmosphere without being frozen; he cannot enter the thunder-cloud without receiving in that conductor—his body—the shock of electricity. Those privileged souls which, flinging off the clay of this world, force their way upward till they become like bright stars in the firmament, almost approaching the angels; those beings—who, from the rock of their own shipwreck, hold forth the light to future genera-tions—have fed the divine splendour burning in the lamp of their own brain with tears from their eyes and with blood from their hearts!

WE are now drawing near the end of Lord Byron's life—a life as short as it was stormy. It became impossible for him to reside in his own country. He travelled to various places, by chance, as it were, as if following the flight of his own wayward thoughts and desires. An artist as he was, southern climates were those most congenial to his ardent imagination. In the limpid atmosphere, under a brilliant sun, breathing the aroma of flowers, a spectator, if not a sharer, of exalted passions, he satisfied his aspiration to realize poetry in life, or to exalt common life into poetry. He passed from England to Belgium, and from Belgium to Italy. His first visit was to the field of Waterloo—a sad picture, where the iron sceptre forged by Napoleon I. was broken, and his giant genius forced to succumb to the cannon of the enemy. Lord Byron was naturally enamoured of greatness—great beauty, great ideas, great passions, and great crimes. His purely original genius rebelled against all that was vulgar and commonplace. Old, useless customs, imperious social laws, tormented him as the waves and winds torment one shipwrecked. If he had been able, he would have torn his body from the laws of physical gravitation, and his mind from the laws of social gravitation. And in this violent struggle with contending forces, so powerful and so necessary, he destroyed both mind and body, drinking in large draughts the sweet poison of eternal dreams, though the cup was deadly.

He was naturally excited on seeing the battle-field, suggestive of the brain wherein, from the cradle tended by the plebeian Letitia Ramolino, had been re-erected the throne of Charles the Great, which from the Alps had spread to the Pyramids, and from the Pyramids to the towers of Notre Dame, covering the world with its shadow. Byron was deeply moved on seeing the spot where this extraordinary genius, whose Herculean strength supported a falling society, had been lost among the smoke of battle raised by the English forces—the place where he showed power almost worthy of a god, to be baffled by the stubborn perseverance of man.

From Waterloo, where the blood of the defeated troops of Napoleon lay fresh, Lord Byron went to the Rhine, and passing up the river he entered Switzerland. That country is everywhere rich in historic recollections. The greatest men have gone thither to breathe the pure air of the mountains and of liberty. Especially the shores of Lake Leman, where Byron remained for some time, are replete with recollections of the men of the eighteenth century— those men whose philosophy was a revolution, and whose revolution shall be the key of our philosophy of history.

I have visited the house occupied by Lord Byron near Geneva, as I, a humble pilgrim of liberty, always seek those places made famous by heroism or by genius. I saw, on the border of the lake, on a vine-covered hill, half-hidden in foliage, like a mysterious nest, the modest habitation where so many shadows, that will fill up the annals of the human family, crowded together in his brain. In front, the Jura raises its violet-coloured chain above the forests; from the foot of the Jura to the shores of the lake are stretched meadows of perpetual verdure, whose uniformity is relieved by dark trees and white hamlets; below, the tranquil surface of the lake repeating the purity of the heavens. At one end Geneva, raising its spires and slated roofs; at the other, the picturesque villages of the Canton of Vaud; behind, the immense ridge of the Alps, enveloped, like an army of white and changing phantoms, in a snowy mantle, upon which the golden light throws so many lovely and brilliant colours—a beautiful spot, calm as an eclogue, yet grand, majestic, and in perfect harmony with the spirit of the poet.

On those shores many of the great ones of the earth took refuge, and they have bequeathed to humanity ineffaceable traces of themselves. Every stone there speaks of Rousseau—of that grave and melancholy writer who lent to reality his own sadness—of that eloquent prophet who transformed reality with his aspirations. There Voltaire laboured many years, contemplating a small corner of the lake visible between the dark foliage and the lofty summit of Mont Blanc, seen against the pure sky in the distance. There Gibbon finished his history of the "Decline and Fall of the Roman Empire"—commencing where the empire was at the height of its power, and concluding in the regions from whence the barbarians assailed the empire. With this magnificence of nature, amid these recollections and these spectacles, and with the conversation of Madame de Staël, who then resided on the shore of Lake Leman, Byron, in some measure, amused his thoughts, and tried to forget his ungrateful country.

But ultimately Italy was the centre to which his ardent nature tended. The passage of the Simplon invited him to the country of the arts. He crossed over and went into Lombardy. In that journey he felt the inspiration which produced "Manfred"—at the roar of torrents bursting from inaccessible heights, and dashing against the rocks; at the sharp cry of the solitary eagle on the naked crags; at the sound of broken trees hurled violently down the defiles, and flinging around showers of crystal water like a rain of diamonds; at the contrast between the deep shadows of the valleys, where the profundity of the abyss is lost and hidden in the darkness; in sight of the lofty mountain peaks, where the mind approaches the Infinite, and seems renewed by the contemplation of immensity, and is drawn into intimate communion with the vivifying spirit of Nature.

Lord Byron remained some days at Milan. He compared the beautiful Italian city with our own lovely Seville, and gave the palm of beauty to Seville. In La Scala of Milan, he saw for the first time that fine observer, that acute critic, that scrupulous physiologist of Italian society—the famous Sthendel, whose intolerance towards my philosophic convictions, and the literary school to which I belong, cannot conceal from me his real merit. Sthendel afterwards remarked that, having closely observed Lord Byron while he listened entranced to a fine piece of music, he found in the expression of his countenance, in the breadth of his forehead, in the changing light of his eyes, in the curve of his lips, all the signs of great genius. In fact, the Apollo Belvedere did not shoot his arrows with so much majesty and impetus as Byron shot forth the inspiration of his soul from his oceanic eyes.

At length he determined to settle in Venice. The lagunes, the sea, the marble palaces, the wondrous pictures, the mysterious gondolas, the nocturnal adventures, the historical recollections, the poetry in action—all these harmonized wonderfully with the state of his mind and his peculiar genius. Venice was like the external form of his soul—sublime, romantic; sometimes gay, and sometimes melancholy; sensual, and yet monastic; neither a daughter of the earth, nor a child of the heavens; passing quickly from the disorder of an orgy to the desperation which approaches suicide. The soul of the man and the spirit of the city comprehended each other. Both suffered and both wept. Both sought forgetfulness in the arms of pleasure. Both sorrowed for their country. Both doubted the benignity of the Almighty, and both cursed the injustice of men. Both plunged into the excesses of life, hoping to find rest in death. Venice was the sea-shell in which, as in a native home, the soul of the poet unfolded.

He went then to Venice, turning aside to visit the tomb of Juliet, immortalized by the tragedy of Shakspeare. There, in an ill-kept garden, solitary as a ruin; forsaken, like a heart without love, is the tomb which the pious tradition of the people—always faithful to the worship of martyrs—declares to be the last resting-place of the unfortunate Juliet. When the lark salutes the coming day, expressing the praise of all creatures by her joyous canticle, she knows not that the stones, though mute, join in her morning hymn to the Creator and the light; but the poet, who makes himself a part of all time, turns aside to draw a counsel, a souvenir, from that fountain of divine inspirations.

Arrived at Venice, he took up his abode in that fair town, where he lived from 1817 to 1819. Only once he left the city of the lagunes to contemplate Rome in her severe majesty, and Naples in her voluptuous gaiety. He soon returned to Venice, where the excess of sorrow and the exuberance of pleasure accommodated themselves equally to his genius, distracted by troubles and torn by contending desires. But not even there did his enemies allow him to remain tranquil. During his exile, insults were continually hurled at him across the sea, from his country. It cannot be denied that Lord Byron's life in Venice was a succession of orgies, and of all sorts of disorder. But it is also true that he sought death in pleasure. He swallowed the poison of dissipation, finding it sweet to the palate, though corrosive to the stomach. How often in life we see examples of such suicides! Powerful emotions, sleeplessness, wine, pleasures, and the bitterness they leave in the soul, end by destroying, as if they were of glass, the most vigorous organizations. To these causes must be added his extreme sensitiveness; fasting, which he carried almost to the total reduction of his strength; and meditations indulged almost to delirious exaltations, in those solemn moments in which the greatness of his soul and the inspiration of his genius were in harmony.

About this time there was a grand Carnival in Venice. It was the policy of Austria to encourage pleasure, because pleasure destroys the recollection of liberty. Every tyrant knows that virtue is his enemy—his Judith. Unhappily, in this, Venice conspired with Austria. Even in her degradation her children danced madly, as if seeking in the dance a fatigue—and in fatigue, death. Many Eastern fanatics die thus at the feet of their idols. They seek suicide in the cup of their orgies. It is needless to say how much those grand buildings, so full of souvenirs, contribute to the mad pleasures of the Carnival—those spacious saloons, filled with graceful statues, which stand out from the smiling pictures; those gondolas, which appear a shadow and a mystery; those lustrous dark eyes of the Venetian women, which beam now softly, now severely, through their black masks; the saline air of the lagunes, which offers with the eternal echo of the kiss of their waves a fit accompaniment to the giddiness of the dance, and to the voluptuousness of music. I remember, one night, at the mouth of the Grand Canal, when the melancholy rays of the moon shed a soft splendour over the scene, I looked upon the islets with their white marble spires, and the palaces with their sculptured walls, extending into the pure and silvered water, and from a distant gondola there came an air from the "Lucretia" of Donizetti; and with the music there passed before my imagination those Venetian festivals in which the wine-cup and the poisoned bowl went together, and death and pleasure were in the dance.

The friends who visited Lord Byron at this time, did not recognise him. His wasted form and his pallid face gave him the appearance of a corpse, animated only by the brilliancy of his fatally beautiful eyes. Pleasure was consuming his existence. Among his passing affections was a lovely woman of dark complexion, black eyes, and sanguine temperament. Tall in stature, and robust as a Venus of Titian, she was sensual as a Bacchante; but capable of love and of self-sacrifice. This was Mariana, the mistress of the house in which Byron lodged; a married woman and the mother of a family, but ready to leave all for the sake of the poet. Light affections have but little sympathy for profound sentiments, which, even when aware of weaknesses and defects in the beloved object, consider them as an infirmity, worthy of tender care and attention. Byron soon discovered that Mariana was both violent and jealous. One day, while he was speaking to the sister-in-law of Mariana, the latter came in and gave a blow to the poor girl. Another time she sold a jewel which Byron had given her, and which he purchased again, in order to present it to her a second time. Love of this kind is but of short duration, yet nothing is so insatiable as pure love. Sensuality is neither satisfying nor constant. Pleasure, and pleasure only, means disgust and weariness. In the purity and devotion of a real affection, there is the assurance of eternal love. The abyss of the heart can be filled only with the infinite. But the voracity of low desires is quickly over. Byron soon left the house and the lady, and went to reside in the Palace Moncenigo, about the middle of the Grand Canal of Venice.

This was the scene of the adventures of Margherita Cogni, the well-known Venetian baker. There are some who have compared her to the Fornarina; but between the only love of Raphael (or at least the preferred love), and this fancy of a few days—between that fountain of inspiration, and this source of disgust —there was an immense difference. In Venice there are people of the lower class who sell oysters in the market, and who nevertheless like to have their ears soothed by the Italian translations of the poet, and to listen to stories of his life. Margherita was a woman of the people, in the bad sense of the word; a woman who could neither read nor write; a woman accustomed to tyrannize over her family almost in public, who concealed neither a fold of her soul, nor a throb of her heart, and consequently did not trouble herself to put any restraint upon her actions.

Lord Byron sought with much anxiety a burial-place among those lovely islands. Floating along in his gondola, he went about the Venetian Archipelago to choose a spot where to plant a willow-tree, of which the branches, drooping over the waters, should be a shadow for his tomb, erected under the azure sky of the south, close to the Adriatic. But, as if wishing to hasten his repose in the dreamless bed, he gave himself up to the study of different races, to the plastic art, to the intoxicating songs of the Carnival, to orgies without intermission. Often turning away weary from a festival, he wandered among the tombs, and met Margherita, who at this time exercised much influence on his life.

The boiling Venetian blood flowed in her veins, and excited her passions. She was tall, her shoulders broad, and her arms robust; her face was handsome and her head vulgar; her eyes seemed to consume like a flaming fire. She loved almost to folly, but was jealous to madness. She caressed Lord Byron, and she maltreated him. She met him with the smile of an angel, and she struck her nails into him with the ferocity of a tigress. The golden pin with which she confined her hair served her for a stiletto. She was a woman to bring forth a race of gladiators. She might have wrestled with any vigorous Englishman, and have won the victory. Her peculiar eloquence was interlarded with shameful expressions. Her ideas were no clearer than those of a primitive savage. Her passions were as ardent as a giant volcano in eruption. Her character was formed by the wind of the lagunes, and her soul was opened by the southern sun; there was something grand in her whole being, although it was a brutal grandeur. In the Palazzo Moncenigo, Byron had collected horses, numbers of cats and dogs, parrots and all kinds of birds, and this woman; like a wild Eve, in a strange paradise, angry with Adam, intoxicated with wine and pleasure.

But notwithstanding her ferocity, Byron deceived

her. One day there was a terrible uproar. The parrots uttered indescribable noises, the cats mewed, the dogs barked, the furniture flew in pieces, the Venetian mirrors strewed with a rain of little crystals the pavement of the palace—everything was in commotion, as if struck by a hurricane, or shaken by an earthquake. It was caused by Margherita, who had encountered a rival, and had with her a terrible battle, which was sustained on both sides with vigour and heroism. Imagine the fascination exercised by that powerful nature in the wasted frame of the poet, and his deep disgust. Her glance put new fire in the cold blood of those almost exhausted veins. Her violence and her unexpected blows pleased him like a food tasted for the first time. He laughed at the impassioned letters, written by a public scrivener for a charge of twelve sous apiece, and dictated by the baker's wife on her return to the market with her basket on her head.

One night, at a masked ball, Lord Byron gave his arm to a lady of respectability, Signora Contarini; he was covered by a black domino, and quite concealed by his mask. Margherita arrived, insulted the lady, and with loud vociferations snatched away his mask. On another occasion she quarrelled with her husband, whose flesh she tore with her sharp nails. In the middle of the night a loud knocking was heard at the door of Byron's house, when every one was sleeping; at the same time Margherita's husband appeared, and demanded his wife. The police interfered, and the woman was brought back by force to her forsaken home. But she soon left it again, and took refuge in the Palazzo Moncenigo, with her lover.

There she assumed the command of the household, but she exercised her power in a most tyrannical manner. She tried to copy the air of a great lady— wore a splendid dress, a Parisian hat, costly jewels, Flemish lace, and the train of a princess. And in this costume, and wearing gloves, which greatly incommoded her, she would catch up a stout stick, and, flinging about her arms, apply it all round, from the dogs to the servants. It was wonderful that she made an exception in favour of the master, though nothing prevented her from reviling him.

Lord Byron was very fond of the Lido, and of swimming in the Adriatic. He constantly rode past that beautiful tongue of land which forms the Lido, where the rich vegetation is watered by the sea. When tired of being on horseback, he went to the water, plunging into its depths like a skilful diver. All over Venice he was, as we have said, called "the English fish." One evening the sky became overcast, the wind arose, tossing about the waves, and Byron was in the sea. Poor Margherita ran to the feet of the Madonna, invoking all the saints, and promising masses, rosaries, and other offerings to the heavens in a strange litany, now and then interrupted by maledictions. When night approached, and the

poet did not return, the woman remained as if petrified
on the marble steps which descended into the Grand
Canal, holding out her arms towards the sea, half dead
from anguish.   But when he returned, she screamed,
cursed, and vociferated, saying, "Was this a time to
go to the Lido, dog of the Madonna!"

There was one advantage from the residence of
Margherita in the household—economy, though she
carried it to excess.   She counted on her fingers, but
her arithmetic was always correct.   Brought up in
the market of Venice, she knew the proper price of
everything; and as Byron had scarcely any appetite,
she bought very little food, often leaving the servants
hungry.   They, being accustomed to the former magnificence of their master, could not endure the strange
tyrant who condemned them to forced fasting.   Thus
there was one plot among them after another to oblige
Lord Byron to dismiss her.   This was not difficult,
for in the excited state of his mind he soon felt contempt for the flower whose aroma he had once enjoyed.
In loves of this nature novelty is the sole attraction,
but soon comes the sad conviction that there can be
nothing new in pleasure already exhausted.   To the
irritable condition of the poet's mind, the domestic
machinations against Margherita caused much uneasiness, and to these were added her own follies.   She
intercepted his letters, and not knowing how to read,
she went to the first scrivener, and paid him to read
Byron's secrets for her.   This, and the aversion which

he now felt for her, made Byron decide on ridding himself of Margherita. At the moment of departure she flung herself in a fury, and seized a knife, as if wishing to kill herself. They did not conduct her to the gondola, but dragged her to it. There she wrung her hands, and roared like a lioness robbed of her cubs, her eyes flashing fire. The night had been chosen for the separation, in order to avoid as much scandal as possible. Suddenly, on turning one of the numerous corners, Margherita threw herself into the water, notwithstanding the intense cold. Wet to the skin and shivering, her long hair hanging on her shoulders, her face deadly pale, her eyes wandering, her lips livid and contracted, convulsive sobs bursting from her bosom, she cast herself at the feet of her lover, imploring pardon. But he was inexorable.

He had descended nearly to the bottom of the abyss. In such a life it was easy to lose even con-science. After such nights of dissipation reality was more sad, and his heart more desolate. A great change was essential, and this could only be effected by love—a pure love. A beloved companion could calm the tempest of his thoughts with her smile—could purify his immoral life by her example. Nothing is so chaste as a pure affection—it is alike beneficial to the body and the spirit. To love de-votedly, to fix one's heart on a pure-minded woman, to watch for her glance as for a star, to consider her heart as a refuge, to blend two lives in one which shall be like a reflection of Heaven—this would have been safety to the poet, fallen into the mire of dissipation. The struggles of Parliament, the glory of poetry, the enthusiastic admiration of society, distant voyages, and the sublime spectacles of nature—the recollections of history in the places where great scenes have been enacted—Greece with her antiquities, England with her liberty, Spain with her tales of romance, Switzerland with her mountains, Italy with her works of art, and the East with her love-songs— had not been able to satisfy the heart upon which pleasure fell like a poison, and which, in the immensity of its suffering, broke forth into poetry. His passionate emotions could alone produce such a sarcasm as "Don Juan."

The Countess Guiccioli, the pure love of the poet, appeared at this juncture. What gave rise to this passion? I know not any definition of this love so precise or so profound as that which the psychological poet, *par · excellence*—Shakspeare—gives of the love between Othello and Desdemona. Othello says,

> " She loved me for the dangers I had passed,
> And I loved her that she did pity them."

Teresa, as the beautiful Countess Guiccioli was called, saw Lord Byron's sorrow in his face, and resolved to redeem the poet, to snatch him from the abyss, to rekindle inspiration in his soul, and love in his heart—to strengthen him by virtue, and to crown him by a glorious death. Byron was disgusted with life, and Teresa was scarcely acquainted with it. Educated in the gloom of the cloister, the notes of the organ, the clouds of incense, the waxen tapers burning at the feet of the Virgin, the litanies of the nuns —all this had filled her mind with the poetry of the convent, with that mystic and undefinable love which, at the first contact with the world, is ready to change into a violent passion when it meets with a suitable object on which to fix itself.

Her parents had made her miserable. Consulting neither her heart nor her inclination, they took her from the convent to marry a wealthy old nobleman, the Count Guiccioli. Teresa carried the romantic exaltation of her early years, and the vague longing for true love, into the arid soil of a *mariage de convenance*. This sad position led her to seek consolation in reading, particularly the poetry of her time. This was the period when Madame de Staël and Monsieur de Chateaubriand began to popularize in their works the shallow loves and unhappy attachments which amused that age, and from which neither of them dared to depart; they feared to adhere to the old ideas and to follow the new; they cherished fantastic delusions, which left on the heart their corrosive venom.

Teresa read and re-read all these works ; her imagination became exalted ; she suffered ; she seemed in a dream to converse with shadows, and wrote verses addressed to these phantoms without form, to these ideas, without reality and without object, that be-witched her brain, filled with the most romantic inspirations. Her hero, the hero of her girlish fancy, the hero born in the convent, and secretly nurtured in the reality of a cold and cheerless marriage, the ideal hero becoming more real every day as her delirium increased—thanks to unceasing and injurious reading—this extraordinary person did not exist, or if he existed, he was Lord Byron—the only one capable of kindling reality with the light of poetry.

Teresa and Byron were both in Venice at the same time, and did not know each other. Teresa infirm of mind, and Byron infirm of mind and body; the one eighteen years old, on the threshold of life, the other worn out with dissipation, and, though still young, on the borders of the grave. In 1818 Byron first saw her, but did not then understand her. She was with her husband, to whom she had not been long married, and to Byron she appeared at that time to be one of those numerous women who please the eye for a moment, but who say nothing to the heart. During the spring of 1819 they met one night at the house of the Countess Albrizzi, whom Lord Byron called the Staël of Italy. They were both present against their wish. Teresa was weary of festivities, and Byron was tired of women. The Count Guiccioli was annoyed because Teresa was at the ball, and the Countess Albrizzi almost forced Byron to be pre-sented to Teresa. They saw and loved each other.

A mutual glance was sufficient to make those two souls understand each other, and to unite them for ever. Neither of them ever remembered which said the first word, or made the first declaration. They were two halves of one soul. Byron, amidst all his vices, had searched for Teresa; and Teresa, through all her dreams, had sought for Byron. They met like two shipwrecked creatures tossed by the same wave; they met without any hope of making their love lawful; she, wedded to a wealthy old miser, and he to a most intolerant Protestant, who had made them mutually miserable—like two cold brazen walls between two hearts of fire. They passed over these barriers for the sake of each other.

Nothing is more dispiriting than living with a woman who is always melancholy and desponding. Many biographers assert that the Count favoured the love of Byron for his wife. I never wish to blacken human nature when I can discover any rational motive for actions that at first sight appear inexplicable. Probably the Count observed that his wife's melancholy departed with the presence of the poet. And he might also attribute this preference to their mutual love of literature. Delighted to see dissipated a sadness which darkened his own life, he was, at first, an innocent accomplice in his own calamity.

But very quickly he became aware of the real state of the case, and he endeavoured to separate the lovers; but separation, which is a remedy for passing fancies, is but a stimulant for deep sentiments. The Count quitted Venice, and went with his wife to Ravenna. Her thoughts were continually with Byron, and she was unable to bear up under the sadness of absence. She became alarmingly ill, and Byron hastened to Ravenna—being summoned to her side, for she was believed to be dying. On the 8th of June, 1819, he was standing by the bedside of this woman, who was dying of love. On seeing him enter, Teresa revived, as the tender violet expands at the kiss of April. All her physicians agreed that there was no cure for a malady of sadness and languor. The presence of the poet was enough to bring back the colour to her cold cheeks, the light to her eyes, already closing in death. That same day Teresa was able to go into the garden, and leaning on the arm of the poet, under the waving branches of the pines, amongst the bay-trees and myrtles, she spoke of her recollections and of her hopes.

But the health of Teresa was only re-established at the cost of the Count's happiness. Though Italian manners at that period were extremely lax, it is at all times scandalous to see a husband accompanied by his wife, leaning on the arm of her lover. Guiccioli once took a dagger, intending to stab Byron, who was reading "Corinne" to the Countess under the trees. But his own irresolution, and the composure of his rival, disarmed him. The Count, with difficulty, resigned himself to his part in society, which, though tolerating evils of this nature, always punished them by malignant glances and whispered observations.

Byron spoke of an elopement, and Teresa recalled the expedient of Juliet, who, clothed in the costume of the grave, took a narcotic, shut herself up in the family vault, and waited till her lover should, with a look or a kiss sent through the grating, convert the funeral pantheon into a paradise. But notwithstanding the romantic nature of Byron, he wished to show his affection in society, in the light of day, in the glitter of the world as well as in the bosom of Nature; as a thing to be proud of, as a virtue in a life till then given up to vices, and henceforth fixed in one passion chiefly nourished by sympathies of mind and similarity of taste for intellectual pleasures.

It is touching to read the lines written by Lord Byron on a blank leaf of the volume of "Corinne," which Teresa left in forgetfulness in a garden in Bologna. That simple love of the heart compared to the hyperbolical love mentioned in the book, appears as a lily of the field beside a false flower. He says—

"AMOR MIO,—How sweet is this word in your Italian language! In a book belonging to you I can write of nothing but my love. In this expression, 'Amor mio,' is comprised my whole existence. I know now that I live, and I fear the future. You will decide my destiny: my fate is in your hands; you who are but eighteen years old, and who but two years ago quitted the seclusion of the convent. Oh! if the heavens had

10

but given you to me then; or, if I had never seen you married! now it is too late. I love you, and you love me—at least, you appear to love me. This will be—no matter what comes—a consolation. Doubtless it is I who love the most, I who can never cease to love. Think of me sometimes, when the sea and the Alps divide us; but this cannot happen, at least, not unless you command it."

And after having written this letter, as if he understood that being is defined by a comparison with nothingness, and that love from its melancholy is allied to death, he went to visit the cemetery, to study the dreams of the dead in the silence of graves, and the grief of the living in the inscriptions on the tombs.

Eventually the Count Guiccioli retired, although accidentally, from his house, and left the lovers together. From Bologna they set out for Venice—for the country part of Venice; to one of those beautiful and distant houses from whence can be seen the Alps and the Adriatic, and between the Alps and the Adriatic, Venice, like an immense fleet of crystal and coral. There Teresa inspired Byron, being at the same time the muse of love and the muse of Italy. There, with her natural eloquence, she described to him the shadow of the past, the hopes of the future, and the sadness of the present. There she inspired him by her smiles and by her tears with prophetic ideas of the restoration of Italy, realized in our days and before our sight as a miracle of the faith of this age. There she purified him from ephemeral passions, leaving the only passion of true love. She withdrew him from orgies and extravagances which exhausted him, teaching him to employ his nervous activity more usefully in the study of humanity and in the struggle for the people's independence.

So much happiness could not continue, considering the delicate and difficult position of Teresa's husband, Count Guiccioli. I acknowledge with all the writers of that period, that Italy was then indulgent, too indulgent, to breaches of fidelity in married life. What I positively cannot admit with these writers is that the Italians learned this toleration from the Spaniards. " *The healer of his own honour; for a private wrong, a secret vengeance,*" is a saying which teaches all ages the horror with which crimes of this sort inspire the Spaniards. Where the Tetrarch of Jerusalem was born, there is no room for the Sigisceo of Italy. But notwithstanding Italian toleration, everybody in the case of which I am writing should have been on the side of the husband. Count Guiccioli, blinded by his ruling passion, avarice, forced public opinion to go against him. In the first place, the journey of Teresa and Lord Byron to Venice was made with his consent. Afterwards he wished to constitute himself the agent for receiving the money of the poet, in order to gain in gold what he had lost in honour. In the end came the proceedings for divorce. After the action for divorce, which was lost by the Count, there came a

Pontifical brief pronouncing the separation. Teresa joyfully abandoned her palaces, her equipages, society and riches for the love of the poet.

About this time Teresa's family were exiled. Her father, Count Gamba, belonged to those powerful provincial Romans who may be called the Aragonese of Italy. The love of liberty and of country which prevailed in this family received the common reward of such affections—exile. The Gamba family, to which Teresa returned after her legal widowhood, took refuge in sweet Tuscany, in the solitary town of Pisa, in that convent city, in that cemetery city, so congenial to great sadness. Lord Byron was also there.

The chief merit of Teresa was that her love for the poet was not egotistical. She loved his glory more than his person, and more than his glory his virtue. She restored and elevated him, drew him out of the mire, and placed the crown of purity on his brow. And then, when she had recovered this great heart, instead of keeping it all for herself, she gave it to humanity. She perceived that Byron did not belong solely to the order of men who are thinkers, but also that he was one of those capable of action. He was indeed a Grecian hero by virtue of his statuesque features, a Northern poet in right of his lofty sentiments; in one hand he bore the lyre, and in the other the sword. Instead of withdrawing him from exalted thoughts and actions, and confining him within the narrow sphere of worldly pleasures, she showed this

Achilles the field of battle, and told him it would be more worthy of his heart and his head to struggle for the rights of the people. She preferred to unite his soul with hers on the altars of sacrifice, to the enjoyment of vain and idle pleasures, and all the satisfactions of self-love and of pride. Teresa awakened in the bosom of Lord Byron the love of virtue and the love of glory which he had so often depreciated and cursed. She taught him to love Greece and Italy—those nations whose men of genius shall be for ever counted among the great ones of the world. In fine, she showed him how to die. And teaching him to die for many, instead of living for himself alone, she secured to his name the most glorious of transformations, martyrdom, and to his immortality the noblest of all temples—the heart of the people. Teresa would have been herself immortal like Heloise, like Isabel of Segura, like Sappho, if she had preserved for ever, under the pines of Italy, by the shores of the Arno, the glorious widowhood of the love of Byron. At twenty she was one of the muses, and at sixty-eight she was a wealthy old marchioness who flung an ill-considered book upon the poet's grave.

We now approach the end of Lord Byron's career. Here we conclude his life and begin his death. Here the frozen clay of error falls off melted by the fire of faith, and the wings of his soul expand to their utmost extension. Henceforth his life becomes a poem, the poet a hero, the sepulchre an altar, and death, immortality ! Here he bade farewell to the woman so fondly beloved, and betrothed himself to liberty, the eternal spouse of great souls, the fruitful mother of heroes. Here all the clouds which overshadowed him evaporate, all his vices are forgotten, his doubts are dispersed, his passions have departed, and the hare-brained trifler of London, and the libertine of Venice, and the despairing poet, is transformed into one of the martyrs of humanity, redeeming the errors of his life by the holocaust of his death. Many knew how to live better than this man, but few die like him, in travel undertaken in defence of liberty, in a struggle for Grecian independence, at the feet of that ideal nation, that mother of the arts, the true country of his soul, which will for ever name him with Homer, Æschylus, Pindar, Miltiades, and Aristides; those men who are the stars of the horizon of time—Greece will eternally count Byron among her poets and her heroes !

The leaves of Lord Byron's life were sadly falling. His daughter, Allegra, a child born in trouble, died at the age of five years. The poet ordered her grave to be made upon the hill of Harrow, on which he had written his first verses, and had received the pleasant kiss of the pure country breezes. Shelley, the metaphysical poet, like Byron, exiled from his native country, and like him wandering through the world, had just died in a terrible tempest, less stormy than his own perturbed imagination. Byron took his body and burned it on a grand funeral pile, upon the sterile sand, on the sea-shore ; throwing into that burnt sacrifice quantities of incense, which mounted in a cloud of smoke to the heavens, like an offering of aspirations and of orisons, bearing with it the spirit of a poet who believed the heavens to be a vacuum, and always denied that from the body of flesh which perishes could proceed a life lasting for eternity.

What remained for Byron? To die also, but to die for an idea, to perish for the faith of his epoch. In the midst of the silence imposed by the Holy Alliance upon Europe, the voice of a people arose demanding liberty. That heroic people was the Spanish nation, the same which ten years before had showed all others how to fight for independence. The voice of Spain had penetrated two sepulchres, that of Greece and that of Italy. The three peninsulas of the Mediterranean, the peninsula of men of genius, the peninsula of warriors, and the peninsula of navigators arose at the first whisper of liberty, as if to renew those paradisiacal and historic times, in which the most illustrious citizens lived like a choir of priestesses and muses, illuminating the human conscience with their own light, and filling the air with their canticles.

But all these hopes were fleeting as dreams. Upon Spain fell the misery of the French intervention, and upon Italy that of Austria. The people of Greece alone remained standing—the men of Thermopylæ and of Platæa, those who taught letters to humanity, those that have flung the silken cord of the arts around all nations, who have sculptured the human form in its severe beauty, who have revealed the conscience with Socrates, and who still preserve in the ashes of ruin all the warmth of poetic inspiration.

Lord Byron, who went over Greece, musing upon the laurels of Apollo on the borders of her rivers, the choir of priestesses of Dodona, the shores of Cephissus in the plains consecrated by the traces of Demosthenes and Plato, the ruined Acropolis where had been converted into shadows the statues of Phidias, the heights of Hybla and of Hymettus, crowned eternally by the gods—Byron did not alone meet in that country the recollections which arise like bright insects in swarms from the scattered ruins, but he also found powerful races, in whose classic features shone the reflection of ancient inspiration, and whose nervous hands could wield the arms of Epaminondas and Themistocles; people heroically determined to sacrifice themselves upon the sepulchre of their fathers, sooner than endure longer to see all their glory dishonoured in the chains of infamy forged by Turkey for their country, the country of heroic deeds, for their mother, also the mother of genius.

Let us reflect. Byron was rich, and he renounced his riches; beloved, and he forsook her whom he adored; a poet, and he laid down his harp young, and he stifled his passions; crowned by his genius, and he withdrew from glory: he left all these and went to fight and to die for one of the most righteous causes of humanity—the cause of Grecian independence. While in Italy, on the shores of the Tyrrhene Sea, under the shadow of the pine trees, breathing the aroma of orange flowers, beholding the wondrous works of art, in which he learned the perfection of his style, beloved by a woman who in herself united beauty and talent, he might have let his days run on in contented serenity, singing like a bird near his new nest, in that garden of happiness.

But no! He preferred the fight, the stormy sea, the harshness of winds and waters, the field of battle, the shedding of blood, the miasma of pestilence, death for his brothers, a sacrifice for humanity! Believe in his scepticism, you people of commercial England, you who cursed him, you who, crammed with beefsteak and drunken with beer, belch forth, as Sancho observed, the vapours of your digestion upon the aureole of genius! His life was evil to you, to whom moral egotism is so easy because you are devoid of passions, and to you a sterile Protestant faith is natural, for you have no imagination. Fling him from you as unworthy of England, and he will arise with his sword and his lyre, will traverse the divine shores whence sprung the arts, will convert the great among his countrymen, will go to die for Greece, and will have for country all humanity!

We shall sum up his works in a final observation, the climax of this poor history consecrated to one of those men of genius whose writings have given us the most consolation in our sorrow. It was in the month of April, and the day after Easter Sunday. Nature revived with the butterflies, with the lengthening days, with the gentle warmth so delicious in the spring of southern climates. The Church chanted the resurrection of the Saviour. Byron foresaw the resuscitation of Greece. Doubtless the struggle, the uncertainty, the clashing against life's impure realities which wore out his soul, the trouble, the pestilential miasma consequent upon the war, exhausted him and made him bend and fall upon the banner of liberty in which he had wrapped himself to die like Cato or like Brutus—under the shadow of the republic. He was scarcely six-and-thirty years old. He bent before death like a tree loaded with fruit and flowers. It was a lovely morning, and the sun darted his first rays among the last dewdrops, and the birds intoned their chorus, as if Nature consecrated a hymn to the poet's victory. In his delirium he fancied he scaled the walls of Lepanto, and in reality he surmounted those of eternity. He said, "Farewell! farewell!" as if losing himself on other shores; and his last word was "Farewell!" as if consoling his weeping soldiers and his afflicted friends, assuring them of the continuation of his life in other lands.

CONCLUSION.

AFTER having thus reviewed the life of Lord Byron, let us pause a moment and contemplate this marvellous genius in his connexion with others. As there never was in the world a poet so independent and individual, so never did any life contribute to unfold a character, nor a character to unfold a literature, like that of this noble Englishman, born for happiness and tormented by so many calamities. I do not believe that genius is solely composed of nerves and of blood, of the sap which it absorbs from the earth where it is born, of the sun which illumines and fertilizes its brain. Genius is, above all, a powerful interior individuality, with innate faculties, elevated and enlarged by study and by the clashing of life with a great power: genius is a spiritual creator. All true artists, whatsoever their class and condition, have the wonderful faculty of thinking and of embodying their thoughts; the lively fancy which impels them to a work as long as the labour of the creative forces of Nature; the profound capacity for analysis, which makes their ideas like a microscope, with which the most minute objects are visible to them, though hidden from the vulgar; the investigating examination which lightens up the most distant object in space as with a telescope; besides that exquisite sensibility by which, in the kindling furnace of the heart, is easily mingled both joy and sorrow.

Few men have possessed these great faculties in such a large degree as Byron. He raised himself at one flight to the most sublime regions of the spirit, in which all appeared to him expanded and glorified. He descends with an observation acute enough to enable him to relate the smallest peculiarities of life, and to discover the almost imperceptible touches of light and shadow in the universe. He experienced the invincible necessity of producing, of creating, of scattering his writings with the same reckless generosity with which the star pours forth its light, and the nightingale her canticles. He had, above all and before all, sensibility, that extreme susceptibility which is moved and ruffled at the lightest breath, that changes its shades at the least reflection of light, that foresees the future in the universe and in society, and which, being one of the choicest gifts of Nature, is also one of the greatest torments of existence.

But if he possessed this first and most essential quality of genius—sensibility—he certainly had also those peculiarities of his race, which were to his character as necessary and fundamental as colour to a drawing. The fiery Norman blood flowed wildly in his veins. Restlessness was his habitual condition. When he did not meet with actual troubles in life he formed them in his own mind. When action did not offer him sufficiently violent emotions he sought them in his passions, and if he could not invoke them by his passions he had recourse to his imagination It was a necessity for him to live upon the brink of an abyss, to stand on a tottering pedestal, over a boiling and foaming wave, lashed by the hurricane and stricken by the lightning flashes. His imagination was his continual torture. A darkness which seemed eternal fell upon his soul, so that at times he saw evil in every-thing. He believed himself desolate, and that which appeared the most evil and the most abandoned was himself; hence that irritability, those doubts, those strange contrasts, a fragment of Heaven appearing at the sight of a group of pine-shaped clouds, a suppli-cation coming after a blasphemy, as the soft breeze after the hurricane.

But he was not only Norman by the race from whence he sprung, but English, perfectly English as the nation in which he was born. What is the peculiar characteristic of the English people? Per-sonality, individuality. The Englishman insists that the entirety and totality of his person shall be legally sacred, that his house shall be a safe refuge from all his fellows; that his own conscience shall be the only medium between time and eternity, between the earth and the heavens; that his property shall be his standpoint, and that his life shall unfold itself at his own cost and risk, thanks to the spur of his activity, exciting his inclinations and feeding the fierceness contained in the principle of his own responsibility. Byron, above all men, had a distinct personality. Whatever impeded the growth, the unfolding of this individuality irritated and wounded him ; faith, laws, customs, limits of nationality, prejudices of race. He desired to live alone with his own conscience, his own reflections, and the imaginings of his own spirit thundering like a god, and almost expecting to see natural laws bend before his omnipotent liberty of will. No people ever hated a man as the British people hated Byron ; and yet no race was ever more faithfully represented in its characteristic qualities, and, above all, in its haughty individuality, than the English people were represented by Byron.

But with the Northern and essentially English qualities of which I have spoken, Byron had others which were entirely Southern. Our sun had poured forth his rays on that spirit of the poet, had imprinted on him his fiery seal. His was a British personality wrought in the marble of Paros, under whose seeming immobility the embers of divine warmth were concealed. Over these stones waved the red flowers of the oleander, on the borders of torrents, as if to crown him with laurels.

The combination of different qualities explains the rapid changes in Byron's style, and the formidable antithesis of his thoughts. But at the same time, it explains his culminating faculty—the quickest, intensest, and most imperious—sensibility. He was totally without the British phlegm. An emotion passed so forcibly through his whole being as to leave behind a burning scar. It appeared as if the social world only communicated with him by means of heated irons, whose contact made him groan, howl like one in torture, writhe and foam like one seized with epilepsy. Light does not so cruelly hurt the eyes which have but just recovered their sight as the society of his time wounded Byron.

Yet he, nevertheless, loved these emotions. He believed that to live was to feel everything, to experience everything; to pass through the different gradations of the warmth of universal life; to plunge heavily in the depth of the ocean like the fishes, to scale the snowy peaks like the eagles, to roll among the dry leaves of autumn, to trample on the snows of winter, to languish under the burning sun of summer, to hover like the butterfly among the spring flowers, to be a pilgrim wandering continually from the Alhambra to the Vatican, from the Vatican to the Parthenon, from the Parthenon to the Pyramids; to be the orator who wrestles in the tribune, and the brawler who fights in the streets; to be the aristocrat, the noble who rejoices in the remembrance of his blazonings, and in the pride of his long descent, and the democrat, the man of the people who protests against all tyrannies, and demands complete liberty; to be by turns a cenobite and an epicure, chaste and voluptuous; sceptical and believing; a criminal and an apostle; an enemy of humanity and a philanthropist; an angel and a demon; as if his spirit embraced all things and all ideas; as if his being was the abstract of all life, his personality the protagonist of the grand scene of the Universe, of the great tragedy of history.

He had also another remarkable quality, he referred the entire world to himself. The great power of certain men of genius to oppose their ideas and their sensations was never shared by Lord Byron. He sung what he felt; the cloud passing over his conscience, the spark touching the harp of his nerves, the love of his heart, the doubt of his mind, the hope of attaining his wishes, according to the state of his health, of happiness, of pleasure, of sorrow, experienced in his life which was his poem. From hence, as Henri Taine has justly observed in his admirable work, "The History of English Literature," the monotony, the uniformity of his characters, who are all of them touched with the same infirmity as the poet. But from this, also, arises the lively colouring, the force of expression, the marvellous aroma of sentiment, the vigorous reality which breaks forth in Byron's verses, reproducing all the being of the poet in each one of those cadences, which exhibit the beatings of his heart. And nothing so much attracts us—the children of an age of over-excited sensibilities—nothing so much attracts us as the pulses of a vivid existence.

And being thus sensitive, few men are so symbolical, few better reflect their epoch. For what was the condition of thought in those first years of this century, which are represented in the works of Lord Byron? Uncertainty. We had flung aside the old beliefs, and had not yet adopted the new. We had passed from liberty to reaction, and from reaction to liberty, by rapid changes. The Revolution had completed the ruin of a society, and upon these ruins arose the spectre, the skeleton, of the Middle Ages, with the Imperial crown upon its brow, asking for vengeance and for conquests. The people, in their trouble, desired to unite and to mingle all—religion and philosophy, democracy and aristocracy, ancient authority and modern constitutions—in the Pandemonium of eclecticism and of dogma. The spirit without faith complained of its sterility to the heavens, and wrestled in the coils of the serpent—Doubt.

From one extremity of Europe to the other there vibrated an incomprehensible genius, which rose from the lowest to the highest, raising a tempest of troubles, which only served to increase the darkness; a genius, now sombre, now flashing; from one side, Robespierre with his cannon upsetting kings and establishing despotically the Social Contract with the people; while, on the other side, Charles the Great, anointed by the Pope, surrounded by a horrible military

11

feudalism, re-erecting thrones and privileges, reconstituting the ancient Holy Roman Empire. The heavens which La Place beheld full of worlds, but void of spirits, were re-peopled by Chateaubriand with angels of tale, whose lips bore not the ancient simple litany, but the maxims of a rhetorical academy. English liberty placed itself at the service of the Holy Alliance. He who dug the grave of Poland, half-mad and half-enlightened, imagined himself the Baptist of universal liberty, and died of rage and ambition, without knowing where to go, or what to do with his hundred millions of serfs. Despots invoked the blessing of the Holy Trinity upon the scaffolds of Hungary, of Venice, of Milan, of Naples, of the divine and beautiful Greece, given over to the Grand Turk to satisfy his love of power and of pleasure. All the northern kings promised liberty when they required the blood of the people, and all forgot liberty as soon as the generous blood had produced the day of Waterloo. Literature waned, like everything else, in this universal uprooting, for literature is highly sensitive, and represents the times better than any other social element. It no longer knew whence to draw its inspirations. The fountain of Helicon, which had fertilized the republican spirits of the ancient world, was cursed in the name of liberty; and Gothic castles, which had beheld serfs trampled in the dust, were rebuilt in the name of liberty; while, at the same time, there passed through the dry bones of the martyrs of liberty, in Greece, in Italy, and in Spain, the galvanic action of rapid revolutions.

Where shall we seek for the representative of this moral crisis? Who shall be the Dante of this Inferno, in which circles of fire are entwined with circles of ice? Lord Byron. Read his poems, and there we shall find the embodiment of the spirit of the age. It seems as if the distracted spirit of his time had brought him its troubles, between insane laughter and heart-broken sobs; between supplications and blasphemies; between the accents of sublimity and the indecencies of buffoonery; sometimes intoxicated with grand conceptions, and sometimes drunk with wine; with the cruel tortures which are always produced by the vacillations of doubt and uncertainty.

No one has ever expressed the circumstances of his time so plainly as Lord Byron, who simply described the condition of his own mind. Enclosed in his own independent individuality, impatient of every yoke, incapable of bringing his soul to the direction of thoughts which did not proceed from his own conscience, he believed that in the bosom of his being was found the principle of his life, of that which could raise him above men, to breathe and live in a freer air, carry his imagination by a supreme effort far from humanity, there to remain immovable as in his centre of gravity in the immense heavens which he beheld full of hope, peopled and re-peopled with the light of his ideas, transforming himself in the infinite as the cold iron is transformed by the contact of fire into a burning mass; but the mortal clay repressed his flight, and then, turning against himself, he dashed against the confines of his narrow cell as a prisoner bird against its cage, kindling his blood with the violence of his maledictions, striking his claws into his bosom to tear out his heart, and changing himself into a melancholy shadow, like an angel who, with his harp in his hands before the Creator, when the worlds spring forth into being in the immensity of space, should suddenly find himself alone, dumb, exiled, his wings clipped under a funeral shroud of thick darkness in a deserted planet of ice.

There is no tragedy comparable to the tragedy of Byron's own heart. We must ascend to Jeremiah to meet in universal literature a poet who could like him send his voice from the tombs, repeat like him the elegy of ruin. The sorrow of Thamo, the pilot of Plutarch, in whose ears the god Pan murmured his agony by the Cape Miseno, was less poetical, less profound than the grief of Byron on crossing the shores of Greece, and beholding her forsaken of the gods, and peopled by slaves. Foscari could not love Venice as Byron loved her, could not feel the lamentation of the weeping Adriatic lagune as he felt and repeated it, when beside the Palace of the Doges, and the historic and sombre Bridge of Sighs, raised like a catafalque over the silent canal whose dark green waters flow beneath the city, resembling the outline of a corpse. He wept as the Roman tribunes wept over Rome's desolation. Of ideas he knew but the shadows, of history he felt but the catastrophes of life, he tasted but the bitterness. Our doubts, our sorrows, he touched so pathetically that our hearts overflow at seeing each day more distant the liberty of our soil, more narrow the road of progress, more Utopian our noble aspirations towards virtue; this disenchantment of thousands of men who wished to raise an altar for their theories, and have but erected a scaffold for themselves, who wished to extend their country throughout the universe, and have only attained exile, that sharp pain like a poignard in all great European reformers, has had its poet in this genius of disenchantment.

It is true that his position and his family honours contributed much to his success, that is, his hereditary dignity, his nobility, and his seat in the House of Peers. But it is also true that he made his own sorrows those of his age. His was a strange history and genealogy. His uncle had killed one of his relatives. His father stole his first wife and deceived his second, the mother of Lord Byron. She died of a stroke of apoplexy, brought on by a fit of passion. The friends to whom the poet had given his first affections all died young, desolating his youth. The woman for whom he felt his earliest love married another, and the recollection of this childish passion filled his heart with bitterness. He scarcely met, on the day that he first entered the House of Lords, any one to receive him and to welcome his rising glory. Criticism was severe upon him. He set out on his travels, and the ruin of his estates obliged him to return again to his country. He became enamoured of a celebrated authoress, and this love was to him a fountain of disgrace and of calamity. He married, and his wife abandoned him. He had a daughter, and this daughter grew up, and was educated far from the heart and the influence of her father. He had a country which should have counted him her pride and glory, and his country cursed him. In Italy he became transformed by the ardent kisses of her sun; he felt the duty and the necessity of action, took ship and went to help Greece in her struggle for liberty, and, scarcely arrived there, he died!

Can anything be more sad than this history? This man is like some hero of antiquity, condemned from birth by a cruel fatality. He resembles one of the gladiators of old brought from the Grecian mountains, young and beautiful, with his soul full of poetic fire, and his body a model for the sculptor, distinguished by emperors, caressed by the Roman ladies, and yet whose destiny it is to divert the people for a day with his death agony between the claws and the teeth of a wild beast! In vain try to evade the fatality which pursued him, in vain try to fly from his torments and his sadness, like Orestes from the Eumenides. The earth is his scaffold, life is his torture, inspiration is a crown of fire, love is an insupportable chain; each literary jewel which issues from his hands turns against him; each day brings him a new trouble, every good action turns to a thorn piercing his heart; his mother treats him with bitterness, his country with abhorrence; his own friends calumniate him, his own wife refused him her tenderness; and after having travelled through Europe, and having expended fruitlessly the emotions of his life, he met no other balm for his griefs than a death drank from the cup of heroes, a death at thirty-six, which resembles a noble suicide!

Lord Byron cultivated the three kinds of poetry: the lyric, the dramatic, and not to say the epic, I will say, the poem which is really distinct from the epopee. But as his character is eminently subjective, as his personages are all emanations of his own spirit, formed by the exhalations of the sentiments which battled in the ocean of his heart; his poetry, the poetry proper and peculiar of his genius, is the lyric poetry. The greatest philosopher of modern times has declared that lyric poetry is the most subjective— the poetry of Lord Byron is the most lyrical with which I am acquainted. He does not represent the world, like Goethe, in itself, in its existence, in its laws and phenomena; he represents it as it appeared to his soul, such as it seemed in the abyss of his thoughts. He is self-possessed on enter-ing a theatre. Nothing more uniform and monotenous than his dramas; nothing less dramatic. Each of his characters may be called a choir which intones a hymn, an ode, an elegy. The dialogue has scarcely any animation, because it is one-half of his idea speaking with the other half, a portion of his heart discoursing with another portion. All his dialogue is connected in one thought, each personage disappears in one soul; every action is blended in one life; in the thought, the soul, and in the life of Byron. And as one life, be it ever so grand, revolves upon one idea only, his dramas are not suited to the stage, wanting movement and variety. All the grand Oriental poems are of the same order, such as the Book of Job and the Apocalypse, in which immaterial and material beings support harmoniously a dialogue with the inspired prophet, who beholds them in ecstatic visions, and lends them the rhythm of his own ideas.

Byron's first poems, those which were so cruelly criticised by the *Edinburgh Review*, scarcely announced the poet, then in the dawn of his fame. They are subjective, but wanting in grandeur. Had he been happy, he would have been lost in the choir of so many poets who have gently rippled for a day the stagnant lake of common life. Byron, being unhappy, distinguished himself among all other poets, as Satan is distinguished among all angels. His poetry, sometimes tranquil, but always illuminated by a ray of lightning, has much that fascinates. The temper of his verses is so stormy, that the attention is not allowed to wander from the sublime confusion. Byron's grandest poem is " Manfred." Henri Taine compares it with " Faust," and says that " Manfred" is the poem of individuality, and " Faust" the poem of humanity. I should call " Manfred" the poem of sentiment, and " Faust" the poem of ideas; " Manfred" the poem of nature, and " Faust" the poem of history.

Both poems represent the disenchantment which is produced within the limits of human existence. Faust himself is weary after having thought, and Manfred after having lived. The one dies, as becomes a German doctor, after having studied medicine, alchemy, the theological sciences and philosophy, and having found them but ashes. The other expires after having felt, struggled, and loved in vain; after having ascended the gigantic ladder formed by the Alps, without finding anything more than the piercing wind eternally moaning, the white frost falling, the pines amid the snow-flakes, the cold desert of crystal fatal to life, the profound abyss where light is extinguished; beneath, men are like insects; above, the eagles fly in endless circles, breaking the immensity and the silence by their cries of hunger; a spectacle which reminds him of another desolation, the moonlight night in which he trod the ground of the Colosseum, the ruins overgrown with nettles, and heard nothing but owls, whose melancholy cries were an elegy over the ashes of the martyrs and gladiators of the past.

To dissuade Faust from suicide came the sound

of the Gothic bell celebrating the morning of the
Resurrection, mingled with the voices of the eccle-
siastical choir; but to save Manfred there was needed
the real and powerful hand of a deer-hunter, seizing
him upon the verge of a precipice. The one, after
having proved the emptiness of real love, invokes
Helen, the classic beauty for whom lovely Greece was
deluged in blood, and proud Troy was burned; from
whence sprung the refinement of Art, eternal mother
of gods and men ! The other, after having also tasted
the nothingness of loves and ambitions, longed to
behold the nymphs of nature, she who sleeps in
everlasting snows, she who weaves her hair in the
cataract, she who sighs in the movement of the pine-
trees, she who possesses above the clouds a palace of
opal, created by the uncertain reflections of the day-
dawn, and she who bathes her fair form in the limpid
bosom of the ocean, and whose long hair of sea-weed,
interlaced with pearls, reposes on pillows of shells and
corals.

So " Faust" went over the East; with its theogonies
saluted the classic statues of antiquity, descended the
abyss of human thought, in which the web of material
life is woven by original or mother ideas, mounted the
cupola of the Gothic church which sends to the heavens
the aroma of incense, the hymn of the organ, the
vibrating echoes of supplication ; and " Manfred" has
passed from the feudal castle to the mountain, from the
mountain to the war, from the war to the chase—for

"Faust" is the thought of universal history, and "Manfred" is the action of universal life. In the poem of the one, all ages speak; in that of the other, all beings. In the one poem all writings are glanced at, from the Creation of Light in the Bible, to the making of paper-money in the coffers of the Jews; in the other poem, we find the essences of all elements, from that which raises the waters to that which draws tears. Between these two poems, the one of which embraces thought and history, while the other comprises life and nature, there should be a third to comprehend society and its struggles. Perhaps the age has reserved this great glory to my country—at least, I almost gathered this from the magnificent vestibule designed by the hand of Esproceda, and which is called "El Diablo Mundo," a work not perfect, nor finished, as the construction of our society is still imperfect and incomplete.

The poem of Goethe and that of Lord Byron, both end in death. Both works keep near to the protagonist, his inseparable companion—Evil. But Byron, with his remarkably distinct individuality, bears the evil like a cancer in his body and his conscience; carries it shut up in his mind, adhering like a fiery skin to his flesh; diffused like a corrosive torture, like boiling lead in his blood; painted with all its horrors and deformities in his retina, like two suns of death and darkness, which spoil and devastate. Goethe is a philosopher who observes evil, and accepts it in the limit of nature and of human life as an inseparable companion of good, as the antithesis which determines the thesis, as the shadow which follows the light, as the fever which results from the excess of life, as the sting which extracts the honey : as sorrow which is apparent, as doubt which creates, as the negation which defines and affirms.

Byron *feels* the evil, and Goethe *thinks* it. In the sphere of sentiment the contradiction of good and evil exists. Byron goes in a stormy cloud where two opposed electricities contend; both of which shock his nerves with their powerful rays, and kindle his blood with invisible fire. Goethe, immovable as the Jupiter of Phidias, protected by the bronze of human life, placed in the heights of history, sees with indifference the evil roll by as a cloud, which obscures certain portions of the earth, while refreshing and invigorating the others; like a doubt which for a moment disturbs weak spirits, but steels and prepares for the truth those which are vigorous; like an irony which leaves solemnity for ever with art, and also gives it those various and discordant tones, without which the harmony of beauty could not be attained, those touches of shade without which the colours in the picture of the soul could not be produced.

When one thinks superficially, when not inclined to the serious study which should enter into our life, we are apt to say, " What use are these poems, ending one in the sepulchre and the other in eternity ?" But we are blind of heart and of spirit, when we are offended with these great works of grief and of martyrdom, against these grand poems which for one age are phantasms, and for another are ideas. Without contradiction we cannot have the truth, as we cannot have life without labour and struggle. The history of science is a prolonged history of different echoes. So when a genius which demands is born, there appears another which replies. Without the despair of Job, we should not have had the balsam of the Gospel. Without the maledictions of the Prometheus of Æschylus, we could not have sat at the banquet of Plato. Without the scepticism of the Sophists, Socrates would not have revealed to us the secrets of the human conscience. Without the irony of Voltaire, who perverted a world, the prophets of another world would not have arisen crowned with new ideas, in the Constituent Assembly to confide to the hurricane and the tempest the divine germ of the rights of man. We enter on the truth by scepticism, by despair, as we enter into life by sorrow, with tears in our eyes and sobs in our bosoms. He who is born and cries not, is born dead. The age which doubts not is an age which asks not; and we should importune the truth with questions, as we should come to God with supplications. By one of these poems, we have arrived at the knowledge that men, reptiles so feeble to mount or to descend the ladder of life, are one with the universe; by the other poem, we *know* that this im-

palpable and invisible spirit, like the breath of a corpse
—this human spirit is yet *one* with all history, *one*
with all ages, and may aspire to eternity.

Both poets draw from created things, from clay
they extract honey. After having read them, after
having agitated your heart with their sorrows, shaken
your intelligence with their scepticisms and your faith
with their denials, you deduce the moral lesson that
neither life nor truth can really be found in grossness,
corruption, and discordance : they are there on the eternally serene heights of immortal essences ; and as after
the shades of night have departed the world becomes
renewed, brighter, and more joyous, the sun deepens
the colours of the plants and gives voice to the birds ;
after having passed in the spirit through those profound caverns of thought, you behold, as it were, the
face of God, unfolding the creative power, giving a
living faith with His light, invisible, but penetrating
to your soul. In these poems there are two leading
ideas, one plunged in obscurity, but which is heard
in the tempest, like the moaning of impotent creatures
wallowing in evil ; and the other, which looks to the
light, repeats the harmony of the stars, and keeps the
sight fixed in the contemplation of the Supreme God,
like Murillo's paintings of the Conception. It will,
perhaps, have happened to you in life to pass into a
thick cloud when wandering over mountains, to feel
the darkness falling like a winding-sheet over your
brain, the lightning flashes like the scourge of death

by your side, and after conquering the hill and
mounting to the summit, you see the blue heavens
above your head, the resplendent sun reflected in the
light, pure covering of snow, and on one side the cloud
in a rainbow encircling you. It is thus with great
works of art. When Byron's unhappy Manfred has
finished his strife with the elements, when his unquiet
spirit snatches him towards the invisible world, when
alone there remains of him only an immovable mass,
I leave the book, my heart oppressed with sorrow,
my brain heated by excitement, and, by a natural
contradiction in the soul, I behold Immortality, like
the Virgin Mother, presenting herself to the dead,
now new-born, and showing them with her rosy
fingers, like those of the Aurora of Homer, the ethereal
mansion of eternity, hidden among the crimson clouds
of heaven, and illuminated by the presence of God.

Lord Byron's was indeed a strange genius—Norman,
Saxon, British, individual—and, in spite of all these,
universal. When he describes the palace of an
Albanian Governor, the marble court, in the centre of
which a fountain plays, shaded by cypresses, their dark
branches entwined with jasmine and roses ; the army
of slaves and of soldiers, some Greek, others negro,
all clothed magnificently, fully armed, and strong in
their temperance ; when he applies his ear to the wall
to listen whether the heart of the poor Mahometan
woman beats wildly in the prison of the harem, if
she sighs oppressed by silence and solitude, any one

would believe he was reading an Oriental poem. But soon his eyes become suffused, his heart in commotion, the tempest which hung over the cradle of his race persecutes him, the clouds of the North overwhelm him, the wind whistles in his ears, accustomed to the roaring of the waves, to the wild cry of seamews; spirits of darkness, like obscene birds of the night, rise in flocks through the dark caverns of his soul, and then, by the lightning flashes of his mind, he describes the day in which the sun did not visit the earth, and men kindled all combustible matter to illumine the obscurity, till they all died buried in ashes; gigantic recollections of that Scandinavian Apocalypse inspired by the eternal darkness of Polar nights, and of which Northern bards have sung. Presently the air becomes clearer, the moon arises, extending her veil of silvery gauze; the coasts become visible, and show their outline; the fine sand appears gilded and adorned with brilliant and opal-dyed shells; the blue water, lightly rippled by the breeze and moved by the plunging of the dolphins at play, with the light wings of the seagull casting a passing reflection; in the fissures of the valleys the rose-leaf blooms among the stones with the vine and fig-tree; on the distant horizon the sky and the Mediterranean are blended, each beholding the beauty of the other, and mutually exchanging reflections; and in that solitude of voluptuous enchantment Don Juan and Haydée change caverns into palaces, and abandon themselves to the infinite happiness of a love inspired by youth and hope, without other witnesses than the roseate dawn, bright as the cheeks of a Grecian maiden on receiving the first kiss of her lover, and who, careless of the future, loses herself in the present, as if love formed the whole of life and will not cease till death. Surely he who describes this must be a Southern poet?

The course of things has changed; the whirlwind of events which we can scarcely comprehend impels poets all over the earth to change distinctive poetry— the poetry of race, into universal poetry, the poetry of humanity. Byron was not the only exile who went to ask inspiration from the Alcazar of Seville, the gigantic skeleton of the Colosseum, the ruins of the Parthenon. Chateaubriand travelled from the sepulchres of Jerusalem, where repose the ruins of ancient society, to the cataract of Niagara, which rocks the cradle of modern society. Goethe went from the forests of the North—a pilgrim of the religion of art— to the Greek marbles under the triumphal arches of the Vatican. The genius of Victor Hugo seems to have had its cradle in Spain, and to look for its sepulchre in England, since he is Oriental in his likeness to Calderon, and Western in his resemblance to Shakspeare. Hugo Foscolo, with his Grecian blood and his Italian poetry, sung among the mists of the North Seas. The breezes of the Rhine caressed the infancy of Heine, and the Seine wept his sorrows, as if in his genius alone could meet the two opposing currents, stained with blood. Mazzini writes his social prophecies from London. Quinet meditates upon the Apocalypse of the Revolution on the shores of Leman, and before the Alps, on that small spot of earth called Switzerland, which liberty has converted into a world of faith and hope, into a refuge of virtue and of conscience. All great poets are not merely phantasms which Nature creates in order that they may chase away pain and misfortune. This choir of mysterious and of celestial birds, which bring the nourishment of the ideal in their beaks, and the echoes of infinity in their verses, go through the world wafted by all breezes, drinking all the juices of Mother Earth, hearing all the poems of history—to form, in fact, the Iliad of the future — the Iliad of labour instead of war; the Iliad of right instead of the Iliad of privilege, the Iliad of humanity, in which each people shall form a choir and intone a canticle. When a poet of such marked individuality, and of such pure Saxon origin as Byron, was able to turn his genius from its natural bent and to attain to higher and broader flights than common, what cannot the children of more humanitarian races do and attempt? They are gifted with a more flexible character, and have their consciences more imbued with the sublime conceptions of an ideal brotherhood. The great genius who lived to repeat the aspirations of all peoples, and who died young and unfortunate, among those who were the first imitators of liberty—the true poet of history, the artificer of human personality, the revealer of the conscience—deserves to be accounted in the book of human progress between our prophets and martyrs. He often wandered from the right path, but he was the echo of an uncertain age. Of him history may write—"I forgive thee, for thou hast loved much." And this age, the commencement of this century, which beheld the Apollo-like head of Byron, crossed with sunbeams and with shadows, could exclaim, "This is my resemblance—this is my symbol!"

END OF THE LIFE OF LORD BYRON.

VICTOR HUGO.

VICTOR HUGO.

—

ROMANCE is certainly one of the most beautiful phases of modern intelligence; although in its tendency it appears to be a revival of the Middle Ages, in its proceedings and its methods it destroys the ancient artistic traditions which ended with the reign of Aristotle in the sphere of art, as Bacon, Luis Vives, and Descartes concluded with the same despotic reign in the region of science. Aristotle held a very singular place in history. A representative of the ancient position, above all before Plato, who represented idealism; an indefatigable commentator of nature, a believer in experience, a prodigious observer even more than a daring investigator, he became the founder of a theological school. The Moors metamorphosed him with their dreamy and mystic ideas, and three centuries were barely sufficient to admit of man's becoming acquainted with him. In the sphere of art, Aristotle never preached the three vigorous unities proposed by the masters who professed to continue his doctrines, and doubtless classic scholars respected his poetic pieces, as the Moors respected his metaphysics. And from this threefold adoration of Moorish theologians and classic scholars resulted a false Aristotle, a kind of oracle that imposed his despotic dogmatism upon reason and fancy. The philosophical schools of the Renaissance finished with the Aristotle of the theological schools, and turned to the arts. The Italian poets of the sixteenth century were Aristotelian, so were the first founders of the Spanish theatre, and so was French poetry; and later, there appeared a Church which held a literary Aristotleism with its gospel, which consisted of the works of Boileau, and of these three—Corneille, Racine, and Voltaire.

The man on the Continent who dared to revolt against this poetic convention, to recover the undefined rights of nature, and to defend the spontaneous creation of the imagination, deserves a place among great reformers, among the friends of art and of liberty. This extraordinary man was Lope de Vega, the admiration of all ages for the inexhaustible fecundity of his genius; capable of creating in the infinite space of moral nature as many types, and as many relations among those types, as material nature can produce in its inextinguishable life. Excluded as he was from all communication with the modern spirit by the native intolerance of the Spanish race, and by the tyrannical policy of the House of Austria, he opened for himself a breathing place—a window, as it were—in the arts, from which he received light from Heaven. Thus, while nothing else seemed to flourish in the country, whilst the profession of arms declined, and population, politics, science and industry decayed, the arts advanced so far as to produce, in the seventeenth century, our first great painter Velasquez, and our first great poet, Calderon. The romantic spirit of the age created the Spanish theatre, with its richness, its animation, its variety, whence we have derived metaphysical ideas of the first magnitude, as in "Life is a Dream;" perfect social types, as in "The Alcalde of Zalamanca;" passions as pure as that represented in "The Slave of her Lover;" tragedies like "The Physician of his Honour;" and comedies, which so clearly describe life and society, that we still feel delight in their reproductions, since they form, with their beauty and vigour of conception, one of the brightest collections of art in any age.

To the Latin nation, where romance held its greatest empire, Victor Hugo went in his childhood—to Spain. The warm kiss of our southern sun still burns on his Titanic brow. There is something of the rude harshness of our soil in his genius; there is much of the hyperbolical part of our character in the great outlines of his works. This journey of Victor Hugo into Spain was analogous to that of Madame de Staël to Germany. The great authoress brought the ideal romance of the North, and the great author the practical romance of the South. The one became inspired by the sad and profound dreams of Jean Paul Richter, and the other by the simple verses of romancists, and by the ideas of Calderon, infused in the conscience like those streams of *materia cosmica* which are called nebulæ, and from which, almost continually, a new planet is suspended like a drop of light in the immensity of space.

Victor Hugo returned from Spain disposed to set on fire the temple of the gods of ancient art. Classic poetry reigned in France from the time of Louis XIV. without any interruption. The people in Ninety-three ignored the existence of such a glory. But had they been aware of it they would have sought to destroy it, in their eager desire for change. The Academy and the Court were then at Versailles.

The principles of Victor Hugo's poetry may be summed up thus:—1st. That the spirit of the ancient school is to lessen the essential part—the idea, so as to confine it in the narrow mould of petty formality; *we* elevate all idea on all form. 2nd. That tragedy is a dead body without spirit and without blood; let us substitute for this ossification art and the drama, and give it life. 3rd. Nature loves contrasts, and places light by the side of shadow; society also loves contrasts, and puts tears and laughter near each other. Let us reproduce in the picture, art, society, and nature; let us extend life with its contrasts in the theatre. 4th. This separation between art and life proceeds from an aristocratic school, which has promulgated a code of false laws; let us substitute for this arbitrary code liberty in art, a genuine inspiration, a real conscience.

These revolutions cannot be made hastily. This reintegration of all being in itself is one of the greatest difficulties ever conquered in history. The ancient world puts morals in positive codes, changing like the course of events and the foundations of societies. Socrates placed the base of morality in the human conscience. The philosophy of the Middle Ages placed the laws of truth in a conception foreign to all life, beyond all reality. Descartes placed the laws of truth in reason. The classic authors put the laws of art in academic codes remote from the inspirations of fancy. Victor Hugo put the laws of art in inspiration, in the light which belongs to the spirit. No one can deny it this unfading glory. And from the moment in which he has the first glimmer of an idea, he realizes and makes use of it like a warrior who rushes to conquest. "Notre Dame de Paris" is his poetic spirit in action. Conceived under the shadow of Gothic towers, like a mysterious bird whose nest should be perfumed by incense, before seeking in space the aroma of universal life in the infinite, it is ready to expand its wings and fly towards the heavens. Quasimodo was romantic art, grotesque and hideous materially; but beautiful in that he was life's essence, in the moral part which looks to eternity, in the recesses of the spirit. Captain Febo was classic art, beautiful in person, empty in being, without a spark of the divine light which is concentrated in that focus of moral life called Quasimodo. La Esmeralda, lovely in form and in spirit, is the art of the future; that which will come forth from the battle and proceed from the union of two ideas, from the synthesis of two contrasts produced by human reason—which society receives with its great mechanisms, unique and capable of combining with all its powers. Febo loved Esmeralda with the sensual and passing passion of antiquity; Quasimodo with the profound love of the spirit, for whom the sepulchre is the cradle of true life. Claude Frollo is the spirit of the middle age, which desires to kindle the new life, the new art, but who, detained in the darkness by his beliefs and his vows, dies tormented by the inextinguishable thirst of pleasure, by the desperation of unsatisfied desire, by the warfare of an unregulated nature with the sting of excessive voluptuousness, which consumes him in its fires. Modern art is poetry in action.

It became essential to take the new school to his battlefield, the theatre. It was for this he wrote "Hernani." From thenceforth his dramatic pieces were inspired by the spirit of the Spanish theatre. It is a statue chiselled from the same quarry as "Garcia del Castañar" and "L'homme riche d'Alcalá." Ruy Gomez de Silva is valiant, generous, noble, but implacable as the father of the Cid. Doña Sol is the beautiful Castilian, whose light, whose idol, whose only and exclusive passion is love, in which she concentrates her whole existence. The two feeblest personages in the drama, in my opinion, are Charles V. and Hernani. The former, on feeling the imperial crown upon his brow, becomes changed in character; and the latter also changes when the Order of the Golden Fleece is placed upon his neck. There is certainly in this a great want of poetic logic, and of that logic which is the more severe and inflexible, because it unfolds itself by the regions of the absolute. In art, in the greatest elevations of the spirit, the air is more pure, as it is on mountains, which are the highest points of our planet. An internal change would have been more logical than this sudden change, owing to external accidents.

In reality Victor Hugo, who is the first poet of his time, is not the first dramatic poet. Sometimes his genius is too great, sometimes his wings are too much expanded to find free action in the small enclosure of a theatre. But while acknowledging a certain inferiority in Victor Hugo as a dramatic poet, I cannot deny the merit of his works. What elevation of sentiment! what profundity of ideas! what accents of passion! what marvellous harmony in those verses which are made in a language so flexible, so sonorous, and so robust as the Spanish, the immortal language of romance! And when " Hernani" appeared, it was wondered at, like a comet, and announced a war in the heavens of poetry. The Pleiades of young romancists applauded it as the central point towards which eventually they should concentrate all their forces. The classic writers arose against that continual hyperbole, against that contempt of all academical conventions, against those personages whose greatness they called extravagance, exaggeration, the result of a wandering and inflamed imagination. Each representation was a battle. The hissing obliged the performers frequently to interrupt the dialogue. Madame Mars did not dare to repeat the verses as the poet had written them, and trembled before those audacious innovations as violations of all the acknowledged rules of good taste. Even Lemaitre could not understand why people gave money in the pay-office and hisses in the theatre; rushing to support them by purchasing tickets of entrance, and then condemning the performance with protests and tumults. Victor Hugo remained unmoved in the midst of the tempest, with his thoughts bent on the necessity of reform, and his eyes fixed on the eternal justice of the future. If he had been present, as I was, at the later representation of his drama; if he had beheld the audience profoundly moved, giving to him something more than applause—a tribute of tears; if he had listened to the beatings of those hearts which relieved themselves in an enthusiastic burst of emotion, he would have seen that after thirty-five years of struggle the red comet had been changed into a planet, inhabited by the souls of the new generation. And he, from that fair isle where his companions are the unfathomable ocean and his own conscience, on hearing the echoes of the applause borne by the breeze, saw the image of immortality, so dear to genius, shedding a drop of honey into the bitter cup of his exile!

But while speaking of his works I have insensibly forgotten to speak of the poet himself. I wish to make use of this disorder, which, if it is contrary to artistic rules, in compensation takes from both writer and reader some of the fatigue which usually accompanies labour. Victor Hugo's face is bright and animated, like his mind; his head is large and spherical; his forehead broad, like a heaven destined to contain many stars; his eyes small, but deep as the abyss of his thoughts; his nose aquiline, his beard is snowy white, and his whole expression indicates the culminating qualities of his spirit: athletic powers, indomitable energy, the countenance of a warrior, who retains his Olympian serenity in the midst of the rudest shocks of battle. On presenting a master-work to the public, instead of the laurel crown so dear to an author, he was met with hissing. This would have overcome one less vigorous than the soul moulded in the bronze reserved for the greatest human intelligences; but Victor Hugo bore it unflinchingly.

He has not the grace, harmony, nor proportion of those poets who have studied antiquity, and who have sought to reproduce in their verses the marbles of Paros. On the contrary, it is evident that his models were taken from the exaggerated though sublime literature of the East; and that his favourite study has always been the poets, particularly the Book of Isaiah. From hence those brief sentences, those sudden flashes of a style which resembles lightning, those unexpected antitheses, those touching contrasts, those melodies of the idyll—sweet as honey, yet cutting as the edge of a sword. For these reasons the classic school of Germany never admired Victor Hugo; on the contrary, it totally opposed his views, though he undertook a revolution equal in point of fact to the revolution of the romantic school in France. Goethe could not read " Notre Dame de Paris ;" he found it inflated, disproportioned, hyperbolical, false, removed from the eternal laws of reality, contrary to the strict harmonies of art. And Henri Heine, though he has greatly admired French literature, says that Victor Hugo was deficient in the three grand qualities of French genius —taste, grace, and clearness. On these points I will not contend. But genius is varied as nature. You will not search for the serenity of Raphael in the Titanic works of Michael Angelo ; you do not seek in the Book of Job for the tender elegy of the Œdipus of Sophocles. But you will not refuse a tribute of approbation to the genius of a great author because though wanting in some qualities, he has, instead of them, others still more sublime.

Great qualities cannot exist if not accompanied by great defects, for the light of the soul is only made visible by shadows. Imagine a perfect spirit possessed of all conceivable powers in a complete harmony and a just equilibrium—and what you would have in reality would be either a weak and infirm creature, a being with reason but without reality; or a very crdinary individual, without any of those strong touches, those extraordinary and peculiar qualities, which characterize genius. Victor Hugo is great, sublime, serene as the Moses of Michael Angelo, which appears seated on the *cuspis* of the earth, resting after an athletic labour, but disposed to continue, like the Creator who cast by a word the golden halo of the first light upon chaos.

Let us describe his life in a few words. Son of a General of the Empire, Bonapartism was during some time more than a political belief in Victor Hugo—it was a poetical conviction. The poet of strength should worship the genius of strength; the athlete of poetry should bow before the gladiator of war. He was filled with a delirious enthusiasm at the tempest of blood and fire which spread from the Alpine peaks to the Pyramids, and which swept from the Kremlin to Cadiz, sowing in its course death for that generation in a hundred battles, and the breath of life for future generations in the principles of the Revolution !

Moreover, Victor Hugo was for some period a

Legitimist, because of the education he received from a tender mother, who belonged to one of those French families ever faithful to ancient traditions. He shows the condition of his mind in an ode dedicated to the consecration of Charles the Tenth, that last glimpse of the antique monarchy then about to expire. When his mother died his genius was lost in his sorrow. In his grief he cut out of an obscure rock a deep cavern, where, like a new Cyclops, he made with his hammer a deformed statue, the sight of which drew from his breast heart-rending sighs. It was "The Han of Iceland," the first apparition of the ethics of ugliness, as many writers call the canons of romance. That sudden apparition in the midst of the correct forms of David, of the measured style of Chateaubriand, and of the works of Madame de Staël, different kinds of art at that time in fashion, must have produced the same effect as the invasion of the barbarians, the sons of the forest and of nature, in the last scenes of the Empire. They came naked, when Oriental customs had clothed the lords of the earth with heavy silken mantles, and with heavier gold crowns; they shouted with their brazen lungs, while the smoke of orgies deprived the Romans of their voices, so that they could scarcely chant the song of their pleasures.

At the age of twenty Victor Hugo married a young girl of fifteen, who brought love to his heart, peace and joy to his home; a ray of light in the tempests of his soul reflected from the heavens upon the griefs of his life—an angel who often became his guide in the bitter hours when he found the world a desert—a wife who sought from virtue the secret of happiness, a mother who kept for herself the aloes of existence, and divided the honey among her children.

They resided in the street of Notre Dame des Champs in Paris, among luxuriant trees, in a small house artistically furnished, where beautiful children played, where the wife divided tender words and sweet smiles among numerous friends, where birds warbled in the garden, and poets sang in the salon. That was a sacred legion. The men who afterwards intellectually directed France, swore to put down the idols and the powers of the classics. Afterwards, many of the friends who at that time formed the legion of innovators, abandoned Victor Hugo, but he alone refused honours, whilst those who exiled him sought honours, crosses, gold, places in the Senate, and pensions from the Revenue.

In 1830 Victor Hugo established himself in the Place Royale, where he reigned for the space of twenty-two years. His house was like the tabernacle of his genius. The sentiment of colour, the culture of art, a taste for contrasts, manifested themselves in that tapestry-covered salon, filled with arms, statues, urns, and with pictures, which gave enchantment to the sight and elevated the place into a spiritual temple.

There met together the romantic spirits of the age. The most celebrated lyric poets, novelists, dramatists, critics, went to receive the word of command, the signal for combat, counsel for a work, applause after a victory. There the words of their enemies were repeated, whom they proposed to persecute, to annihilate by force of talents, of grace, of ingenuity, using all kind of intellectual arms, indefatigable in a struggle, and determined to hoist at all cost the standard of victory.

Victor Hugo attempted everything, for to him so much was possible. As a historian he admirably sketched the character of Mirabeau, a genius whom he somewhat resembles in his ambition for tempestuous phrases and Cyclopean descriptions. As a critic, he wrote the Introduction of Cromwell, which was the poetic gospel of the new school, a gospel dictated with the inspiration of a prophet, sustained with the impetuosity of a warrior. As a novelist, he wrote those wonderful pages of " Notre Dame de Paris," in which we see the death of the Middle Age and the dawn of the Renaissance, in which the novel sometimes takes the grandeur of the epopee, in which the genius of Victor Hugo at sight of the press coming from the earth armed against the Gothic cathedrals, which incline as the cedars before the hurricane, begins to unfold his wings to fly from the refuge of his ancient beliefs, and to place himself on the arid and volcanic rock lighted by the ray of the Revolution, where is found written the decalogue of the rights of man.

It is common to all reforms to excite great hatred, and the inheritance of all reformers is to have bitter enemies. The lovers of the ancient school cannot tolerate the perilous novelties of the poet. To them his language does not appear to be French, his style is not literary, his versification is not dramatic, his personages are not theatrical types. They look with repugnance on the rehabilitation of Thisbe by filial piety, of Lucretia Borgia by the holy virtue of maternity, of Marion Delorme by love. That rawness of expression, that simplicity of type, that turning to the world and to nature, after the dryness of the characters and of the conventional language of the classic school, appear a series of daring offences, of buffoonery, of literary heresies, which revolt against all prejudices, and wound one's sensibilities—in a word, those habits of thought which have become a second nature.

But the great poet, without heeding these arrows, which rebounded from his bosom of bronze, continued to give glorious days to his country and immortal works to letters. In his most valuable books, which are his collections of lyric poetry, we can never sufficiently admire the flexibility of his genius. By the side of the epopee, the idyl; near the combat of heroes, the play of children; after the beatings of a heart which is bursting with sorrow, the rays of a star bathed in eternal light; beside the metaphysical, impalpable idea which proceeds from a volcano of passions, the butterfly of summer, which flutters among the petals and the aroma of flowers.

The genius of Victor Hugo is especially visible in
the animated and varied picture he draws of Naples;
where the vine twines her garlands and hangs in
rich clusters from the poplar; and the lemon-tree
contrasts its emerald verdure with the fainter green of
the olive; and the Eastern heavens, which shine like
the serene look of angels, covering the painful recollections of antique tyrannies, and a city of enchantment, of brightness, and of beauty rises by the side
of other cities, corpses, shrouded in petrified ashes as
in a winding-sheet; and above the azure sea, rise—like
Nereids crowned with pearls and flowers—islets as
beautiful as antique statues, and as gladsome as
the antique Naiads; whilst in the midst of this festival
appears Vesuvius, with its cone of lava like a funeral
catafalque, always sending from its dark bosom the
sound of eternal warning.

Advancing with the age, there came a transforma-
tion in the spirit of the poet. The dreams of the
Middle Ages fled from his soul, and left an entrance to
the ideas of our age. The oratorical genius, not less
uneasy and not less admirable than the poetic genius,
boiled in his conscience, and struggled to issue from
his lips in torrents of grand ideas clothed in majestic
language. The ancient monarchy, after having been
decapitated on the scaffold of the Place de la Révolu-
tion, after having long remained like an immovable
trunk, having many times sought a new existence,
sometimes enduring a *coup d'état* like that of the 18th

Brumaire—again in foreign interventions, like that of 1815—again in the barricades of 1830—the ancient monarchy fell again, and vanished like a shadow in the person of Louis Philippe. The people regained their sovereignty with the Republic and universal [male] suffrage.

The most eminent men in France were sent to the Assembly. It was impossible for the people to forget their great poet. Victor Hugo entered the Assembly, and from thenceforth devoted his burning and prophetic words to the cause of the people. The discourses of the great writer were marked by the same characteristics as his verses—force, enthusiasm, wonderful antithesis, astonishing inspiration. But many persons who heard him at that time have assured me that in his mouth glowing words lose much of their energy, and that, neither for the manner of pronouncing them, nor for intonation, does Victor Hugo merit the name of orator! I cannot judge, for I never heard him. But no matter how they may have been delivered, his speeches, whether well or ill spoken, will remain in French literature as models of the truest eloquence.

The *coup d'état* drove him from France. With his liberty he lost his country. From that time he wandered through strange lands, lonely and desolate; for exile, which is always accompanied by melancholy, is doubly sad for those who have once enjoyed a great popularity, who from having been honoured and beloved, are compelled to pass their remaining years in silence and retirement. Then the genius of Juvenal awakened in Victor Hugo. His satire became cutting and bitter. The grandiloquence of the prophets seemed united to the grace of Heine, and produced satirical pieces, sometimes in prose and sometimes in verse, which merit a place beside the compositions of Dante, near the gloomy figures of the condemned which Michael Angelo left intoning an eternal *Dies iræ* on the walls of the Sistine Chapel.

At length he decided to settle in one of the islands of the Northern Ocean, under the wing of English liberty, in face of that beloved France whose coasts may be seen from the flowery shore which the waves surround with their white foam and salute with their ceaseless music. There he has written in tranquillity, and with an inspiration which seems inexhaustible, those splendid poems called " Les Misérables," as " The Legend of the Age," more or less feeble in some parts, but grandiose and colossal taken as a whole : where the most beautiful figures of the past and the loveliest ideas of the future pass in prophetic visions, sketched with the firm fingers of genius, and with that warmth of colouring which is the secret of artistic power, and accompanied by the music of verses engraved eternally on the human memory, as breathing the aroma of immortality reserved for *true* poetry.

Our age is an age of prose. The pressing necessity to create for ourselves a better society than that enjoyed by our fathers, and to completely subordinate Nature to our dominion ; these reasons have caused all the activity of our time to expend itself in politics and in industry. Those men who, like Victor Hugo, raise their souls to the horizon of the beautiful, will be in the future as admirable as the Sphinxes of the Desert are at present ; they teach us that in the midst of ruin, in the midst of the troubles which encompass us, we may always preserve as an inextinguishable light the artistic inspiration in the human conscience.

We should not conclude the biography of the great French poet without speaking of one of these inspired poems, which is sweet and tender as the breezes which kiss the valleys of Provence, in which favoured land Victor Hugo was born ; a prayer, energetic and grandiloquent, now rapid as the rushing of the waves which break against the rocks of Jersey, now prophetic, patriotic, sublime as the voice of genius, as the echo of the holy ideas that surge in the mind of the poet and scatter themselves in sonorous verses, which are a torrent of faith, of charity, and of love. " *La Prière Pour Tous*" is perhaps one of Victor Hugo's compositions in which the most brilliant qualities are pre-eminent, and in which we admire the Christian poet, the friend of the people, the loving father, the apostle of humanity, who asks his daughter to pray for all the unfortunate. These verses have been translated into Castilian by the poet Andrés

Bello, and in the translation they lose nothing of
the brilliance of the images and the rhythmical harmony; so that we may say of this work, as Lamartine said to an English poet who had translated one
of his "Contemplations"—"I admire myself in your
verses."

ALEXANDER DUMAS.

ALEXANDER DUMAS.

I WOULD not believe any one who told me he had taken up a book of Alexander Dumas and laid it down in disgust and weariness. No one would do this. Dumas may be wanting in art, in style, in taste, in ideas, but never in graceful language. This extraordinary writer, while always interesting his readers, seldom obliges them to reflect. In the depths of our souls there remains a drop of the honey of innocence, and a cherished memory of the delights of childhood. No matter how much we have grown in reason and experience, the fables we loved to hear in infancy retain a charm for our riper years. You may have travelled all over gastronomic Europe; you may have sat at the first tables, and partaken of the rarest and most exquisite dishes; you may have lived in that great kitchen, that Babylonian warehouse, called Paris, and on tasting the familiar food of your native land you feel a keenness of appetite like that awakened by the fresh air of the country. Perhaps you have beheld the greatest natural spectacles of Europe — Vesuvius, which sends its volumes of smoke to the heavens; the fall of the Rhine, which flings up its foamy showers; the summit of Mont Blanc, with its eternal snows, and over which the sun casts a rosy light; the Black Forest, with its long rows of dark pine-trees, where the shadows and the silence invite to meditation—yet in the recesses of your memory there is a spot, sacred as a sanctuary, which treasures the land where your early years were passed; the tree, which lent its shade to your cradle; the place where your heart first opened to love; or that part of the heavens under which you breathed your first prayers.

We say that life is sad, yet we cherish the recol-lection of our early years. To the natural curiosity of children, which continues through all our lives in some degree; to the desire of being entertained, and of being separated from the daily realities of life, the pen of Alexander Dumas was always directed, and so successfully, that his works form in themselves not only a library, but a literature. When he was at the summit of his fame, at the period when his imagination was in such vigour that he was publishing ten stories at the same time, filling the magazines of Europe and America, and startling the press by showering his fertile pages like snowflakes from a winter cloud, I read "The Three Musketeers," clumsily translated into Spanish, and published in what was then a most important journal, *El He-raldo.* I can never forget the impression left upon my mind by the reading of that book. The characters are life-like, and stand out in such high relief, that I seemed to see them, to speak to them, to distinguish their features and manners, and even to compare them with real persons among my acquaintances. So absorbing was my interest in the story, that I watched for each new number with feverish impatience to read the end of these adventures, as if they were intimately connected with some one beloved, with my former friends, with my nearest relations, with my own soul.

I am not able to judge of the imperfections of the style because of my own imperfect studies, and of the very indifferent manner in which the work has been translated. I was not then aware that an intelligence so exalted should have furnished ideas more profound, and compositions more perfect. I needed, above all, the opportunity of comparing, and consequently of judging correctly. But that exciting narrative; that flashing style; those personages, so boldly described; those scenes, so marvellously woven together; that ever-increasing interest in the story—all this worked upon my imagination, and by the magic of art the fictitious world was changed into the world of truth, and poetry became as real as society or as nature.

It must, however, be admitted that we need not expect to find in Alexander Dumas that which we

meet with in poets and in writers of the first order—
ideas. Those analyses of the human heart, which
convert a novel of Balzac into a philosophical work,
are opposed to the lightness of Dumas. Balzac
enters into descriptions of life like a naturalist into
the fields, with his microscope and his instrument for
examining insects in his hands, and with a fixed
resolution to study. Dumas comes like a satyr into
the meadows, with the determination to repose in the
shade, to chase the nymphs, to feast upon grapes, to
drink wine to intoxication, to laugh even to delirium,
and to amuse himself and grow giddy with Bacchanalian
verses. This is truly a rare phenomenon. This
man, who is wanting in profundity of thought, is
also deficient in poetic inspiration. We must not
seek in his writings those highly-coloured pictures
and those powerful intonations which are traced by
Lord Byron, nor the immortal irony with which
Henri Heine laughed at his time. To have been
gifted with the poetic fire of the one, Dumas must
have had more genius ; and to have had the uncertainties of the other, more talent. His is perhaps a
remarkable individuality; without suitable ideas,
without relevancy of style; the creator of a world and
of personages, which sometimes resemble the world
and the personages moved by the machinery of an
organ for the amusement of children ; but he is nevertheless always elegant and enchanting, capable of
writing a hundred striking and highly dramatic stories,

without either descriptions or reflections, and with the most slender of arguments.

I have said that Dumas was a distinct individuality, and this word completely describes the man. So excessive were his conceit and egotism that he never troubled himself to conform to the society in which he lived. Without contradicting its ideas he contradicted its habits. He believed that everything was permissible to genius, when in reality all is forbidden to it, since the sword of envy is continually pointed at its shortcomings. He imagined that though deficient in self-respect he could inspire respect in others. He considered life as a matter of small importance, the events of which could be made to turn at his pleasure, as plots, dramas, histories, and romances were constructed by his pen. He never sought to conceal his fickleness, his low delights, nor his ill-temper, and did not scruple to expose his private affairs and his opinions. He collected around him a little court of parasites, whom he fancied would extend his fame; but, on the contrary, they maligned and degraded him. He was garrulous, foppish, feeble, and untruthful, telling many false stories of his travels, to make his own life seem like a romance; and wasted, in injuring his reputation after this fashion, more talent than would have been required to immortalize himself. In many respects childish, society treated him like a child badly brought up. And with those surpassing talents which the French possess for caricature, a satirical publication once represented him with a great lump on his curly head, a tambourine in his hand, and a baby's feeding-cloth under his chin, saying, " Here is a child who gives much anxiety—to his son." It was a sharp dash of Attic salt, for his son was really much troubled by his follies.

In many ways he carried his imprudences to excess. There was at that time in the Parisian theatres a celebrated actress, whose chief talent was silence. Being unable to affect her audience with the charms of language, she tried to please them with her eyes, her limbs, and her graceful attitudes. It became necessary for this mute young person to learn French, in order to revive the interest of the French people, who were already tired of her movements and monotonous exercises, which principally consisted in being fastened to a barebacked horse (like one of Lord Byron's heroes), and going no farther than from the front of the stage to behind the scenes. To learn the language, the actress had recourse to Alexander Dumas; and after some days, on the shelves of all the photographers appeared photographs, apparently taken from life, which informed the Parisian public that Alexander Dumas gave French lessons in his shirt-sleeves, with his pupil on his knee. The affair caused much scandal, though Paris is not very easily scandalized. His family, consisting of his son, a very grave person, and

of his daughter, who writes devout and holy books—
in fact, all his relations, were thrown into great
trouble. His children insisted upon their father
taking up the matter, and bringing an action against
the daring artist. The photographs were condemned,
as contrary to good morals. But Dumas was condemned also, for the photographer produced a letter
from him from Frankfort, asking for the photographs, in order to spread the story throughout all
Germany.

Everything in this world 'passes away, and, like
all else, the glory of Baron Brisse has departed.
Not long ago he was the protagonist of Paris, the
man in the fashion, certainly more read than any other
author. His works resembled those of Victor Hugo,
in that they were written in short sentences; but
these sentences were receipts for cookery, directions
for the kitchen, a sublime chemistry of sauces. This
illustrious personage, who appeared daily in the
periodicals and in the theatres, reminded one of those
men of the Roman Empire who went from banquet
to banquet, using a feather to provoke vomiting, after
which they returned to eat again, crowned with
flowers. In order to facilitate the evaporations of
the wine they devoured great quantities of food;
amongst other dishes, they favoured the eels of the
patrician tanks, fed upon the flesh of their slaves,
raising digestion to the heights of a philosophical
system, gorging and drinking without truce or ter-

mination, till the day in which they were pierced by the swords of the barbarians. I was wrong—Baron Brisse was merely ridiculous, not wicked. Girardin, who at one time tried to excuse him in *La Liberté*, afterwards treated him with much contempt on ascertaining that, trading on the reputation given to him by that journal, he begged hundreds of bottles of wine from the vineyard owners, cows and oxen from graziers, food from hotels, and refreshment from the cafés. In consequence of this he reigned only for a year. And Dumas, the great Dumas, the gifted novelist, the illustrious writer, lyric poet, dramatic author, one of the glories of France, one of the highest reputations of the age, envied the fame of Brisse, and wrote vigorous articles to prove that he himself was a much better cook !

And he who professed to be the Plutarch of Garibaldi, who pretended to have placed a stone on the great work of Italian independence, tells us that he did not visit Italy to admire the pictures, nor to study the secrets of the plastic art in the outlines of beautiful statuary, nor to breathe the perfumed air from the Alpine heights, nor to watch the play of light among the waves of the Adriatic—but in order to improve his knowledge of cookery, to expend the flower of his genius upon the method of preparing Neapolitan macaroni. And descending from dignity to buffoonery, he offered his books and periodicals as a prize to whoever would take tickets for a masked ball. Never did an enemy rob another of his fame with the insane pleasure with which Alexander Dumas stripped himself of his literary crown.

All these faults proceeded from numerous mistakes, and an erroneous conception of life. Dumas imagined that genius could follow one pathway and life another, without mutual injury. He fancied that the ideal could reign above in higher regions, in infinity, without illuminating, without giving vitality to those daily actions whose thread forms the whole web of our existence. And a man of genius ought to feel his own power, and elevate himself to an almost sacred position. In truth, evil mingles continually in all our actions, in every work of our existence; and although in small portions, it corrupts and poisons it as if with a corrosive virus, and the intelligence is deeply penetrated with this uneasiness; the distinction is soon lost between good and evil, the sensibility becomes deadened, and the whole life of the man is given up to the force of his own imagination. He receives no new light upon his actions, for poet and poem, artist and his work, are enveloped in the stupefying vapours of vice, which ruin his judgment. To be untruthful in a book of travels, to falsify fact in a historical work, appears at first sight but a light matter; yet it is much more serious when we reflect on its frequency, and on the enfeebling effect it has on one's mental powers. And, without doubt, a deliberate falsehood deprives a book of all authority, as proving the immorality of the writer. Such a work is useless, or worse than useless, though it may be a laboured creation of thought, though it may send forth rays which flash from the brain through a great effort, if they do not bear with them some of the light of conscience—a higher morality in the customs of society, a little consolation for the troubles of existence. I do not say that art is a moral work like a sermon, or useful as a teaching. Art has for its principal object the realization of a beautiful conception. But let us not forget that art is no exception from the general laws of life, nor is it a wandering comet, separated from the infinite orbit of justice. In this, as in all cases, evil eventually produces deformity.

Everybody believed he had a right to cast a stone at the triumphal car of Alexander Dumas when he entered as a conqueror by the *via sacra* of literature. This would have actually happened in the ancient world, if, when the people anxiously expected the coming of a conqueror—one of their own heroes— instead of seeing him enter clothed with a purple mantle, and wearing the crown of laurels, they had beheld him in the garb of a harlequin, and with an ape upon his shoulder!

Victor Hugo understands far better the nature of genius, and the character of the public. He from an island carved out a sepulchre which is a throne of glory, and from thence he shot forth the lightnings

of his genius, heard the applause brought him by
the waves, and beheld, while living, the glorious
spectacle of his own immortality.

But even if Dumas had been gifted with the profound genius of Calderon, united to the facility of
Lope, the lofty thoughts of Shakspeare, and the
flowing language of Petrarch, the world would think
him a buffoon, not from any want of intelligence, but
from the errors of his own life. The journalists used
every day to say something about Dumas in their
lightest pages; and the *gamins* of Paris called him
familiarly " Uncle Dumas." And yet this man filled
an entire generation with his works. He wrote a
library with his pen, created types which we carry in
our retinas, and profoundly affected us in the theatre
with the overwhelming ambition of Darlington, with
the brutal passion of Antony, with the dream of
Catherine Howard in her pantheon, and the vengeance of Christina of Sweden at Fontainebleau;
pictures full of light and of shadow, pictures which
forcibly represent the boldest types of the romantic
school.

He was a man who always remained a child, one
who compromised in that war of giants the struggle
for the poetry of nature against the poetry of the
academy, breaking the chains of all literary codes, and
loudly proclaiming liberty; ardent and daring even
to folly, like a hero in the war of his age against
past ages; an enthusiast in his opinions, even to the

weaving of crowns of laurel for his rivals and his
enemies. A lover of the drama, he proved himself
able to reanimate the theatre. To accomplish this
purpose he chose pieces of lively interest, characters
of a strongly marked individuality, descriptions of
unbridled passions, which though without the artificial rules of poetic conventionality, followed the inspirations of fancy in its native purity, and were
powerful enough to awaken artistic attention. And
in this struggle he had, as in all literary battles, to
sustain implacable hatred. In material wars they
discharge cannons, and shed blood; in these artistic
contests they disperse calumnies, and slay reputations.
Thus it is no marvel that Dumas was so much calum-
niated. The incomprehensible puerilities of his life
much injured the prestige of his talent. The fever of
creating took vigour from his creations. He was
extremely grand superficially, but shallow in reality.
In his eagerness to produce literary works he brought
them out imperfect. Lope de Vega also acted in this
fashion; but Lope de Vega was born in another age,
and with another genius. The work for humanity in his
time was not so grand as it is at present, and not so
much overcome with its own gravity. Suffering
himself to be carried away by his own inspiration, he
erected figures, personifications, characters, immortal
individualities. His numerous stories still serve for
materials for the theatre. In looking at his inexhaustible conceptions, they seem like a virgin forest,

notwithstanding that three centuries have passed, during which his successors have been cutting them down. Lope left thousands of sketches, which his followers have converted into pictures; thousands of stones scarcely polished from whence wonderful statues have been chiselled. But besides, Lope as a great poet, possessed in a high degree the faculty of combination. His ideas were interwoven in verses of a lightness and a wonderful brilliancy. They were like clear-set diamonds, which shot forth sparkles of all colours. Dumas came into the world too late to possess so great a fecundity, which alone belongs to primitive epochs, during which, above all other necessities, is felt the necessity of producing and creating. Dumas has not left us new types; on the contrary, he has remade the old ones. Dumas did not imagine arguments; he took and adopted them. Dumas did not conceive the perfect plot, which of itself alone so often constitutes a poem.

Dumas was born the 24th of July, 1802. His grandfather, the Marquis Dary, married a negress called Trinnette Dumas. The fruit of this union was the father of the poet, a mulatto. There was certainly in the blood—in the restless genius, in the fecundity of the novelist's imagination—something of the characteristics of his grandmother. And of course, living in an age which cried out with so much contemptuous pride against Dumas for his singularities, his enemies did not fail to observe on the conditions of his race and the colour of his blood. One day Balzac, who was continually pursued by his creditors, complained to an editor who was paying him poorly for a book. The other said, " I pay you the same as I pay Dumas." On which Balzac retorted angrily, " I will have nothing. Keep your money, and give me back my manuscript, since you have dared to place me on a level with that mulatto."

In fact, Dumas showed in his person many of the characteristics of the negro race. He was tall, corpulent, nervous, formed for Herculean labours. His complexion was dark and pale, almost of coppercolour, and his hair curly. He had projecting eyes, a narrow forehead, open nostrils, and thick lips. Self-satisfaction was strongly marked on his countenance; there was irony in his glance and in his smile, something infantile in his whole bearing and his manner, a sort of puerility in his old age, like one of those fruits which never arrive at maturity. And he was the son of a man who led the life of a hero—a life of struggles and of personal sacrifices. The father of Alexander Dumas was at the wars of the French Republic in 1793. The revolutionary hurricane had passed over France, awakening the strongest passions and infusing heroic greatness into the souls of the generation of that epoch. The country and liberty renewed on the banks of the Rhine the marvels of Salamis and of Plataea. The soldiers, almost without food and clothing, intoxicated with the divine idea of justice, excited themselves to a mad enthusiasm with the song of liberty which then resounded in all quarters, set out for the frontier to encounter the regular troops, strong, disciplined, directed by kings and nobles, who appeared to be invincible in their severe majesty. The courage of the people was in-disputable, their determination unflinching, and their victory was the miracle of the age. With them the father of Dumas received the baptism of blood, and entered into the rank of heroes. Rising from one grade to another, and proving his valour in every battle, he was advanced to the post of General, and became one of the companions of Hoche. In the time of the Empire he retired from the army, and lived and died in poverty at the beginning of this century. Alexander Dumas never knew his father. He was born in 1802, and his father died in 1806. At so tender an age it is impossible to preserve the recollection and the image of those who are most beloved ; and doubtless the man born in the free air of America, nurtured among the rude clamours of battle, vigorous as a tree of the New World rooted in the soil of Europe—a contemporary of great epochs and a witness of mighty actions—a hero in those camps from whence proceeded a new idea and a new existence—faithful to a most noble cause, withdrew in a season of servile obedience and of luxury, when camps were like towns and soldiers like ordinary citizens—withdrew from this inglorious life of inaction, living in poverty, being faithful to his convictions, and dying in sad loneliness, almost an exile, preserving the worship of his recollections. The brave father of Dumas, had he lived, would have been a living example and a lesson which would have inspired the poet with nobler thoughts, and led him to higher aspirations.

The early part of his life was devoted to the cultivation and development of his muscular strength and his naturally powerful physique. He was a good horseman, skilled in the use of fire-arms, and active in the chase; a lover of all bodily exercises, much addicted to a wandering life in the country, where he contracted that poetic vigour which afterwards took possession of his mind; and it was thus he preserved the perfect health for which he was remarkable.

Dumas soon felt the desire to be known, which is common to most men of talent, and at the age of eighteen he became a clerk in the office of a notary. A friend of his, a Parisian, who discovered his tastes and capabilities, advised him to make the theatre his profession. Dumas wrote several short pieces, which were sent to Paris, and refused by all the theatres. Not discouraged by these failures, he went to the great capital. His friends procured him letters of introduction to influential persons, amongst them to the generals of the Empire, and others, adherents of the Restoration. Nobody took any notice of him except General Foy, who, seeing the youth had a very favourable testimonial, procured him an appointment in the houschold of the Duke of Orleans, with an annual salary of twelve hundred francs. "To-day I live upon my letter," said Dumas; "to-morrow I will live after my own fashion." And soon he offered a new dramatic work to the Ambigu. Being associated with others in this first-accepted piece, he only received for his own share four francs for the price of representation. Not long after he presented another drama to the Gymnasium, and for this he gained two more francs.

It is impossible to describe or to imagine how much a young man of ability suffers during struggles of this nature. He is aware that he carries the world in his brain, a poem in his language, a great glory in his life, possibly new light for his epoch, and honour for his country. And yet he is unable to attract public attention towards himself, cannot even fix that of his own friends. He has but an obscure name, to which nobody listens. If he dares to show any talent in conversation, he is taken for a pedant. He lays his manuscript upon the table of an editor, or the director of a theatre, and they will not even look at it. He becomes discouraged in the struggle, is exhausted by heart-sickness and despair, often begins to doubt himself, to lose all faith in his own powers, and in his depression and disappointment reaches the point which annihilates his hopes, and is the suicide of his genius. What a stormy life is that of letters! A

Herculean labour to open a pathway; a Titanic wrestle for existence. The world's justice, universal appreciation, is not attained by victory, as on the field of battle; it is won by death, as in martyrdom!

Dumas had previously written a drama of great interest, "Christina of Sweden." His detractors said he took it from some celebrated German memoirs; but the dramatic author must gather his arguments from history and romances, as the sculptor takes his stone from the bosom of nature. Baron Taylor was then manager of the Théâtre Français. Few men in Paris have been so celebrated as this Baron Taylor, and for several years I endeavoured to investigate the cause of this celebrity, without being able to ascertain it. I asked many persons connected with the press, with the Government, and also men of letters, and no one was able to satisfy my curiosity. Everybody acknowledged that he was celebrated, but no one was aware of the reason of his reputation. There was no literary banquet without his presidency, no burial without his discourse, no first representation except under his auspices, no festival or rejoicing without his presence. Baron Taylor laid his protecting hand over the head of young Dumas, and promised to produce his drama in the Théâtre Français. But just at this time there was a funeral, and, as I have said, there could be no funeral of importance without the presence of Baron Taylor—certainly no academic funeral. It was then proposed to bury the

obelisk of Luxor, hewn from the stones of the first
volcanic days of Creation, enriched with hieroglyphics
which preserve the early secrets of antique civilization, gilded by the sun of the desert, sadly placed as
a tree transplanted on the gloomy banks of the Seine,
under the winding-sheet of eternal clouds; and as the
funeral *cortége* was to accompany the great corpse
from the Nile to the Seine, it was impossible for
Baron Taylor to be absent on such an occasion.
Then Dumas saw all his hopes vanish of a representation in the Théâtre Français. A dramatic author
said to him, "Do not fancy you can have your works
represented while you are without fortune." It was
a great cruelty towards the young man, and a real
injustice to the poet. At length, in the following
season, "Henri Trois" was represented.

Then came the days of July; Dumas was twenty-
eight years of age. His impressionable nerves
became more irritable than usual. His enthusiasm
burned in his heart. Recollections of his early
Republican education thronged upon his memory.
The warrior's life tempted and seduced him, as it was
natural that the idea of greatness should take possession of the soul of a son of nature, accustomed to
the liberty of the fields. Dumas heard the booming
of the cannon, the whistling of the balls, the sounding
of the attack, the shouting of the multitude; and he
rushed into the street determined to struggle to the
utmost, like a hunter accustomed to fatigue. There

are many who attribute the almost incredible heroism
of Dumas to political ambition. I do not share this
belief. If he had had political ambition, instead of
the wild and irregular habits of an artist, his manners
would have been marked by the decent gravity which
becomes deep thinkers. If Dumas had been really
ambitious, he would have commenced by putting his
own house in order, and thus proving his capacity for
ruling a republic. I have always believed that men
of great imagination are not suited for the government of the State. Certain qualities are only possessed at the expense of others; the lion cannot have
the voice of the nightingale; and as bodies contain
organs in harmony with the ministry of nature, so
talents have faculties in harmony with their social
ministry. When one ascends to metaphysical heights
in the sublime regions of eternal harmony, and is
moved by the living source of inspirations—bathed
in the pure dew of ideas, and accustomed to things
higher and nobler than those of earth, on suddenly
descending to the lower spheres one stumbles
against all obstacles, and a grain of sand appears an
insurmountable barrier. Imagination, sentiment—
those flashing inspirations, those lightning ideas,
which overwhelm the organism, and shake it with its
mysterious electricity—if one be a great poet, a great
writer, or a great orator; if one have something of
the divine, something of the artist in one's nature,
these qualities will not serve for earthly subjects, for

the dreary realities of political life. Wings are
created for the immensity of the air. On the earth
they but embarrass the footsteps; they circumscribe
the pathway. Plato wrote his " Republic," but can
we be sure he would have been able to govern it?
Demosthenes could inflame a legion with his
eloquence, but can we think he could have directed
it with his tactics? If each individual would but
cultivate his predominating qualities; if he would but
strive for that step on the social ladder which is most
suited to his ability; if he would employ his aptitudes
and his activity in those objects for which they were
created, the world would be a marvel, a chorus of
ineffable harmonies, a return to the blissful days of
Eden. Society has much need of reformation in these
matters. Instead of appreciating so very highly
certain social employments, and despising others as
contemptible, it should esteem them all equally, for
all contribute to the well-being of the world we
inhabit, and to the happiness of the human family.
Men ought only to abhor vice and to punish crime.
They should regard among the most useful and
honourable of social employments that of the labourer,
who fertilizes the earth, and eats bread in the sweat
of his brow, as so much more noble than a life of
wealthy idleness, wasted in sports, dances, banquets,
and horse races? I believe, then, that Dumas,
knowing himself to be a Poet, did not aspire to be
a Minister of State.

The theatre and romance were naturally the vast field of his mental activity. He has been reproached with having had *collaborateurs* in both departments; but I declare that all these *collaborateurs* lost their brilliancy when they separated from Dumas. And I must add, that all of them united do not weigh in the literary balances of Europe half as much as Dumas weighed alone. And as for plagiarism, we should observe that originality becomes every day more difficult on account of the literary riches we acquire by inheritance, and the great activity of the human intelligence during the three last ages of the increasing reign of liberty of conscience. But as to this accusation of plagiarism, Dumas defended himself in a manner the responsibility of which I leave to him, and the appreciation of which I leave to his readers.

On one occasion Dumas said, "Observe that a pirate robs, and that Alexander conquers. In the long run the thief and the hero do the same thing; but humanity rewards the robber with a gibbet, and places a crown of laurel on the head of the hero. The same thing happens in literature: everything has been already discovered; there is no new Columbus, because there are no new worlds. We have travelled all over the world, and we have not found a new continent; in like manner, unknown regions can no longer exist in the immensity of human knowledge. We all live in a well-known land; we all copy, only that as there are pirates and heroes, so in literature there are plagiarists and conquerors. I have not robbed, I have conquered."

The number of those who have pretended to have had a share in the works of Alexander Dumas is almost unlimited. If any credit could be given to his enemies, a single feather would not be left in the wings on which he soared to so high a reputation. I have before me the libel of the pious Mirecourt upon Dumas—Mirecourt, one of the most orthodox of Frenchmen. Here it is:—" Delanone is the author of 'Napoleon,' signed by Alexander Dumas ; Gérard Nerval and Gauthier were the authors of 'Charles VII. ;' Emile Souvestre the author of ' Antony ;' Aniceto Bourgeois the author of ' Theresa,' ' Angela,' and ' Catherine Howard ;' Thealon and Courcy the authors of ' Kean ;' the Count Walewski the author of ' Mademoiselle de Belle Isle ;' Leuven and Brunswick the authors of ' Les Demoiselles de Saint Cyr ;' Paul Meurice of ' Ascanio ;' Mallefille of ' Les Deux Dianes ;' Macquet of ' Le Cavalier de Armenthal,' of ' Les Trois Mousquetaires' and of ' La Reine Marguerite ;' Conilhac of ' Les Mémoires d'un Médecin.' " But we should never finish if we attempted to enumerate the works of Dumas, and those of the many said to be his literary assistants.

For such a task we should require a folio volume ; add to this a list of the most ruinous lawsuits that have ever occurred in the memory of French tribunals. Gaillardet writes a drama entitled " La Tour de

Nesle;" as plot, as argument, as a creation of types and personages, the drama is a work of merit; but the *dénouement* is indifferently written, and, above all, there is in this drama, notwithstanding its interesting situations and warmth of style, evidence of great inexperience, of much want of theatrical knowledge. Jules Janin, the critic of *Le Journal des Débats*, attempted to correct it; but Jules Janin, who knew how to criticize, did not know how to create. He was about to throw away the drama, when Dumas took it in hand, regulated it, polished it, flung over it the golden powder with which he adorned his peculiar style, and the result was a drama which was received enthusiastically. But in consequence of this there followed a lawsuit. Macquet pretended that he wrote "Les Trois Mousquetaires." A new lawsuit. One *collaborateur* demanded seventy thousand francs. Another lawsuit. Dumas founded the historic theatre, which he thought he could support with his historic pieces; the speculation fails, and the creditors fall on him like flies. A lawsuit follows. Merlsem accuses him of literary falsehood, in having published in his periodical, *Le Caucase*, a kind of plagiarism of his books. This also resulted in a lawsuit. It would be impossible to exaggerate the scandals which accompanied these lawsuits.

Alexander Dumas did not go unpunished for the two gravest faults of his life—two faults for which it would have been most difficult to atone. The first was, to take life as a continual jest. Life is itself so grave a matter that whoever falsifies it becomes corrupt. This great gift of life must not be received as false money ; on the contrary, we should accept it as a metal which we are bound to purify in the fire of conscience, and to refine eternally. Each one of us should endeavour to elevate his own life, so that it should be a model for the lives of others. And when, after all this striving, a man has succeeded in thus elevating himself, his life becomes like a lighthouse, that cannot be hidden or extinguished—a star, to which all others turn as to a centre ; but nobody can feel any respect for a person whose conduct is not worthy of esteem.

One day Alexander Dumas presented himself at a ball given by the Duke of Orleans, with a lady whom he had no right to introduce into such society. The Duke said, " I believe, M. Dumas, you have brought your wife to my house?" To escape from such an embarrassing position, which would have betrayed ignorance of, or an indifference to, all social propriety, and in order not to fall into disgrace with the Duke, Dumas was obliged to marry. But he immediately separated from his wife, promising her five hundred francs a month for income. This, however, he never paid; and one day the woman went to him and complained of this neglect. " Ah !" he said, " so you do not find five hundred sufficient? Then I will allow you one thousand." Of course, according to his manner of performing his promises, he might have given her a million daily without difficulty.

At another time he quarrelled with Louis Philippe, because he put off giving him that red *bouton* of the Legion, for which Frenchmen would make almost any sacrifice. Dumas wrote some bitter epigrams against his ancient protector, which, as may be supposed, deprived him of the King's favour. He afterwards petitioned the Duke of Orleans to intercede for him. One day, when Louis Philippe was at the Trianon, his eldest son concealed the poet behind a curtain. When the King passed, the Duke of Orleans withdrew the curtain, and Alexander Dumas appeared kneeling, with his hands folded in supplication. " Schoolboy, schoolboy," said Louis Philippe, pulling him sharply by the ear. Alas! is it for this that God gives a glowing imagination, and places a lyre in the hands of those privileged beings we call poets!

I have said that informality was one of the faults of Dumas, and now I must add that a commercial spirit was the other. I do not believe he was the plagiarist his enemies assert. I do not say that all his works were written, during his thirty years of activity, by *collaborateurs*. On the contrary, I have already observed, that separated from him his *collaborateurs* achieved nothing brilliant. Perhaps comets are loose hairs from the sun, which fall from his fiery head; when united to the great focus, they form with him, the light; separated from the fountain of light, they are but wandering filaments, *materia cosmica*, which soon vanish—a gas, a splendour, nothing. But Dumas did not content himself with producing, he was not satisfied without creating, and living with his creations. He desired to realize an extravagant luxury, such as Providence scarcely ever permits to persons of great genius who possess so much wealth in their own intelligence. This obliged him to make enormous outlays. To meet these expenses he was forced to enter into obligations, and these obligations led him to absurd associations. From these associations many supposed he received his light; but they were in reality but atoms in that whirlwind which I will not call ideas, but fantastic creations. The sublime privilege of genius should be to aspire not to gold, but to glory; not to ephemeral enjoyments, but to immortality.

Probably but few men have been born with so many and such brilliant qualities as Alexander Dumas. His dramas are somewhat deficient in finish, but they are highly interesting. His novels contain nothing ideal, but much that is enchanting. Had he taken time for reflection, he would have produced some perfect work. With such great rapidity this was impossible. His creations are meteors when they might have been stars. Here we find a poet of a wonderful imagination, of an extraordinary power, fallen in the mire of the Parisian streets; punished for not having considered life as a reality, art as a religion, genius as

a ministry, the world as a tribunal, and history, that
conscience of humanity, as a judge.

We should remember that the earth is a temple
filled by the Almighty, that each individual is a
priest, that each profession bears a divine character;
that we should employ all our powers in the development of great ideas, and that responsibility grows in
the same proportion as merit, in the measure in which
the sovereign faculties increase, in the way in which
applause and glory become greater. If there is a
life replete with moral lessons, it is surely that of
Alexander Dumas. His punishment was a great and
salutary warning.

EMILE GIRARDIN.

Emile Girardin.

WHEN I take a newspaper in my hand, and glance over its columns; when I consider the diversity of its matter, and the riches of its contents, I cannot help feeling a rapturous pride in my epoch, and a thrill of compassion towards the ages which were unacquainted with this powerful channel for human intelligence, this most extraordinary of human creations.

I can comprehend societies without steam engines, without the electric telegraph, without the thousand marvels which modern industry has sown in the triumphal path of progress, adorned by so many immortal monuments. But I cannot understand a society without this immense volume of the daily press, in which is registered by a legion of writers, who should be held in honour by the people, our troubles, our vacillations, our apprehensions, and the degree of perfection at which we have arrived in the work of realizing an ideal of justice upon the face of the earth.

I can understand the monastic life, even to the isolation of a man who renounces the intellectual pleasures of society and the delight to be found in family affection, in order to consecrate himself to religion, to science, to charity, to meditation, to idleness, if he will, in one of those moral islands which we call monasteries. But I cannot understand this man resigning the reading of newspapers, giving up his daily co-operation in thought with the brain of all humanity, his sympathy with the hearts of his fellows, the mingling of his life with the great ocean of human existence, his interest in the agitation of its waves by the breath of new ideas. The ancient Chinese had a powerful institution—that of historians. Shut up in a palace surrounded by gardens, the Chinese historians devoted themselves in silence to the task of writing down daily events, with the severe majesty of the judges of those times, of the dispensers of immortality. Beside the celestial dynasty of Emperors was placed this severe dynasty of tribunals. They formed something more than a magistracy, they were a priesthood, and they dealt with all as if they were the representatives of the human conscience, and the emissaries of the divine justice. Their ministry consisted in engraving on immortal pages, to be preserved as the heritage of generations, the most important acts of the Empire. No people ever honoured their priesthood as the Chinese, who have lived in perpetual infancy, honoured these historians.

I think that modern peoples ought in a similar manner to honour their journalists. For these exceptional witnesses know what rays 'of light cross each other on our horizon ; these public judges prescribe rules which form the judgment of the human conscience upon all actions. The passion of parties is of small importance ; without it perhaps we should not be able to comprehend this prodigious work, which, like all human works, necessitates the steam of a great passion to set it in motion. The studied silence upon some subjects matters little, nor the partiality shown on others, nor the injustice, even to falsehood, so often manifested ; for from this battle of spiritual forces results the total life, as from the shadows we perceive the harmony of a picture. It would be better if we had not these evils, so we should be more happy if we had not either physical infirmities or moral misfortunes ; but it is as difficult to rectify society as nature, and its laws are as complicated as the mechanical laws of the universe, and at times as fatal. And it is a fatality of the social organism that progress encounters obstacles in the great efforts designed to advance it ; the past, with its errors, rises against all kinds of advancement, and makes the utmost efforts to destroy it. But from the cloudy and intricate world of falsehood arises a luminous ether, which forms the world of truth. However, if all the different institutions, of which people are so proud, were one day called to judgment, and if each of them showed both the good and the evil they have done, perhaps not one of them could retire from the trial as pure as the press, and none would more justly merit a blessing from humanity.

What a wonderful work is a newspaper—a work of art and science! Six ages have not been enough to complete the Cathedral of Cologne, and one day suffices to finish the immense labour of a newspaper. We are unable to measure the degrees of life, of light, of progress, that are to be found in each leaf of the immortal book which forms the press. We find in a journal everything, from the notices relating to the most obscure individuals, to the speech which is delivered from the highest tribunal, and which affects all intelligences; from the passing thought excited by the account of a ball, to the criticism on those works of art destined to immortality. This marvellous sheet is the encyclopædia of our time; an encyclopædia which necessitates an incalculable knowledge—a knowledge whose power our generation cannot deny—a knowledge which is as the condensation of the learning of a century.

When I picture to myself Athens, I fancy her resplendent with her legions of sculptors and poets; with her assemblies where each discourse was a hymn, with her singers, with that theatre whence were visible the bright waves of the Mediterranean, with those processions in which Grecian virgins, crowned with flowers, danced to the music of the citherns;

with those statues, which almost realized the perfect idea of plastic beauty; with those Olympic games, in which snowy steeds drew in gilded cars the players armed with lances, as Jupiter with his lightning; with her schools, in which were taught at the same time, metaphysics, gymnastics, music, and geometry; with all her life, which was the divine worship of art and beauty! But, alas! all that luxury and civilization saddens me. It was worthless, in that it had no newspapers; and for sake of the newspaper let us cease to be inhabitants of a city, and be citizens of the world.

Labourers of the press, modest and obscure writers! You have never been able to measure the great importance of your occupation, because you live in the midst of it, and consider it almost as a portion of your own being. But, alas! without you the most illustrious personages would be lost, the most glorious works would be as bells sounding in space. You bear to each individual the sorrows of all others; you bring to the afflicted the hopes of all humanity. Your pens are like the electric wires, which unite the most distant regions of our planet. Your ideas resemble the atoms of air in which our souls respire; they are the moral atmosphere of the globe. It is necessary to weigh well all the gravity of such a ministry in order to exercise it with becoming grandeur and dignity. It is one of the most sublime works of which the human understanding is capable. Let us speak of one of the soldiers of the press.

Near the Arc de l'Etoile, in the Avenue du Roi de Rome, there is a magnificent house, inhabited by one of the first journalists in the world. His name is Emile Girardin, and I shall endeavour to describe him in this imperfect and incomplete sketch. After having portrayed his life, I shall describe the writer I have known in the capital of the world, where his writings are approved by some, condemned by others, but are universally interesting. Emile Girardin is remarkable for having done two very difficult things ; he has called public attention to himself, and after having strongly attracted it, he has fixed it permanently. Let us narrate his history.

His birth was singular. He neither knows the year nor the day in which he entered the world, being the child of unlawful love. When in his daily battles with the pen this misfortune was cruelly flung in his face, he, who in this matter was blameless, said to the Imperial journalists, " Truly my mother was not the only great lady who in the time of the first Empire had children which did not belong to her husband." He himself is uncertain whether he was born in 1802 or in 1806 ; whether his name is Emile Girardin or Emile Celamothe. France takes great interest in all her illustrious men. But this does not prevent them from being annoyed; on the contrary, the smallest actions of their private lives are publicly discussed. Proudhon desired a law of *habeas corpus* which should protect homes from the entrance of bailiffs, if not a law of *habeas animam* which should protect private lives from the attacks of biographers.

Girardin is now sixty-six years of age, and is in his work what Thiers was in the Assembly, for he has preserved all his youthful fire, all his constancy, all his talent for improvisation, all his energy in labour.

His education suffered from the misfortune of his origin. One of the greatest evils of illegitimate connexions is the necessity of hiding the children—the great pride of the heart, the most precious treasures of holy and lawful affection. A child, which is the glory of a virtuous mother, is changed by immoral parents into a source of remorse in the conscience, and of dishonour before society.

The parents of Girardin concealed their son in a small house on the Boulevard des Invalides, which was then an exterior suburb of Paris. There he was educated, on the banks of the Seine, among the beautiful avenues which adorn the neighbourhood of the city, and the sombre but majestic monuments which record the history of France.

He passed his first years in a strange school—what may be called a house of baby-boarders. A good woman, Madame Choisel, nursed children confided to her by wealthy families. Some of them were legitimate, which is not singular, since French mother

16

have contracted the detestable habit of deputing to others the holy task of the rearing of their offspring. Madame Choisel never admitted more than ten little boarders. In the same house there was this boy and a girl, the afterwards celebrated Teresa Caburrus, a woman of extraordinary beauty, whose grace and talents had so much influence on the events of the beginning of this century, and whose artifices so much contributed to the fall of the Republic.

The life of the boy Emile was then happy. His parents procured him whatever could satisfy his childish desires. They seldom visited him, but they showed him much affection on those rare occasions, though they concealed his name and his abode. Sometimes a young lady of rare beauty went to see him, in a carriage lined with crimson satin, and lavished upon him her caresses often mingled with tears. Sometimes a tall young soldier, of distinguished appearance and severe countenance, who recommended the boy to the heads of the establishment with solicitude and an air of imperious protection.

Madame Choisel and her husband naturally wished to penetrate the mystery which surrounded the child's cradle; but the city is large, and the investigation of affairs of this nature is difficult. And at that time the society was not founded which now exists, with suitable organization, offices, and advertisements in the papers, the business of which consists in ascertaining the particulars of other people's lives, and in paying agents to follow those persons whom some friend or enemy has an interest in concealing.

The noble pair who felt so much anxiety for Girardin put gold into his hands, but often left sorrow in his innocent heart. The good Madame Choisel burned with impatience to discover the name and position of these mysterious personages. And as there is no place which is unfilled, so there is no doubt which is not resolved, no secret which is not eventually discovered in society, where justice is, in the end, the prevailing power in the ceaseless mechanism of the universe. At last the lady disappeared altogether. Emile was left without the brightness of the eyes which kindled hope in his soul, without the kiss of those lips which left upon his own the sweetness of maternal love, so needed in childhood. This moral eclipse darkened his early years. And later, when the mysteries of life were made clear to his intelligence, he thought that some new fault had restrained his mother from visiting the child of her first error. As to the soldier, he still went occasionally to visit his son, but never alluded by a word to the absence of the lady.

Who was this tall military man who had the manners of a prince? Girardin did not know, and the owners of the house in which he lived were in equal ignorance.

At last the mystery was solved. In the suburbs of Paris there is a royal residence rising upon a wooded hill on the banks of the Seine, which looks at that part like a river of Switzerland, from its graceful windings, its broken-up borders, and its bright waters. Marie Antoinette bought this beautiful country mansion, and the purchase of St. Cloud was as fatal to the dynasty as the purchase of the Queen's celebrated necklace. Napoleon the First and Napoleon the Third both enjoyed this palace of St. Cloud, which from its vicinity to Paris unites the advantages of the capital and the pleasures of the country.

One day, when Monsieur Choisel was passing through the shady avenues of St. Cloud, he saw the Emperor's carriage approaching. Everywhere there is a natural curiosity to see the Chief of a State—him who holds in his hand the rights of men and the happiness of the people. It was still more natural to wait and contemplate that extraordinary genius who, over heaps of corpses, had mounted the ruined steps of the French throne, and placed himself on its summit, with the eagle of Jupiter on his sceptre, the laurels of Cæsar on his brow, the mantle of Charlemagne on his shoulders, the dictatorship in his hands, the world for an audience, kings for lacqueys, and for a slave—Victory. At the carriage door of Napoleon the First there was the mysterious protector of Emile, who was a General in the Army, and who filled the pompous position of Chief Huntsman in those Byzantine dignities with which the first Napoleon delighted to compose his Court. From that period Monsieur and Madame Choisel called their young ward " Baron."

But the proximity of his father to the Emperor was likely to be fatal to the future journalist. Napoleon, who considered his troops as an embellishment, and who regulated alike diplomatic treaties between nations and matrimonial alliances between the families of his partisans, insisted on the marriage of the Chief Huntsman. This was the greatest misfortune of Emile Girardin. Marriage caused that Chief Huntsman to forget the son of his early affections. The boarding-house became the abode of an Egyptian veteran ; former caresses were changed into cruelties ; luxury gave place to poverty ; and at the age of fourteen, shut up in a poor cottage and without any liberty, the afterwards brilliant writer seemed dying of sadness and debility, like a bird without air, or a flower without sunshine. His life was saved by a journey to Normandy. The keen air gave vigour to the enfeebled frame. He beheld the toil of the tillers of the earth, and hardened the hands destined to direct one of the lightest, most flexible, and most delicate pens in all modern literature.

After four years Girardin abandoned the life of the country—a life of labour, rudeness, and poverty, but beneficial to his health. When he laid down his spade he took up a book ; and in his few leisure moments he wandered into the woods, reading as he walked. He was entirely self-educated; hence arose those qualities which have never deserted him—the independence which he carried to caprice, and the self-satisfaction which amounted to egotism.

He soon broke through the servitude of his life in the country; for being a man with a real vocation, he felt himself too feeble for labour in the field, but strong to work intellectually. At the age of eighteen he left Normandy, and went to Paris. The peasant lad, by a miracle of his own will, was to be changed into a writer. Paris is an ocean where much is suffocated, but where also those who are skilful social sailors steer safely among the waves and winds. His first idea was to seek his father, and for this purpose he went to the abode of his childhood. Madame Choisel was unable to give him any information. He then went to see the veteran who had sometimes ill-treated him, the soldier of the Pyramids. He advised him not to raise a scandal. After a series of bitter disappointments he cultivated the truly exceptional faculties with which he had been gifted by nature—talents for the arts of writing and composition, which he carried to an extraordinary degree.

That year, 1824, was the epoch of the Restoration— a rule half absolute, half parliamentary—and at that period the Palais Royal was the centre of Paris. This immense building was always crowded with people, filled with shops, cafés, gaming-houses, and idlers ; it was a sort of Babylon of labour, and also of vice. To the indecencies of the place were, however, added reading-rooms and libraries, where the young literary men assembled. In this centre of ideas Girardin began to expand the faculties needful for his moral struggles.

At last he met his father, who had lived in obscurity during the adversities of the Empire. Although since his marriage he had been so cruelly neglectful of his son, he was not insensible to the appeal of the youth to the heart of his father. Nature recovered her voice and her rights. The General found for his son a position in the office of one of the Ministers of the Restoration. Then Emile Girardin wrote a book, which was partly a history of his own life, and to which he gave his own name—"Emile." It has throughout an accent of bitterness, a mocking scepticism, a spitefulness, a contempt for the most current and most admitted maxims and principles, that must give an unfavourable idea of the author, and this so much the more as he has brought forward all these theories as the code of rules for morality in practical life.

Girardin does not belong to the number of those men who have an ideal in their consciences, which they endeavour to realize by strict morality, and at a great cost in their lives. Girardin has always looked more to the real than to the ideal ; and rather than the combination of moral laws, he has regarded those mechanical forces of society by which so frequently enter crime, error, and injustice. He was not born with one of those easy temperaments destined to worship the imaginary or the platonic ; he was born for battle, and in the battle he has often been stained with mire and blood.

To live and struggle in a city so material as Paris, and in a society so egotistical as that of his time, money was essential. To possess a fortune — a splendid fortune such as he desired—the labour of a writer would not suffice; commerce alone could supply this necessity. The temple of gold is the Bourse ; the Bourse is the heavens from which fall the silver raindrops of sudden fortune. Girardin collected together some small savings which his father had intended for his majority, left the office in which he had been engaged, entered that of an agent of the Bourse, and thus proudly reached the door of the temple of fortune. But he was ill received ; Fortune turned her back upon him, and he was ruined. Then he retired and sought his father, who coldly rejected him. He knew not where to seek an asylum. The army surgeons declared his constitution too feeble for military service. Then, without name, without protection, without fortune, without friends, without family ; unable to follow the honourable career of a soldier, disenchanted with his dearest illusions, disappointed in his most cherished aspirations ; wounded in heart and mind, abandoned to the buffetings of fortune in the great city of Paris, where solitude in the midst of tumult is more sad than the solitude of the desert, there came into his mind, like a cloud that should cover his future, like a refuge from the storm—the terrible idea of suicide.

To combat with a great example the desperate resolve of suicide—to comprehend by a great example the miracles of the will, we have but to remember the poor youth so nearly shipwrecked in the year 1824, whose eloquence now flashes over Paris, and whose writings have a thousand times excited all Europe. His first desire was to possess a name, and for the future he signed " Emile Girardin." His second resolution was to engrave this name in the annals of the press : he wrote a book. His third resolution was to gain for himself an official position, which is often a ladder on which to ascend to rank and fortune.

Then he thought he would found a newspaper, without money and without contributors—a newspaper destined to reproduce and condense the contents of other journals. He gave this weekly sheet the name of *Le Larron*. As the result of his first efforts in the press, he had to fight two duels. In one he was wounded ; in the other he gave full satisfaction to his adversary on the field—it was his brother. Though both were of the same blood, sons of the same mother, they did not know each other, from their difference of name. Then he renounced the editorship of his first newspaper.

But he was born for the press, and he could never abandon his field of battle. The Restoration was losing itself daily in reactionary shadows, and Girardin established an opposition journal, which had distinguished patrons in the Court, amongst those members of the Royal Family who saw the power of the dynasty expending itself against the rocks of undisciplined and retrograde politics. Girardin's newspaper, with a strenuous opposition, contributed to hasten the catastrophe. Nothing was saved of the ancient monarchy. One of the members of the Royal Family was placed on the throne, saluted by the tambours of the National Militia; one who recognised the dogma of the people's sovereignty, written on the barricades with Republican blood.

The era inaugurated by the Revolution of 1830 may be called the mercantile epoch. The ancient *régime* was overturned, and the new one was not yet victorious; it seated itself on the throne of the sovereign, and profaned the altar of justice. All rights were bought and sold as in a vile auction. The *franc* was the number, the measure, and the ideal of all things. Money was the only monarch of that utilitarian society. If one wished to be an elector, he must give gold; to be a deputy, gold; to be a senator, gold; to be a juror, gold: and the gold, which is from its nature incorruptible, is a social corruptor when it fills the place of conscience, when it becomes the only dispenser of right. Girardin then established a newspaper of useful knowledge, at four francs a year—a journal which was the germ of the press, which on account of its cheapness we may call general, that later and on a larger scale was invented by the same journalist. At the same time he showed his great economic and administrative abilities, founding aid societies among the labourers, agricultural banks, and professional schools for the poor. He convinced the numerous subscribers to his *Review*, that by adding another franc to the four francs paid annually, they should, by the invincible power of association, be able to effect those marvels, of the force of which Fourier had so extreme an opinion as to declare, that if the world would give up the isolation so common among individuals, among classes, among nations, among races, which is at present its principle of war and its law of hatred, and would enter freely into the harmony of association, it would be able to pay with the produce of hens' eggs the National Debt of England.

But Girardin was soon disenchanted with these humanitarian dreams. His capital idea was to amass a colossal fortune which should give him a gigantic influence. Then he armed, so to speak, a society to establish another and a greater journal, *La Musée des Familles*. He was the inventor of those monstrous advertisements with huge letters and gaudy pictures, with notes of admiration and interrogation, which occupy the corners of the capital of the world, which every trade and business has copied in a greater or less degree, and which gave him the title of "bill-poster," or "placard man." With these means he published an almanac, called *l'Almanach de France*, which brought him a large profit. Then he fought his third duel with an editor who accused him of having betrayed the Government.

Time passed on, and in the year 1836 Girardin established *La Presse*, a purely commercial under-taking, although advocating a political principle. It was half the price of other newspapers, and contained double the amount of printed matter. The entire press was ready to destroy him on this account. One cannot provoke the anger of newspapers without raising up enemies. One cannot create such formi-dable enemies without exposing oneself to a dangerous struggle. The journals began to fling their darts at Girardin. Among these journals was one which had risen above all the others by its honourable reputation and its stoical character, edited by the illustrious and never-sufficiently-mourned Carrel, who spent his entire life in the defence of liberty, both by the sword and the pen. Girardin and Carrel fought a duel, and Girardin killed the most popular tribune of France. This death has cast a dark shadow upon the life of Girardin, and has for ever separated him from the

French Republican party. His bullet wounded the heart of all the youth of France, and pierced the front of the Liberal press.

After that he fought no more duels. One day he called the writer Bergeron a regicide. The latter went to the theatre (where the director of *La Presse* happened to be with his wife, the beautiful and *spirituelle* Delphine Gay), he entered the next box, which was unoccupied, in the middle of the representation, and, attracting the attention of the audience by a loud cry, gave Girardin a violent blow, awaiting a return with crossed arms and threatening gestures. Girardin arose slowly from his seat, placed himself on the other side of the box, far from the attacks of his adversary, and sat down quietly as if nothing had happened, remaining till the close of the performance. The next day he brought his quarrel before the tribunal.

La Presse never had a sufficiently fixed colour, never a strongly defined opinion; it turned to all winds from a false idea, from a false conception which Girardin holds of life, and another erroneous conception and idea which he entertains of politics. Girardin forgets that writers, orators, publicists are only great when they convert their whole lives into stars which revolve around a grand idea. From *that* they receive their light, from *that* their power, from *that* their true existence; for this idea is their sun. But when writers, when orators become the centre of their own universe, when they only value politics for the lustre reflected upon themselves, and ideas merely because of the brilliance they impart, then they lose the right to be public teachers; they forget the service of humanity, which is their only title of glory, their only pledge of immortality.

Wherefore wish for the gift of eloquent language? To display it as a courtezan displays a necklace of pearls and diamonds? Why desire the power of the pen? To attain a position which is more easily arrived at by even the lowest commerce? Oh! no. The pen and the tongue should serve humanity, should convey another ray of light to the focus of the human conscience, should bear another stream to the ocean of intelligence.

Girardin's false political conception has a double aspect—it is of action and of doctrine. Girardin desires such a complete independence that he will not ally himself to parties, so that they owe him nothing, and he owes nothing to parties. This is a fatal error. In politics we can do nothing alone and abandoned; we require the sacred legion of those who believe as we believe, of those who think as we think. Philosophy is a science more speculative than practical, and certainly great philosophers have always founded a school. Well, political schools are parties—they are armies which require discipline, abnegation, sacrifices for principle. It is only thus that those plants of a

new life can flourish which are so difficult to accli-
matize in the world.

Girardin's conception of political ideas is not less
erroneous than his conception of political conduct.
He says he loves liberty, and I believe it. But he
forgets that we cannot demand liberty from powers
which are alone founded on its destruction—which
are alone supported by its ruins. If Girardin had
reflected that liberty has its suitable forms and
ideas, he would not have supported the candidature
of Napoleon Bonaparte to the Presidency; he would
not have demanded liberty from the Empire. The
Bonapartes have no traditions of liberty except traditions of Dictatorship. How is it that a man who
foresees so much does not comprehend this simple
truth?

So the political career of Girardin has been like the
web of Penelope. He has laboured, like the Hebrew
of antiquity, seven years for Leah and another seven
years for Rachel. He has fought for the Empire and
for Liberty. But at the end of his days he is left
without either Leah or Rachel. He is deprived both
of the Empire and of Liberty.

Few men have been possessed of more brilliant
qualities, few have occupied a more exalted position.
Editor of *La Presse* during the Monarchy of July
and the Republic, also editor of *La Presse* and of
La Liberté under the Empire, his pen has cried so

loudly on the paper that it has been heard amidst the fury of the tempest, amidst the clamour of the battle, being certainly one of the most animated organs of this immense mechanism of modern society. But this is not sufficient. To make any intellectual structure durable, above all the inspiration of faith is wanted; to arrive at the choir of immortals, above all the heroism of faith is essential.

DANIEL MANIN.

Daniel Manin.

—

WHEN I arrived in Paris, one of my first impulses was to visit the spot where repose the ashes of all those who have obtained any worship from my heart or my intelligence. Great men lose much when beheld closely, in life's sad realities, where the mingling of a thousand little accidents lowers the moral stature, which imagination always lifts among clouds of glory. But in death all merit is acknowledged, and all greatness is justly measured. As the wind disperses dust, so death clears our vision, and enables us to see much which has been hitherto concealed.

The human race has a genuine reverence and admiration for great virtues. The thought of being forgotten, which so often accompanies that of death, does not trouble those men who have deserved well of their country and of humanity. Whatever there is in them which is changeable or accidental, caused sometimes by physical ailments which cast a sombre shade over their ideas; sometimes by the fiery glow which hot blood imparts to their opinions; sometimes

by disorders of the nerves—those ever-vibrating
chords of human life; all this is dissipated in death,
which carries with it all doubts, vacillations, and de-
partures from the right path of life.

Injustice, hatred, and envy never cease to torment
the living—even the best, for these are, like other
troubles, the penalties of perfection. Labour is impossible without strength; life without sorrow; glory
without drawing by its own heat from the mine of
the earth the black vapours of envy. But death is a
transfiguration; the tomb is a Tabor; the shades
which seem so gloomy when we behold them with
the eyes of flesh, are eternal splendours when seen
with the eyes of the intelligence. Decomposition,
ruin, cold, darkness, the sepulchre, are for souls as
the circle of shadows in which nature is enveloped, to
make more visible the stars of night.

Thinking thus, my first visit was naturally to the
dead, those whose memory I revered. Among them
was one whose battles in the city of Oriental dreams
and Greek poetry had attracted my attention from
childhood.   And, although then a boy, I had divined
in the relation of the events which appeared daily in
the Journals of 1848 the eminent qualities of that
tribune of independence, of that dictator of liberty.

And what days those were of 1848! We live much
in these times. Every post brings us a new surprise and
a new hope. The spirit glows like a heaven crossed by
innumerable meteors in a night of summer. It seems

as if the universal judgment is about to be celebrated,
as if God is coming in the clouds armed with justice,
placing on his right the elect, the people ; and on his
left, among the condemned, tyrants. Warsaw, Pesth,
Milan, Naples, Florence arose from their winding-
sheets and turned to the light. But among these
cities there was none whose life had been so illustrious
as that of Venice, and whose death had been so much
deplored.

And among the numerous tribunes, heroes and
martyrs, which the ardour of that creative age produced, there was none of such perfect integrity as
Manin. He appears like the personification of severe
justice arisen in the city of legends. He seems to
have in his character the conscience of the juriscon-
sults of ancient Rome, and the patriotism of Grecian
heroes : as if the spirit of the lost Romans, who
escaped the barbarians, and the lost Greeks who
escaped the Turks, had taken refuge among the
lagunes of his country. But to the grand qualities of
the antique character, Manin unites laws of life and
of conduct, which can alone engender the moral principles of modern philosophy. To arrive at good by
the means of good ; to rule human nature by ideas
more than by compulsion ; to govern a people as the
conscience governs life ; awakening in them, with the
voice of duty, a perfect morality ; never to sully a
great cause by a crime, not even for the welfare
of the country—these are the saving principles of

Manin's politics. Unite to the energy of Danton the conscientiousness of Socrates, and you will have the dictator of the lagunes—the man of Venice in 1848—Daniel Manin.

I visited his tomb in the cemetery Montmartre in Paris, by the pale light of funereal heavens, during the dismal days of November, when nature is wrapped in dead leaves, when the swallows quit this scene of general mourning, when the busy hum of insects has ceased, and when the heavens weep. He reposes in the tomb of Ary Scheffer, the melancholy painter of the Beatrice of Dante, revived by his brush, with her eyes lost in the contemplation of celestial truth, and her heart beating under her white tunic, the holy personification of Italy. I could have asked those sepulchral stones if within them lay also faith, valour, political integrity, all the public virtues which are so much required in our generation to reconquer the good. The silence replied to my unspoken question, and led me to meditation. To enable us to separate from all society, we must have a point of support, which is an idea; and a force, which is the energetic will of certain men. Manin acquired this moral greatness which is his glory and his title to immortality, as he identified himself with the desire which passed from the rocks of Thermopylæ to the sacred walls of Saragossa, as an immense bas-relief on the altars of patriotism—the idea of national independence. Talent, virtue, language, science, family affection, the respect inspired by a noble life, were so many other forces placed by this man at the service of his country. He sacrificed to this cause his fortune, his happiness, the dear companion of his life, the sweet daughter of his heart, his home, his country; he lived in the darkness of Paris, and died young and broken-hearted : but he sowed in these furrows of sorrow, watered by the blood of his soul, immortality for himself and glory for his country.

Some time ago, Paris, that capital of the European Continent, wished to exhibit the deep feeling inspired by the independence of Italy. And remembering that it contained an Italian treasure—the bones of the great patriot—it went, on the day of the commemoration of the dead, to carry crowns of everlastings to the tomb of Manin; groups of writers and of workmen—the moral and the material army of liberty bent their heads in silence before the stones which covered those honoured remains. In vain the police endeavoured to prevent this manifestation. Paris showed that she had not lost the antique worship for Italy, which had moved her to send, like a Spartan mother, her beloved sons to die at the foot of the Alps for Italian liberty. The day in which the great city was to lose this deposit confided to her hospitality was one of general mourning, destined to demonstrate as in all solemn moments, how many deep thinkers among the multitude this town conceals beneath its apparent indifference, as Mount Etna hides its fires

under its snowy mantle. The bones of Manin were
furtively taken from French earth and conducted to
the Italian frontier. A commission of those French
writers who had deeply moved the conscience of
Europe in favour of Italy, followed the remains of
the hero, in its journey to his country. It presented
a magnificent spectacle in the defiles of Savoy, among
the alpine declivities, on the borders of precipices,
among seas of snow ; this funeral *cortége* which lost
itself in the clouds of the mountains, accompanied by
the prolonged lamentation, formed by the movement
of the air among the pine trees, or the falling of
cascades from the rocks. I have never been able to
see a great mountain with its hills, from whose luxuriant slopes come the streams which fertilize the
fields ; with its girdle of woods and its pyramid of
snow, without regarding it as a great monument raised
by the Almighty, on which is ineffaceably engraved
the recollection of eternal things. And if anything
is eternal in the world it is heroism, it is sacrifice.

Death is cold and implacable. The bones of the
hero did not stir in his coffin when it passed under the
clouds of the Alps, or into the bosom of Italy, on feeling the soft air of the valleys, the rays of the southern
sun, the echo of that language as melodious as the
purest inspirations of music. It was observed that
neither Piedmont nor Lombardy manifested the
enthusiasm due to the remains of the hero. After the
misfortunes of Italy, the provincial and the municipal

spirits of the country awakened but slowly. The history of old and of new governments has taught us how difficult is the establishment of liberty, and how little durable it is if it be founded while local institutions do not exist with their separate life and independent organisms, such as those of the municipality and the province. Notwithstanding that the imperious necessities of the times, and the irresistible force of circumstances have forced Italy to become an Empire, she always preserves the federative principle in the essence of her political organism. But this should not be a reason for regarding her nationality with indifference, for the country has been built upon the bones of many martyrs, and is splendidly adorned with the crown of genius. We cannot then forget a man whose glory is so universal that he belongs to all humanity, though his lustre is more particularly reflected upon Italy.

But as the hearse drew near to Venice, an air of sympathy and enthusiasm passed through the towns and villages. The crowns which by-gone ages decreed to heroism, the palms of martyrdom were showered upon the coffin of Manin. The multitude ran to the borders of the railroad to do homage to the most sacred thing on earth—the remains of an organism which had contained the principles of virtue and of genius. In Peschiera—formerly a nail in the cross of Italy—the soldiers saluted from the walls and massive bastions, the triumphal procession of the dictator.

Truly, nothing so much predisposes to heroism as the example of martyrdom. When wars or struggles for independence are spoken of, Spain, never weary of sacrifices, is always mentioned. And our ancestors, the powerful Castilians, when they went to expel the Saracens from the enchanting gardens of Valencia, bore at the head of their army the body of the Cid, which though cold and still in death gained battles by the recollection of the virtues and of the glory which it excited.

In Verona, when the body of Manin passed, the people flung themselves upon the funeral car, to detain for a little time in their fields those ashes so dear to their country. At last they arrived at the mouth of the great lagune, where presides the lion of Mark ; of that lagune which is the emerald set in the wedding ring which unites the mysterious East with the land of the West. There the bier touched the soil made famous by the glory of the man whose remains it en-closed. By the side of the coffin were borne those of the wife of Manin, and of his daughter Emilia. A pale and tremulous youth mounted on a mule and clothed in mourning, with sorrow in his face and tears in his eyes, came slowly forward in the midst of a general silence only interrupted by sobs, to kiss the three coffins. It was the son of Manin, who since the last war of independence had suffered from the pain of an Austrian gunshot wound, received in the field of Brescia, where he fought to accomplish the last wish of his father by the side of Garibaldi, seeking to crown Italian liberty with the eastern diadem, called Venice.

It is said that poetry is dead in our time. But does not all this appear like the reading of a page from Grecian poetry; is it not remindful of those great days of Thermopylæ, of Platea, of Salamis, of which Herodotus has written and Pindar sung? Is it not like to that which has been described by Æschylus in his dramatic pieces, which is still repeated by the chisel in those bas-reliefs designed to be shrines to the two greatest ideas of human excellence—those of liberty and of patriotism? Sorrow is not extinguished in the world; the infinite thirst for justice is not slaked, and is insatiable. Our children will labour, as did our fathers, as we labour ourselves, to erect this work of progress that will never be finished as space is never finished, but is infinite as the universe. And future generations will read with wonder in their struggles for the conquest of better worlds the history of all these exiles, of all these martyrs who have known how to renounce the caresses of fortune, the pleasures of the day, the affections of family, the delights of home, because they craved above all to mount a step higher in the infinite ladder by which humanity ascends with so much effort to its transfiguration in the bosom of justice.

Truly Venice deserves all the sacrifices made upon her altars by Manin. This city, which is unique in the world, rises on the moving sand of the lagunes, changing as the flowing waters, yet constant in her unwearied efforts to present her offerings in the temple of civilization. Peopled by the Latin race which fled from the invasion of Attila, and by the Greeks who took refuge from the Byzantine despotism and the scimitars of the Turks; given up to labour during the darkness of the Middle Ages when the rest of the world was devoted to the cloister and enslaved by superstition; owning rich fleets of vessels which came in laden with the products of all countries, and bore in their swelling sails the airs of distant regions; with the Adriatic in the foreground, the green fields around, and the snow-crowned Alps in the distance; furrowed by those canals into which the sparkling sea pours its foaming flood, repeating beneath the dark walls of its palaces the wondrous play of light from the incomparable heavens; showing long lines of marvellous workmanship from the delicate tracery of Moorish architecture to the pure severity of Grecian columns; from Byzantine arches whose massive grandeur seems eternal, to Gothic cupolas whose light chiselling is lifted towards the heavens; by her arts, by her riches, by her lagunes peopled with ships, by her ancient glory, Venice is one of the first of cities.

Venice decayed by slow degrees. Her aristocracy, like all privileged bodies, lost all political feeling when the period of right arrived—the time of democracy. Her commerce lost its ancient importance when the

Portuguese doubled the Cape, and the Spaniards discovered America. The revolution found her aristocracy on its throne of the lagunes like a mummy in the Pyramids of the desert. One day Bonaparte entered Venice. The future military dictator of the plebeians was met with the hatred of the mercantile nobles, like that which Scylla felt on the soil of Athens for the Greek democracy. And after having robbed them of the Lion of Mark, which he sent to the Invalides in Paris, and of the four horses taken from the portal of the great Basilica, and placed by him on the Arc de Triomphe du Carrousel, he delivered up to Austria the remains of the Oriental city, like the wreck of a vessel rotting on a sandbank. The last of the Doges, the Augustus of that Rome of the Seas, sold in the nineteenth century for a fallow deer to the Germans, shrunk from taking an oath to Austria, as if he heard the voice of past generations, and already tasted upon his lips the gall of ignominy reserved for him by history. But Napoleon was cast in the bronze of destiny. His words were decrees. His treaties were the basis of a new Europe. That man who was so perfectly acquainted with the mathematics of strategy was quite ignorant of other and higher mathematics— the astronomy of nations. He rent in pieces with his spurs the map of the Continent, and with the fragments he endeavoured to form new countries. Nothing was ever more arbitrary than the delivery of Venice to Austria. Those who, like Noah in the Ark, saved themselves in the lagunes from the incursions of the Huns in the fifth century, were to fall in a later age at the feet of the Croats. Nothing could be more antagonistic than the Venetian genius and the Austrian genius, nothing more opposed than the Oriental city, like Venus surrounded with doves, and that vast brutal empire supported by bayonets. Napoleon imprisoned Venice.

But it is impossible to measure, even in thought, the point to which the resignation of a people will arrive. No one can estimate the numerous devices of despotism, nor the resources of obedience. It is frightful to calculate the burdens which tyranny will heap on the shoulders of a people. Every race has had an Egyptian bondage, and all have wanted a Moses.

The man destined to save Venice was Daniel Manin. In his life and in his death all future generations will learn to believe that history acknowledges and sympathizes with all great sacrifices. No one should despair, like the last Roman in the last night of the ancient Roman liberty. No effort that is made for good is lost. No great idea sown in the conscience is sterile. Thomas More, amidst the clamour of war in the sixteenth century, fancied in Utopia the religious peace of Protestant and Catholic nations. But the Utopia of the sixteenth century was the international pact of the seventeenth century, written in the Peace of Westphalia. And Manin left his country, lived in sorrow

and retirement, beheld the death, first of his loved wife
then of his daughter: lost by sad degrees all the
branches of the tree of his existence, died in exile,
slept ten years in an ungrateful foreign soil, and afterwards Venice set the bones of the martyr in the
diadem of her glory. We can advance to highest
virtue only by the path of disinterestedness, without
looking for recompense, without even hoping for the
satisfaction of seeing our work accomplished; for even
this legitimate gratification is a luxury unworthy of
the grand moral austerity which is exacted by all
apostleship. But the laws of moral nature cannot fail
of accomplishment any more than the laws of physical nature; and I, who am certain of immortality, I,
who do not believe that death is complete and eternal,
I comprehend the reward reserved to the martyr, I
behold him dwelling in spirit in independent Venice,
feeling in his bones the warmth of life at the caress of
the breeze rising from the lagunes, entering like an invisible and beneficent genius into its home freed from
oppressors, hearing the loving words of his family,
mingling his spirit in a divine effusion of faith with
the spirit of the present and of coming generations
whose chains are broken, and rejoicing in his sacrifice
and sufferings.

Perhaps we should say nothing of the life of this
man. All interest disappears beside these words—he
lived and died for his country. But let us briefly
consider some actions of his life. Manin was born

six years after Austria received from the hands of
Bonaparte the dead body of Venice. He belongs by
blood to that Israelitish race which has always been
so tenacious of its belief, a race of exiles and of prophets. In his childhood Venice passed from the possession of the French Empire to that of the Austrian
Empire, according to the usages of war between despots. After 1815 Venice fell into the grave opened
by Austria, and the lagunes of St. Mark ceased not
to confide to the winds the eternal lamentation of a
city in serfdom. Manin heard daily from the lips of
his father (an advocate, who was also his teacher), a
double malediction against Austria which enslaved
Venice, and against Napoleon who had delivered her
into captivity. The moral atmosphere by which he
was surrounded developed the natural strength of his
character, and filled him with an undying hatred of
tyranny.

Jurisprudence and philosophy were his favourite
studies. At seventeen years of age he was already a
doctor of laws. In 1830 he opened his career of advocate in the district of Mestre, at the entrance of the
lagunes. In the same year, the shock of the French
revolution passed through Venice, like galvanism
through a corpse. Manin, who did not wish to connect
himself with secret societies, thought by seizing the
arsenal to emancipate his country. But the revolution was like a flash of lightning in Italy. Venice
took no action, and Manin concealed his desires and

his projects in the depths of his soul. Seven years later he endeavoured to convert a railway company into a band of patriots. This Society was dispersed by order of the Government, but it left a bond of moral union among the Venetians. In 1847 a scientific congress was assembled. There spoke the orator without a tribune, the advocate without a cause, the patriot without a country. With great ability he converted economic questions into political questions, and with utterances of the most unquestionable logic, he darted sharp arrows at the heart of tyranny. Austria preserved a shadow of popular representation, in order to conceal by this means the fetters of the people. Manin wrote a kind of memorial, which was apparently an invocation to this shadow, but in reality an appeal to the people. Afterwards, in connexion with Tomasseo, he edited a protest against a publication of that time. As was to be expected, he could not approach a tiger ever so gently, without being exposed to his claws. Manin was arrested. There was no substantial charge against him. His motto had been legality and publicity. The advocate had not yet developed into the tribune. The judges absolved him from crime, but the police put him in prison as dangerous. Spielberg, with all the horrors of expatriation added to those of captivity, was henceforth his abode.

Soon after this great events occurred. The word "liberty" was spoken by the Pope. A new hope, infinite and universal, dawned in all hearts. Ancient and modern Rome seemed reconciled, the Tribunes and the Popes to be united ; liberty and the Church to form together a new moral world; and it appeared that the social promises of the Gospel were accomplished in a day, uniting the people in the bosom of humanity, and humanity in the belief in One God. That which the painters of the Renaissance had done in the sphere of art, and with the world of the past, the union of two entities, the connexion of the Christian idea with the pagan idea, was to be the work of Pius IX. in the social and religious sphere, in the world of the future—the union of two beliefs and of two dogmas, the reconciliation of faith with reason and modern liberty, in the eternal precepts of the Gospel—all this was to be accomplished. These aspirations thrilled through Europe, raising a flood of new ideas. Italian patriots imagined that Italy would not only recover from her long humiliation, but that she would claim the predominant moral government of the world, through her Councils and her Popes, as in classic ages by her Senate and her Cæsars. Garibaldi returned from America, determined to serve under the banner of Liberty and of the Gospel. Cities which had long been at variance, restored the trophies which recorded their ancient victories over each other, wishing to confound all old antipathies in the love of country. Above the federalism of the provinces arose the unity of the national soul. And a touching ceremony was solemnized in a church in Venice. There were two societies so much at variance that many times they reddened in their quarrels the waters of the lagunes. Both went to a church, and kneeling, implored pardon of Heaven for their fratricidal conduct. And when the priest praised God and dismissed them, and the bells rang out in melody, the chiefs of those two bodies advanced, and holding each other's hand before the altar, swore an eternal reconciliation for the love of their country, and in the hope of her approaching liberty.

But the time of struggle had not yet come for Venice. Manin was of opinion that this important event must be preceded by two others of equal gravity—by a revolution in Paris, and another in Vienna. These two events took place as he anticipated. The Austrian authorities so much dreaded the echo of the battle at Vienna, that they liberated Manin and Tomasseo who had been imprisoned for heading the agitation. This state of affairs could not continue without great peril to the country. One morning Manin called his son to his side, and took leave of his wife and daughter. Then he set out for the arsenal, intending to drive the Austrians from Venice. His efforts were crowned with success. Venice was free on the twenty-second of March, 1848. The lagunes resounded with cries of jubilant rejoicing for the city now free as the winds, which so long had borne to the waves her lamentations.

Manin proclaimed the Republic. This form of government had many advantages for Venice. It was the tradition of centuries. It was a record of the time when the city was united to the Adriatic in happy nuptials. She united two things which are rarely seen together, the rewards of commerce and the inspiration of the arts. Her senate was equal to that of ancient Rome in grandeur, and for its brilliancy and prestige it resembled the House of Lords in England. Her reputation was sacred in all the provinces with which she formed contracts, and was vigorous till the day of her decline. And her power was so respectable, that before Charles the Great there was existing a federation of seventy-two islands presided over by twelve greater islands, whose vessels carried to her shores the germs of modern commerce.

Venice is situated at the entrance of the Hellenic seas, and before her is the garland of islands which stretch as far as Asia, from whence have come to conquer and embellish the moral world philosophers, poets, sculptors, and others famous in art and literature. It was natural that, newly risen from her bed of ashes, Venice should attempt to found a federation after the manner of antiquity, where liberty should reign supreme, and the law be the realization of right, and the constant pride of the citizens, each of whom should be master of himself; natural that she should convert them into heroes ; a nation wherein the artistic democracy of Athens should be united to the wealth

and grandeur of Carthage, and to the struggles of
the sailors amid the waves; the propaganda by the
people of all new ideas and discoveries thus continuing
the traditions of those Italian cities of the Middle
Ages; of Florence, which invented bills of exchange
and wrote the pages of the Divine Comedy; of Genoa,
which founded the banking system and inspired
Columbus with his poetic dreams; of Aosta, which
brought forth followers of the great metaphysician,
St. Anselmo; of all, in fine, who left a track in the
future whose lustre shall not be extinguished whilst
there remains in the human conscience the worship of
great thoughts and the respect of glory; a historic
footprint in which Venice can read her enduring power
over the Adriatic, the resuscitation of her ancient
institutions without the revival of her aristocracy, and
give to the world an example of the Greek coalition
which taught us the arts, literature, and heroism.

Manin, then, proclaimed the Venetian Republic.
His first thought was like his first desire—to leave
the Dictatorship at the point in which the revolution
had triumphed. Venice without Austrians was a
thing so great as to satisfy a hero and to immortalize
a life. But he was unable to relinquish the command
of the city. The perils which encompassed Venice at
the establishment of her independence were far less
than those which were essential to her defence. Italy
desired her liberty and hated Austria; but she was
not acquainted with the political measures the most ·

suitable to carry out this great design; she knew not with what stones to erect the altar of the country. This nation, which has been distinguished among all others for her political genius, was like one intoxicated, overcome by the old wine of her recollections in the festival of her new existence. She already clamoured because Pius IX. led her to make war upon Austria. She followed the King of Naples, who abandoned her in the most solemn and critical moment. She confided herself to Charles Albert, who was more anxious to save his feudal territories than to benefit Italy. Even in the question as to whether she should or should not call in foreign aid she vacillated. Whilst one political party desired to summon French intervention, another rejected the proposal, so that Italy, like the captain of antiquity, knew how to conquer, but did not know how to profit by her victory.

The clear and practical intelligence of Manin at once perceived the supreme necessities of the situation : on one hand, an alliance of Austria and Russia; to be checked on the other by an alliance of France and Italy. But Charles Albert did not favour this idea, because he feared an inevitable result—the reclamation of Savoy by France as the price of her alliance and as a compensation for the aggrandizement of Italy. Educated in antiquated notions which he had always followed, but foretelling, with the far-seeing ambition of his race, the benefits to be derived from the new, he doubted in those moments in which confidence is most useful and energy most essential. Manin turned to England, demanding her acknowledgment and her moral support in the counsels of the world ; but Lord Palmerston feared to favour the Republican propaganda by the acknowledgment of Venice, a propaganda detestable in his eyes, first, because he was an Englishman, and secondly, because he did not wish to countenance disaffection in Ireland.

It is inconceivable that France was deaf to the invocation of Manin. The French Republic, that wished to outshine the Roman Republic, refused to recognise the Republic of Venice in its cradle. Lamartine, who was at that time at the head of the Government of France, and who had so often written tender and enchanting pages upon Italy, scarcely seemed to inhale the aroma of poetry which arose from the free lagunes, and which seemed to fill with azure clouds of incense the temple of her glory. He treated Italy as he himself acknowledges he treated Graziella. He contented himself with lavishing incoherent words upon her altar, like Hamlet upon the shrine of Ophelia, who died through his fault. Venice remained alone in the world. Then the Republican city was delivered up to the Constitutional Monarchy of Piedmont, and Manin, who would not be counted among courtiers, quitted the government of his country.

But the alliance did not hold. Manin had foreseen its incoherence. A handful of gold, thrown as if to a beggar, and 1400 soldiers, were given by Charles

Albert for the loveliest of his provinces—Venetia. At the end of a few days the King suffered a defeat, and his first act was to abandon his new dominions, drawn to him by liberty, in order to preserve the old, which were the heritage of feudalism. Charles Albert undertook to abandon Lombardy and Venetia, leaving both regions under the protection of Austria. Venice never sanctioned this act. The Republic reappeared amid the lagunes, and Manin reappeared in the Government. If unable to secure the independence of his country, he was determined to save her honour.

The Assembly met, and Manin was declared President of the Triumvirate, the dignity of a Dictatorship being indispensable in the midst of such grave perils. Manin requested the Assembly to give him a vote of confidence, and they gave it by acclamation. He requested the citizens to bring to the Bank all their gold and silver, to exchange them for receipts bearing large interest, and all Venice brought her jewels with heroic cheerfulness. He sent Tomasseo to France to demand her intervention in favour of Venetian liberty. In his febrile agitation, and with his fervid imagination, Venice still appeared the refuge of Italian liberty. He hoped to make of her what Spain made of a very similar city in the War of Independence; what Spain made of Cadiz, the bulwark from whence the Italian flag could extend her maternal shadow, like a great hope, over the whole peninsula. A loan of ten millions of francs was decreed by Manin for the succour of Northern Italy, and subscribed by the inhabitants, who deprived themselves of food to give succour to their country. Eighty-five thousand francs were dispersed daily, and the usual receipts were but two hundred thousand per month. But whatever were his economic operations or his loans, the most wealthy proprietors of Venice became poor in order to bring him the gold necessary for the safety of the country. One day he summoned the Assembly to sanction his financial projects. The Assembly desired to decree salaries to the individuals composing the Government, especially to the President of the Re-public. "I will not accept it," said Manin. "I will live on my own resources. When they are exhausted I will apply to my friends; but I will never accept a salary from my country while I see her, as to-day, reduced to ask alms to ransom herself from servitude."

Yet these great qualities of an honourable man and a skilful economist were not sufficient. Venice needed a soldier. Charles Albert had recovered from his first debility. Hungary had shaken off the yoke of Austria. Piedmont established associations to save and defend the city, which was the capital from whence issued Italian nationality. England proposed that Austria should concede to Venice the title of a free city, though she refused to give her the title of an Italian city. Manin wished to prove that she merited the crown with which European opinion rewarded her, and commanded a sally against Mestre, the key of the

lagunes, the point of union with the mainland, a spot
on which the Austrians had taken shelter.

The Austrians were ejected from Jusina, from the
fortified station of Mangliera, and from their refuge
of Mestre, leaving in the hands of the Venetians five
hundred prisoners and six pieces of artillery, and
with the sad loss of more than two hundred dead.
Hugo Bassi, a young priest, a friend of Garibaldi,
was there. In one hand he carried the host, and in
the other his banner; his forehead bore the stamp
of virtue, on his lips was the eloquence of faith;
wounded and bleeding he ran among the legions of
liberty to comfort and sustain them, reminding them
that sacrifices for the country elevate those capable
of them to the height of religious martyrs in the
eyes of the Eternal. Even boys were admirably
distinguished. Two children of ten years were beating
a drum. One of them fell wounded; his companion
took him upon his shoulders and continued sounding
the attack. The Italian flag fell from a boat into
the water, a marine flung himself into the canal, drew
it out, mounted to the topmast, crying, amongst a
shower of bullets, " Viva Italia!" It is certain that
from the 23rd March, 1848, on which day Venice
declared herself free, to the 29th October of the same
year in which she obtained such signal victories, the
life of Venice was a continual self-sacrifice—a holocaust to Italy. The union of all in these sacrifices
had awakened the idea of human equality in that

ancient land of aristocracy. Poor gondoliers were elected to the National Assembly. One of these, Grossi, spoke like an orator of antiquity. His companions opened little subscriptions among themselves in order to give him the wages he daily lost in his noble occupation of serving his country.

A new Assembly was convened and declared the cessation of the dictatorship of the 17th February, 1849. As the Assembly showed some slowness in the constitution of the new authority, and some of the members manifested tendencies opposed to the policy of Manin, the people loudly protested against these changes. But Manin took his sword, went to the Giant's Steps, and told the people they could enter if they would and outrage the majesty of the Assembly, but they must pass over his dead body and that of his son, whom he kept by his side to teach him to die for the law, after having taught him to fight for liberty. Certainly one may say in reviewing the life of this man, and considering his actions, that he realized the ideal of times hidden in that shadowy future when society shall be governed by conscience, for morality was his sole code, absolute justice his centre of gravity.

But a terible hour arrived, an hour in which all hope of liberty departed. The last days of March, 1849, beheld the fatal field of Novara. Russia drew Hungary into the quarrel. France gave herself up to a reaction, which ended in the foundation of the

Empire. Austria was enabled to narrow the position of Venice, to enclose her in the smallest circle of her miserable martyrdom. Manin implored the Assembly to resist at all cost, if necessary. The Assembly assented. Manin ascended to the highest point of the tower of St. Mark, and there, in the presence of the Alps and of the sea, under the pure rays of the glorious sun, illuminating the sad spectacle of human sorrows, among the grove of columns, of domes, of pinnacles, which compose an aerial harmony whose beauty is increased by the fleecy clouds which hang over the lagunes and the play of light repeated in the waters; near the heavens, like an appeal to the eternal justice, he unrolled the red banner which declared the resolution of the city to defend herself to the last sooner than consent to new indignities. But nothing availed. Abandoned by the world, without allies, reduced in numbers, dying of famine, fired, bombarded, besieged by an army of 45,000; encompassed by a powerful fleet, which deprived her of the possibility of foreign aid; her food and ammunition exhausted, the fishermen's quarter reduced to ruins, the cholera raging with a terrible violence, as if willing to help the besiegers—Manin had to choose between the two horrible extremes, either to deliver up Venice to the invader, or to blot her out from the world, flinging her like a corpse into her lagunes, and destroying the marvels of her arts in a horrible suicide.

The Assembly and the people preferred death. Manin wished to preserve Venice for the world, Venice for her children, Venice for the arts, Venice for the future, Venice for liberty. In proceeding thus Manin was the man of his time, and, like the prophets of Israel, prepared for the future. The suicide of Brutus was conceived by the sentiment of desperation which existed in the bosom of ancient societies. When an institution was uprooted its life was destroyed. Nobody believed that justice would revisit the earth. An implacable theology considered her as dwelling eternally in the heavens. Even patriotism encouraged this idea, which has been transmitted from generation to generation to our time like a sacred inheritance. When life is shut up in the narrow circle of a privilege or of a city, people are apt to conceive that life is finished with the circumstances of existence, with the roof which covers it. So the ancients committed suicide; Cato at the feet of the law, Brutus at the close of the republic, Nero at the end of the Empire, Cleopatra at the departure of her greatness, Demosthenes at the fall of his country. Both the good and the bad destroyed themselves, when the principal object of their lives departed. And the same thing occurred with cities. Without denying the heroism of Tyre, of Jerusalem, of Sagunta, of Carthage, of Numantia, we understand heroism of this nature among peoples who blindly adore the irresistible force of destiny, when they possess neither the hope nor the sentiment of progress; when they imagine the victory of their enemies to be an eternal supremacy; when with the violated boundary of their country they associate their gods, their homes, their laws, liberty, the soul, their entire existence. But in the modern world, in this world of unity and of justice, where all outrages against right have a certain compensation in the weight of public opinion, where the principle of nationalities is as deeply rooted as the principle of justice was in the early ages; where without ceasing to belong to our country, which should be the first object of our lives, we belong to humanity, for which we feel a not less exalted, though a less enthusiastic worship—under such altered conditions we cannot conceive the suicide of a people if we have not lost faith in human progress, and with faith in human progress lost all our hopes. Manin did well to avoid a giddy, tragic, and horrible death in the flames (as many proposed in the madness of despair), in the city of Eastern beauty, which is one of the loveliest in the world.

On the 27th of August, 1849, after six months of a defence that for courage and devotion has no superior in modern history, except that of Saragossa, Manin left the city never to return as long as the Austrians should hold possession of the canals, on whose banks the deserted and solitary palaces look like immense mausoleums. But he had one consolation in this deep distress. He went out after having heroically defended Venice against the Croatians. He knew that all his fellow citizens would have died to keep him under his own roof. He quitted his brave country for a strange land, but he did not experience the supreme sorrow of exile—he was not flung from his country by his country, not cast forth by those who were of the same blood and who spoke the same language; he could dare to denounce tyrants, without danger lest he should also curse his countrymen.

Manin embarked in a French vessel. He felt a lively sympathy with the revolutionary nation, notwithstanding the ingratitude of 1848. His wife and his two children accompanied him. The former died on her arrival at Marseilles. This new sorrow deepened the abyss in his afflicted heart. From Marseilles he went to Paris, and took apartments in the sad little street, Les Petits Ecuries. Having refused all the assistance that had been offered to him by the municipality of Venice on his departure, he lived in great poverty in that large city, where want of money signifies wretchedness. He sought a living by giving lessons in the Italian language. His pupils were scattered over different quarters of the town. He could not afford to hire a carriage; this luxury, so necessary to his health and his business, would have soon dissipated his few francs. In the cold season of Paris, soaked with rain and splashed with mud, this representative of the city once the richest in the world, this Governor of Venice, was the living image of exile.

One day he met a great French artist, and said to him, "My work is not always agreeable. To-day I was giving an Italian lesson to a great lady, when her husband entered, and did not salute me."

But his greatest affliction was the loss of his beloved daughter, Emilia, who died of a very protracted and painful nervous malady. Her natural delicacy, her great intelligence, the love of country which she had learned in her former home, the terrible tragedies she had witnessed for two years, the grief of leaving Venice, the death of her mother, the sadness of exile, and the sight of her old father reduced to misery; the sad recollection of the eternal murmur of the lagunes, with their changing lights and shadows which she had loved, all these things preyed on her health and broke her heart. She died, poor martyr! kissing the hands of her father, and her last words were of her beloved country. What more? Manin collected his last strength, wrote a sacred testament of last counsels to his country, and died also of the moral wounds he had received; he fell asleep, like a labourer who has worked much and well, with a sweet repose in his conscience, serenity in his face, and a vision of futurity in his eyes, certain that those do not die eternally who have sown justice in the earth.

When death comes to a life so great and eventful as that of Manin the hero is transformed into a divinity, an eternal example of virtue, his history into a dazzling apotheosis. Belonging to a family of Jewish

race and of Spanish origin, Manin inherited from the
Jews the virtue of inexhaustible hope, and from the
Spaniards the sublime love of country and the unflinching resolution to sacrifice himself for his convictions. In his private life he was the perfect model
of a father, a husband, and a friend. His public life
raised to a general law the principles which governed
him in his private character. It has long been a very
common error in Italy to separate public and private
morality, to believe that principles of strict justice are
not essential for nations, and need not be adhered to
between republics. Perfect diplomacy has been considered the art of complete deception. Machiavel, to
save Italy, proposed to dethrone the Almighty and to
exalt the devil; to lay aside all scruples as obstacles
to any great enterprises, and morals as a chain which
cramps action; to blot out the line between good and
evil, to draw men to a cause by their passions and
interests, and to govern them by encouraging their
vices; to fling away conscience as a useless burden,
and to look upon crime as an insurmountable power;
to deceive the ally, to betray the enemy, to banish to
the colonies or to extirpate adverse parties, and to
work, at all cost, up to the only desirable end in
politics—victory. These principles, springing, some
of them from the sublime despair of genius, tinctured
with bitter irony; others written as the result of
profound observation of the different forces which
move society, proposed and proffered as the physician

mixes and presents poison to the invalid—these principles forged a chain of politics in Italy whose catechism of liberty was a reaction against priests and professors, who had made the Gospel a catechism of servitude. But Manin understood that the simplest principles of morality are the most fruitful, as well for public as for private life, and that Washington founded an immortal republic and an enduring liberty on the bases of virtue in the home and of justice in the laws; so the Dictatorship of Manin was patriarchal, his stormy government was the Golden Age of the new Venetia. No wonder, then, that the gondolier should chant melancholy songs among the lagunes, asking the land of France to give back the bones of Manin, and that a funeral urn bearing the remains of the exile should have been honoured more than the greatest captain who returned victorious in the city of the waters, followed by a mourning people, accompanied by a chorus of benedictions, surrounded by the representatives of all nations which defend liberty, for this funeral urn contained, not the cold ashes of the dead, but the germ of eternal life—the example of faith and virtue.

ADOLPHE THIERS.

19—2

Adolphe Thiers

(TO 1870).

IF I had never been told I should at once have
known that this man is from the South, that he has
seen the azure of our heavens, that he has heard the
murmur of our Mediterranean, and has gladdened his
eyes in the brightness of our sun. The shores which
extend from Andalusia to Syria are made one by the
mirror of the pure sea in which they are repeated, and
in the similarity of the races by which they are inhabited. Except the Turks, those strangers encamped
on the soil of Christendom, in which they have never
taken root, all the rest of the Mediterranean-Euro-
pean peoples have something of the boldness of the
Phœnician, of the loquacity of the Greek, of the
restless ambition of the Roman, of the bitter irony
of the Provençal, of the mercantile and navigating
spirit of the Catalan, of the grace and genius of the
Andalusian. So all wear a costume somewhat similar ; a shirt blue as the waters, a red cap, which recalls
their glowing horizon ; the throat and chest un-

covered, as in sculpture; the feet bared to the cool waves. And all these people speak among themselves what they call the Frank language, a dialect as we term it, or a *patois* or slang as it is designated by the French, composed of soft and monosyllabic words with which all make themselves understood, and which is most eloquent in the mouths of these musical and oratorical races.

Sometimes on arriving on the shores of the Mediterranean, on seeing its celestial waters with waves of silver foam, the sand which is gilded by the sunlight, the vast horizon, in which is visible the outlines of the mountains bronzed by the changing atmosphere, and which look like huge pillars and columns, this grandeur of nature has convinced me that all these coasts are formed to give voice to orators, inspiration to poets, to be the great palette of humanity, rich in all variety of tints; the eternal studio of the sculptor, the matchless abode of the plastic arts.

The sea conveys an idea of awe and of sublimity. The eye seems to penetrate through that immense profundity. The abyss covered by rolling waves, the thought of which makes one giddy, looks like something animated, like an immense creature in whose moving waters we see the eternal generation of monsters. The mountains surrounding it are opposing forces which have been placed there to resist the invasion of those angry waves, which appear sometimes ready to burst all bounds, and to overflow the land.

The sight of the sea inclines to thought, for the sea is deep, and is an emblem of infinity. Since the first ages of antiquity many have lived under its teachings who have held no intercourse with each other. The branch of a rose tree would sometimes suffice to propel a snow white boat on the smooth waters of the Mediterranean. And the towns upon its coasts have felt its influence, which, from antiquity to the Middle Ages, has in a great measure influenced the drama of history.

I was about to speak of an orator, and I have spoken of the sea. This was because the human voice may be grand, profound, sonorous, beautiful, and tempestuous, and in these qualities it resembles the sea. And no one can speak of eloquence, still less of Southern eloquence, without remembering those celestial waters which formed a background to the theatre of Æschylus, those pebbles on the shore, with which Demosthenes improved his utterance; the spot in which Plato discoursed of the immortality of the soul in undying language, whilst Greek processions passed from their marble temples to the glittering waves, and the rising sun gilded the sacred heights of Hymettus.

If all southern peoples have something Greek in their character, all still preserve something of their mother, Athens. But few of them have so much of this classic land of poetry as the population of Marseilles, for this city was a Greek colony, which in the time of the Romans preserved its renown, exercising the great influence which belongs to the moral superiority of its mother country. Thiers was born in Marseilles, and his nationality is visible in the fruitfulness, the grace, the purity, and the beauty of his images, in the richness of his oratory, in the subtlety of his genius, in the remarkable clearness of his language.

Thiers was born three years before the end of the last century. The French revolution was just over, and at its close the man was born who was destined to do two great things—to write its history, and to represent its fall. He was the son of a poor workman, but did not inherit the sentiment of equality common among his class. By his mother's side he belonged to the family of Andrés Chenier, the gentle poet, who left, with his head on the guillotine, a number of sweet eclogues and of beautiful legends. His mother's family gave him a small annuity, and sent him to the Lycée of Marseilles. In his childhood he was remarkable for his domineering and turbulent disposition, but also for his application to study and for his genius. More than once his temper shamed his intelligence, so much so that he was on the point of losing his education and of being expelled from the college on account of his continual insubordination.

At the age of eighteen he studied law at Aix. There he obtained his first academical prize in a manner which is worth relating. Foreign intervention had brought the ancient Royal family again to the throne. The young student, notwithstanding his constitutional

and moderate opinions, passed for a Jacobin, for a
demagogue according to the Royalists. These composed the majority of the Academy of Aix, almost the
whole indeed, for both Republicans and Bonapartists
had fallen, involved in one common ruin. The eulogy
of Vanvernagues was the theme chosen for the prize.
Thiers presented his essay. The Academy, knowing
that it well deserved the prize for its literary merit,
deferred their decision for another year. Then Thiers
wrote another discourse, forwarded it anonymously to
Paris, in order that it should be sent from thence to
the Academy. Thanks to this ingenious stratagem,
he took both the prize and the *accessit*, the prize under
his assumed name, and the *accessit* under his own name.
This gave fame in Aix to the student, and made him
quits with the Academy, which could not resist the
most terrible weapon in France—ridicule.

We cannot continue the history of this man's career,
which has so much influenced his times, without
describing the great events among which he displayed
his wonderful activity. Napoleon had fallen. No
man ever imagined war with more grandeur, nor
politics with such littleness. He was a Cæsar in the
field, and scarcely the head of a small party in the
cabinet; but he was born in an age which did not
consent to the suppression of nationalities by conquest,
nor of liberty by genius. The communities of Russia,
nationality in Spain, liberty in England, kings at
Waterloo, the ancient *régime* threatened in its ex-

istence, the new in its rights—all worked a prodigious reaction against Bonaparte, and buried him alive in a little island, where the restlessness of his spirit became his scourge and torment. When the Allied forces entered Paris for the first time, nobody seemed to remember the ancient Royal family, over which had passed the scaffold, the revolution, the republic, the dictatorship, the empire. The people soon lose their memory, and re-learn only with great difficulty ideas which they have forgotten. Even Talleyrand himself was moved when that enlightened but half-insane mystic, Alexander of Russia, entered his house, tormented by his spiritualism and his remorse of conscience, and said, "Does France want the Bourbons?"

And, in fact, the Bourbons turned against Alexander, who did not wish the reaction to be completely victorious, nor Napoleon to be entirely conquered. Yet the Bourbons in the second intervention, seemed to have triumphed from the first. There had been great obstacles to overcome. In thirty years a new France had been created. Between this France and the Restoration stood the scaffold ; between the conscience of France and the conscience of her kings there was a philosophy ; between the throne and the people was the decalogue of the tradition in which the throne believed, and the decalogue of the tradition in which the people believed. Besides, it was considered a necessity for restored sovereigns to have foreign armies, to place themselves under the protection of the European powers, to reorganize France, to separate the provinces gained by the Republic, to be like gaolers of the nation, and denying the independence of those whose lives during the empire appeared incompatible with the independence of other people. All this caused open war between the ancient family and the new people.

This war languished a little during the reign of Louis XVIII.—a sceptic, there was small respect paid to his authority; a poltroon, he was unwilling to fight or to move; apoplectic, and he did not like to fatigue his brain by thinking; an egotist, and he took the throne as a pleasure, and authority as a new pastime; a shadow of the last age, of which he retained the changeableness and repeated the errors.

During the reign of Louis XVIII., in the year 1821, Thiers arrived in Paris. The early events of life are impressed on the memory like warm iron upon wax; and it was then he learned the system which makes authority irresponsible by avoiding a dictatorship, and which makes liberty illusory by flying from anarchy and falling into the oligarchy of the middle class, the least generous and the least disinterested of all classes; and in order to reconcile liberty and authority exalts the throne and abases the people, putting them outside the pale of political existence.

Naturally the scepticism of Louis XVIII. was favourable to the development of this system. Thiers went to Paris to be its servant, with his mind full of delusive ideas, and his heart cheered by hope of the future. At that period Paris was melancholy, confined, damp, and dirty. The second empire has applied the pickaxe to the labyrinth of her streets, and if it has not made the city either beautiful or artistic, it has at least made it clean and airy. But there are still some remains of ancient Paris; and among the remnants of the past at the corner of the Rue de Rivoli, near the Hôtel du Louvre, there is a place called the Passage de Montesquieu, and there in a humble chamber, with a poor bed, little light, and no fire, uncertain not only as to the future, but as to the day, Thiers lodged with the friend of his boyhood, his constant companion, the celebrated historian Mignet.

The more active of the two friends was he who was afterwards to become the more famous—Thiers. We are now acquainted with the different qualities of these two men; the one born for contemplation and the study of past ages; the other for the work of government, and for labours in the Senate. Thiers remembered his countryman—Manuel, a man whose character shone brightly during that period of moral abasement, one who well maintained the dignity of the tribune in those times of the restoration of all ancient institutions, and of threats against all innovations. Manuel recommended him to Lafitte, the revolutionary banker and the friend of Béranger, enemy of the Bourbons, an idealist in the midst of banking calculations, nervous and delicate as a woman, but unswerving in his resolutions when they were of decisive and supreme importance.

Lafitte recommended young Thiers to the editor of *Le Constitutionnel*, that journal which has now fallen so deeply from its formerly celebrity. There he commenced to display those talents for which he soon became so remarkable,—quickness of perception, clearness of ideas, brilliancy of style, connexion and proportion between the parts of his discourse and a passion for polemics.

Thiers possesses the peculiar characteristics of the French genius—ease in communication, warm sympathies, a sparkling clearness, an Attic simplicity, and a want of depth, and all these are most valuable for the press. Consequently, he soon gained a very high reputation among his associates, particularly for an article entitled "La Monarchie en France," which showed strong dynastic opposition. But as yet his political vocation had not been clearly expressed, nor was the paper which was afterwards to unfold such great changes, then very decided in its sentiments. However, the essays and articles he wrote procured him an easy position and a complete independence. He was very soon rewarded with the income from one of the shares of the *Constitutionnel*, a journal then much in fashion.

In this improved situation he was admitted into good society. The *salons* of Paris have greatly degenerated.　It is enough to say that Theresa invaded them with her attitudes and her songs full of spirit—of wine.　But in the time of the Restoration, when the sound of battle had been hushed in the murmur of machinery, when the tribune began to resume its eloquence, and the desire of preservation so strong in France increased like a stream freed from icy fetters, then the Parisian *salons* shone as in the first period of their influence.　There was the *salon* of Lafitte, where assembled the Opposition, and also that of Talleyrand.　In his blue *salon* the destinies of France were decided.　There entered, followed by his Cossacks, that Emperor Alexander who ascended the throne by crime; who believed himself destined to bring a new redemption to Europe and a new mission to the human conscience, and who died distracted by moral tortures in a desert, to which he had fled to escape the stings of remorse.　Talleyrand was equal to any difficulty, and was capable of anything.　When a child his nurse laid him down in a field in order to be more at liberty in a walk with her lover, and a pig mangled his legs.　Something of the animal must have remained in his blood, for never was there such a one since the swine of Epicurus.　He was a bishop, and he had no belief in religion; a courtier, and he did not believe in the monarchy; a Constitutional Minister, and he had no belief in political virtue; a Frenchman, and he did not believe in his country.　He showed extreme ingenuity in order to save France in the Congress of Vienna, and displayed still greater meanness at Court to preserve his own influence. But thanks to this influence his *salon* was one of the most sought in Paris.

There Thiers shone, at that time a young man of twenty-five, small and slender, but active. His countenance and manners were somewhat unattractive, but his expression was intelligent, and he had a bitter and ironical smile, like a Provençal satire; much of his face was hidden behind great spectacles, but the broad forehead was visible, in which was perceptible the restless flow of the warm southern blood; he fixed the attention of all by his conversation, fluent, sustained and inexhaustible, which under the transparence of images concealed the richness of his ideas.

But as yet the young man could not have much political influence. To obtain this it became necessary for him to take some decided part, and to endeavour to unfold by greater efforts the energy of his character. A History of the French Revolution, an ingenious but not remarkable work on the exposition of pictures in 1822, a sketch of the actress Belamy; a journey to the Pyrences,—this was the whole literary treasure of the young man; a treasure more valuable for its quantity than for its quality; more for the expectations excited than for services rendered; more fruitful for the future than rich in the present;

the seed of a history which will always be appreciated, and of an eloquence which will always be
remarkable.

Devoted thus to literature by preference, he determined to write a general history. As the French,
according to Goethe, are not learned either in languages
or in geography, Thiers prepared himself to become
acquainted with the globe, and to give a local colouring
to his pages, decided on a voyage of circumnavigation.
Then occurred the great event which was to decide
his political vocation; the death struggle between the
reigning family and the liberties of France, a struggle
which was concluded by the revolution of 1830,
which overthrew the throne of St. Louis, so languidly
restored, to yield to a monarchy of the moderate
kind, which in its turn fell to give place to military
and plebeian dictatorship.

Louis XVIII. had seen his hopes realized, and had
died upon the throne. That European intervention
in France which the republic dissipated like smoke at
the sound of the *Marseillaise*, erecting upon all sides
the banner of liberty, and shaking ancient dynasties;
that intervention to which the people never consented
and which succeeded in placing a king upon the
throne, should at least have preserved the honour of
the country, and should not have accepted a throne
forged with the iron shoes of Cossack horses.

But Louis XVIII. died. A few hours before his
death, he called the Prince his heir, blessed him, and

addressed a dying prayer to heaven that his brother might be enabled to save the crown for the boy. The heavens rejected the petition. Charles X. ascended the throne with the ideas of other ages, and consequently with all the severity of character, and all the inaccessibleness which these ideas counselled. He commenced by a coronation ceremony, half theocratic and half feudal, only suited to wound the sentiment of equality, which holds in France all the intensity of a passion. A fatal error which showed the bottom of his thoughts ! Charles X. had been in his youth perhaps the most gallant among the princes of that gallant Court. His imprudences had many times compromised Marie Antoinette. At Trianon under the shade of the trees, on the flowery borders of those lakes, where the swans disport themselves, the rustic farm is still shown where princes and princesses, dressed as shepherds and shepherdesses, with the labourers of the field represented the Georgiacs; as if disgusted with the evil to be found in high circles by the absence of real simplicity, they were drawn to seek in the mother of all creatures, nature, a holy social equality. But he who was afterwards king under the name of Charles X., and who was then called the Comte d'Artois, was always distinguished by the exclusiveness of his ideas, and also by the vicious habits of the worst of the courtiers of that period.

His face had in it a great deal of royal distinction ;

his manners were aristocratic, his smile was patronizing, he was in fact, a man born for a throne; rather in those epochs which were capable of faith in tradition, of devotion to royalty, of adoring like a Providence absolute monarchy in those exalted and silent regions in which it takes something of the majestic aspect of divinity.

But in those revolutionary times the man of another epoch was lost. To his natural superstitions concerning the monarchy was united a renewal of the beliefs of his early years. This faith of boyhood took the aspect of an expiation. Almost all vices eventually cause remorse and feebleness. This faith wounded the revolutionary principle in its most rooted conviction: the liberty of thought. The force of this principle was so great as sometimes to lead the King to acts foreign to his character. But as he left the press a little liberty during the time of his Minister Martignac, this liberty turned against him and against his political character. Then he invoked inviolability. And he did not seem aware that this had been conceded to Sovereigns in modern constitutions, in consideration of their remaining inactive, and of their renouncing all political individuality. At length he decided to govern, and he named a Minister, Polignac, which was the same as decreeing resistance to everything. The appointment of this Minister decided Thiers to found, in connexion with Armand Carrel (a young Republican) *La Nation*, a bold journal, warm and active, whose idea was to precipitate the reigning family from the throne. Thiers, enamoured of English history and with English institutions, like all the eclectics and professors of his time, wished, like Hampden, to organize a legal resistance against reaction, and was not aware that all legal resistance must presently pass into violence upon a soil so calcined by political excitement as that of France. Thus it happened that his tribune of the press was soon converted into a tribune of the barricade. And his temperament is not of stormy character, for his sharp voice, which was so easily heard in a *salon*, was easily lost in a tempest. Toads cannot sing in the sea: they are the nightingales of the lakes.

And the sea of revolution advanced, encouraged on one side by the wishes of the people, and on the other by the imprudences of the Court. In the smallest matters we can see the bias of public opinion. The royal family thought it necessary to erect an expiatory chapel in the cemetery of the Madeleine, where the bones of Louis XVI. and of Marie Antoinette had been buried in burning lime. On the day of the inauguration of this monument Charles X. had dressed himself in a suit of mulberry colour—for that is the mourning costume in the French Court—and the people said laughingly that the King had gone to the ceremony disguised as a bishop.

At this time the Ministry summoned Parliament, and the Assembly had then come to represent this political formula—a Liberal opposition to the Monarchical reaction. In this work the Assembly was ably seconded by an active press, eloquent, combative, vibrating with enthusiasm, directed by young men who loved the foam of the revolution as mariners love a struggle with the tempest. In this no small part was taken by the nervous, eloquent, and passionate pen of Thiers. At last the King and his Ministers one day determined to break all the chains with which the Opposition had confined them, and they promulgated decrees against the press and the tribune. The King rose against the acts of Parliament, trampled them, destroyed them, and traced the arbitrary limits of his power to the two great conquests of modern times, to the press and to the tribune, to those two points whence scintillate the electricity which gives vitality to language. Then Thiers found that of which he had dreamed lovingly during his whole life. He met the ideal of his political views—a resistance like that of Hampden against the power of the Stuarts. And whilst the people arose like the waves of the sea tossed by the tempest, whilst the revolution sounded like a storm in the distant horizon, whilst the stones of Paris shook as if moved by a moral earthquake, whilst the barricades were being raised—the barricades, those craters of ideas—Thiers, possessed by his Utopian schemes, wrote protests and sent forth manifestations.

But here we must stop to finish the first part of the

man's history, which is extended from the birth to the death of the Citizen Monarchy, and from the birth to the death of the Republic; which contributed to the creation of the Empire, to fall crushed at its base. All the world resolutely declares two things which are undeniable—Thiers has great talents and great eloquence. His versatile talents embrace all sciences, and his gift of eloquence touches all the objects and motives of human activity. From the most minute analysis of politics, he ascends to the most intricate calculations of tactics; from the study of a bas-relief to the consideration of a pretext. For him everything converges to his theme: the State, art, literature, politics, the exact and natural sciences, geography, and æsthetics. He could never be a profound philosopher, though so richly gifted and so fortunate. He could never be an orator to move masses like O'Connell, nor to destroy with the Herculean force of Mirabeau. His language has never had the poetic languor of Lamartine, nor the tempestuous bursts of Danton, that political Titan. But he has always been master of that fluency which enchants us for hours together, like the murmur of a stream in a peaceful and primeval country. And this man of gentle manners has passed all his life in endeavouring to combine in different proportions liberty and authority. He was unfortunate when he thought he had laboured and conquered for liberty. He met a revolution, and when he believed he had laboured and con-

quered for authority he met with a *coup d'état,* the
consequence of his sterile eclecticism.

We leave the history of Thiers at the time when
the prelude of the Revolution of July was heard, a
tempest which had been long threatening in the cloud-
laden horizon. France felt herself humiliated, not so
much by the narrowness of her parliamentary institutions and the restriction of her rights, as because that
both came from foreign hands, reddened in her blood.
The ignominious defeat of Waterloo burned in her
heart like a hot iron. The liberal sentiment, which
had been wounded, arose and sought to inflame the
national sentiment, also wounded by the remembrance
of foreign intervention. Thiers was the chief of a
journal which bore the most radical banner of the
Opposition, and met with a reality exceeding his
dreams.

The true and primitive French Revolution had been
daily degenerating, first, because many of its most
celebrated adherents were dead, and because the Empire had converted the remainder into courtiers and
soldiers. As soon as the men of equality had died in
the agitation produced by the event of that epoch,
the power of the rest being lessened, they thought of
founding an oligarchy. But as the idea of popular
sovereignty was deeply rooted, it became necessary to
give the people some participation (though but apparently) in the Government. This necessity becoming
known, all the reactionary powers combined to give

the people the least possible share in the Government, and to strip them of their rights. To found an oligarchy was the design. Bonaparte desired a military oligarchy; Charles X. a theocratical oligarchy, Guizot a financial oligarchy; Thiers wished for the oligarchy which was at that period the most logical, although always the least glorious, the oligarchy of the middle classes, based on full parliamentary principles.

Naturally, when it became a question of establishing a liberal oligarchy, all eyes turned to England. There are in that country two liberal traditions that should be distinguished—the Puritan tradition, and the Parliamentary tradition. To the first have belonged the most severe and most able men in England, the indomitable Cromwell, whose power was greater than that of kings; the great Milton, who bore, like Dante, his hopes to the heavens in immortal verses, his anger to the infernal regions, and engraved his political ideas in eternal fame; and the names—then obscure, but now brightest in history—the names of those mysterious wanderers who would not submit their consciences to tyranny, left the English coast to seek a free temple to their God, and whose descendants were rewarded by the privilege of being the elected of Providence to found the great model of liberty, the Republic of the United States, a work of conscience which has risen immaculate on the virgin nature of the New World, the continent of the future, as Asia is the continent of the past. But close beside this republican tradition there is the Parliamentary tradition, which has lessened the powers of the monarch and augmented the liberties of the people, in order to favour an oligarchy of the higher classes, of an aristocracy whose art of conservation is admirable; who know how to resist when opposition is feeble, to give way when it is strong : who lay down some of their privilege that they may not lose all, and who always yield in good time, never carrying resistance to reaction, not provoking the ultimate consequence of all reactions—revolution.

These traditions and this ability, these politics and this art led Thiers to the service of the class to which he belonged, the humblest of the middle classes ; but he was sadly deceived, because political oligarchy in Great Britain does not solely consist in art or ability ; it consists, in a great measure, in the position in which it is placed, and which allows it to discern that which is perceptible from all elevations—the distant horizon, the depth of the valleys, the coming of tempests. The English aristocracy is elevated to a territorial height by its possessions, to a historic height by its recollections, to a moral height by its education, to an intellectual height by its political ideas ; and being thus placed, they are separated from those who, slowly and painfully worn with labour and exertion, seek to attain privileges. The middle class in France struggles in the plains formed by the revolution, and for them it was difficult, if not impossible, to prevent the encroachments of the democracy.

But caressing the idea of resistance after the English custom, Thiers was surprised by the revolution of 1830, which vacillated between the Republic and the Constitutional Monarchy in those critical moments of revolutions in which the fate of the people is decided; supreme moments which, in regard to their influence over the future, are worth many ages.

But we come to the revolution and the part taken by Thiers in this event. The ordinances of the King, Charles X., were four decrees :—

First. He suppressed the liberty of the Press, and gave a new organization to this fourth power in the State.

Secondly. He dissolved the Chamber of Deputies, making their nomination illegal.

Thirdly. He gave a new organization to the Electorate.

Fourthly. He convoked a Parliament ruled by these modifications.

The *coup d'état* was complete. The Restoration denied its own laws and destroyed its own institutions. The first movement produced by this blow was one of terror among all those who were within the political organization. The first resistance to which he appealed was a legal resistance. A consultation of lawyers opened the revolution ; a defence of the law was the first explosion of violence. The toga ascended the steps of the tribunals before the tricoloured banner scaled the stones of the barricade. The Bourse was

surprised with this sudden danger, which alarmed
even the most powerful, and certainly the most
cowardly among all social forces, that of riches. The
Three per Cents. sunk from 78 to 72. In the Insti-
tute, Arago delivered a discourse. He who in the
laws of heaven strove to comprehend the mystery
of the infinite, defended the infinite upon earth—
justice in the laws of society.

The discourse which he read that day was full
of terrible allusions to arbitrary power. Marshal
Marmont, who, on the 18th Brumaire, had been an
accomplice in the assassination of liberty, who had also
been an accomplice in the year '14 with the Allies in
the murder of his country, was, in the year '30, an
accomplice in the murder of the law.

But the most formidable resistance was organized
where the wound was most profound—in the press ;
and in the press the periodical at that time the most
combative, if not the most important, was *La Nation ;*
and the most able, if not the most intelligent, writer
in *La Nation* was Thiers. Observe the path through
which the son of a poor workman in Marseilles
advanced to the front scene of the history of France.
The editors confided to him the composition of the
protest. The brilliance of his southern style was
much moderated by temperate protestations of respect
to the law. They hesitated to sign the paper with
their own names, fearing the vengeance of power.
Thiers recommended that the true stamp should be

given to that act of valour, and all signed, believing that they signed their death warrant. The impulse of this fear raised the natural idea in those supreme moments—the idea of armed resistance. Thiers thought that within the law there were efficacious measures, as, for example, the refusal to pay taxes, a means, without doubt, more to be dreaded by power than a revolution, because, though revolution may destroy it by a pistol shot, the refusal to pay taxes lets it die of hunger.

But these legal resistances are difficult to organize among people long habituated to servitude. The violence of arbitrary government engendered the turbulence of the revolution. Force was opposed by force. In society, as in nature, creatures bring forth their likeness. On the 26th, the ordinances were promulgated, and the legal resistance lasted only till the 27th. On that day the people began to fling stones at the carriage of the Prime Minister, Polignac. Liberal journals were distributed by thousands in the streets. These sheets inflamed public opinion, and brought out the profound agitation which had lain tranquil. The compositors leaving their offices, ran to preach an armed resistance, with the excitement they so easily learnt at their work, and gave the first example of engaging in the struggle.

As in the time of the first Revolution, the movement began in the Palais Royal. The stunted trees of the garden may compare with the cedars of

Lebanon, they have seen so many changes. The Rue St. Denis echoes a blow given in the Palais Royal. The first outlines of the Revolution were seen in the first barricades. The pupils of the Polytechnic unrolled the tricolor flag, that glorious banner which had waved from the Alps to the Pyramids, and which had been routed by foreign intervention. The French nation, on flinging off the white flag, in which she had been enveloped since her defeat, was transported as if she had cast aside a funeral shroud, and felt anew the warmth of vitality.

The people rushed into the streets; the revolution commenced. The principal posts were occupied, guns were distributed among the multitude; the Place de la Grève was stained with the first blood of the combat. The drums sounded to the attack, and at the same moment the first shots declared the bursting forth of one of those revolutions which are so well compared to volcanoes, from their light, their fire, their thunderings, their devastations, but which also have their necessary place in social life. In this crisis what was the action of Thiers? He fled to take refuge in the house of one of his friends, in the peaceful and beautiful valley of Montmorenci, from whence he could look upon Paris as a simple tiller of the field looks from afar at the tempest on the ocean. But in this he acted consistently; he had never approved the revolution; he did not practise that which he did not believe, that of which he did not approve.

But he would have been more logical if he had abstained from its fruits. And especially he would have been more consistent if he had not roused an anti-dynastic flag—a banner essentially revolutionary. A dynasty does not fall by argument. A power which is hereditary and permanent does not cease because a pen scratches its sceptre. To show disdain for revolutionary proceedings, it is necessary to avoid the expression of revolutionary ideas. Preaching the fall of the dynasty, and keeping apart from the revolution, Thiers was unfaithful to two causes; he was certainly unfaithful to the established *régime*, with his revolutionary predictions, and false to the revolution with his scruples for order. To overturn a dynasty peacefully is a Utopian idea which was not even conceived by the ultra-parliamentary English. They, in order to put an end to the political life of the Stuarts, passed through two successive revolutions; they invested with the purple a rebellious and ungrateful daughter, most unjustly disinherited the legitimate heir to the Throne, brought over a Dutch magnate as head of their Government, and accepted foreign intervention in aid of insurrection. And all this violence was called a holy revolution by those unwearied readers of the Bible. Thiers, on that occasion, had forgotten his eternal models.

But the revolution prospered. Three principal centres were decided on for the expression of opinions, and for the organization of resistance. We must first mention the central Parliament, the last refuge of the law universally ignored. In this centre Casimir Perrier was conspicuous; a man of an unsteady conscience and selfish character, deficient in a love of liberty, and a despiser of the people, popular notwithstanding because he had opposed the Restoration, and the people always prefer the enemies of their enemies, whatever be the motive of the enmity, to the sincerest and disinterested friends of their rights. Associated with Perrier was the austere Protestant, cold-hearted, of average intelligence, sober in speech, dry and methodical in style, a worshipper of the aristocracy of gold, on whose altars he unhesitatingly sacrificed that which should never be sacrificed, not even for the most sublime cause, nor in the most supreme moments, reputation and conscience. With Guizot was Villemaine, a correct and eloquent writer, but empty and garrulous, who did not hesitate in the Academy to offer the vapours of his rhetoric as incense to the stranger—the Czar, and yet scrupled in the Chamber to forget the mandate of the people sustaining his sovereignty. This Central Parliament was timid.

Beside the Central Parliament was the authority of the Hôtel de Ville. This building is like a royal palace; designed with all the elegance and grace of the Renaissance, although somewhat overcharged by those immense roofs which are necessary in the cold and damp countries of the north, where our spacious terraces and airy galleries could not defy the inclemency of the weather. And this edifice, with its royal *salons*, seems to be for ever inhabited by the genius of revolution. Opposite the abode of the students, in the Place de la Grève, which has given its name to all the associations of the people and of labour; at the end of the Barrière St. Antoine, where were assembled the friends of liberty, those who watered with their blood those thrilling days of the social genesis, the Hôtel de Ville, by historic necessity, was converted into the general quarters of the numerous insurrections, and into the great temple of the revolution. But in the year 1830 it was entered by a nobleman, a gentleman of the ancient régime, a man of pure intentions, of honourable character, of honest opinions, loving the people and popularity, one who had seen the birth of the Republic in America, and passing through all the catastrophes of the French revolution, appeared, among the splendour of so many recollections and the smoke of so many fires, the austere personification of universal democracy. But these *souvenirs* were his ruin. Lafayette, in place of having the boldness of youth and the impulse of hope, had all the slowness of old age, and bent under the weight of his recollections. He converted the Hôtel de Ville into a kind of academy, and revolutionary politics he made use of in historical dissertations. To explain past ages was almost his sole occupation, when the preparation for future times was essential. While he spoke, Odillon Barrot, who by his side represented other ideas and other interests, worked. The greatest force of the revolution was expended in a mere storm of words. The cause which spoke most of right in the eclipse of the monarchy was the most backward in action in the moment for labour. Let us imagine a pilot discoursing of the equipment of a vessel whilst the winds tear the sails and break the planks ; of the accidents of other voyages, and the history of other shipwrecks, and we shall have an idea of Lafayette and the Hôtel de Ville.

The Centre, which had most influence, was composed of two natures, which appeared to be contrary : of two names which seemed contradictory—of a poet. and a banker : Béranger and Lafitte. The poet of the people was the defender of the rights of the people. Béranger has been a contradiction of himself ; sober, he sung of intoxication ; chaste, of light and vicious passions ; austere, of gaiety and chivalry. A son of the people, he chanted the military epopee which deprived the people of liberty, and placed them under an ignominious tutelage, which sacrificed them, poor victims, on battle fields, giving them for a final result, thanks to the irreparable loss of French blood, the restoration of the ancient Monarchy, hailing as a glimpse of liberty and a supreme refuge, foreign intervention. It is impossible to deny the power of the songs of Béranger in bringing about the fall of the Restoration : but it is also impossible to deny the force of these same verses in contributing to the restoration of the Empire. At that period of 1830 Béranger was one of the founders of the absolute rule of the middle class: he influenced Lafitte; Lafitte influenced Louis Philippe; Louis Philippe, Lafayette; Lafayette, the people; and a revolution in its essence democratic, left power with the middle class.

What paper represented Thiers at that time? In the first outbreak of the revolution and during the first battles, he quietly sought refuge in the valley of Montmorenci. And when he knew that the ancient monarchy was about to be overthrown, he went to Paris, anxious to share in the honours of victory and to have a part of the booty, contributing to the nomination of Louis Philippe. He began by a proclamation exalting the virtues of the candidate; this proclamation he threw himself to the impatient multitude. Louis Blanc relates, in his history of the ten years, that the Orleanist proclamation was received with hisses in the Place de la Bourse. After this, Thiers did not reappear in the palace of Lafitte, where the new dynasty was being forged. Without doubt he wished to be in the antechamber of the Court, and he obtained the post of Minister under the new *régime.* Knowing that a commission to Neuilly was contemplated in which he was not included, he ran to Lafitte's palace and complained to the poet Béranger of having been forgotten. "Nothing more natural," replied the latter, ironically, "than to forget the absent." Thiers set out for Neuilly in search of the king for France and of the power for himself. Thiers was poor when he joined *La Nation,* he left it with a crown in his hands for a new monarch. And by a fortune which usually accompanies all those who are sufficiently skilful to remain within the limits of two ideas, on the confines of two parties, the Revolution thought of him as its chief; the monarchy named him its lieutenant. Louis Philippe accepted everything, always preferring the nearest and least perilous course. Utility was his aim, his character was selfish; respectability was his shrine, his god was success, and his life was money; he accepted the monarchy as a lucrative employment. That which he most loved in power was the Civil List. Losing this he conceived himself lost, and while so many men died that he might have a throne, he thought of his receipts.

Thiers did not see Louis Philippe at Neuilly. But he met his queen, the virtuous Amélie, and his sister, the ambitious Adelaide. The former was indignant with the proposition, with the suspicion that attributed to her husband disloyalty to his own family, treason to the King. The latter only asked that proscription of the lesser branch should be avoided. Then Thiers, with that quickness of movement, with that flexible facility of speech, with the air of security visible in all his affirmations, discoursed largely on the irremediable misfortune of the monarchy, on the necessity for Louis Philippe to save from the ship-wreck some planks from the throne of St. Louis, and upon the readiness of the Courts of Europe to support him, alluding to the proclamation in Paris, whose voice then appeared that of the world. He did not omit his usual parallel between the situation of France and that of England.

The battle ended in a victory for the people: the Royal family fled from St. Cloud to Versailles, from thence to Rambouillet and to the coast; the Assembly met, Louis Philippe went to the Palais Royal and rode to the Hôtel de Ville, mounted on a white horse, and preceded by Lafitte, the banker, who went to anoint the king of the money-changers with the blood of the people and the powder of the barricades. Many of the combatants spoke of the death of the new king as a means of obtaining the Republic. But the skilful manœuvres of the middle class turned aside the hand of the people. Odillon Barrot said to Lafayette these memorable words : " This is the best of Republics." Lafayette presented the Citizen King to the people from a balcony, embracing him amid general applause. The monarchy was saved; and the Abbot Gregoire, who had retired to Passy, already very old and infirm, the Abbot who had once said, " the history of kings will always be the martyrology of the people," on hearing of the issue of the revolution, wept with pleasure, exclaiming, " Is it possible? What happiness! a Republic with a king!" And anew commenced, above, the work of the destruction of liberty ; below, the work of the destruction of the monarchy.

The monarchy of Louis Philippe was for doctrinaires the supreme synthesis of politics. Admitting the monarchy as thesis and the people as antithesis, the most difficult but also the most important is to accomplish the synthesis, the middle point which resolves contradictions, tempers its differences, and brings peace to the bosom of antagonists. Thiers thought he could be this synthesis. One of his first cares was to bring some young Republicans to the Palais Royal, in order that they should become accustomed to look upon the new King as their chief, and that the new King should consider the Republicans as the support of his throne. But the interview was not very successful, nor, consequently, was the idea of Thiers very happy. He began by making them wait a long time, which proved that the Citizen King was acquainted with antechambers—those schools for courtiers. Then he spoke to them earnestly of the necessity of avoiding the rocks of the French Revolution. He intimated that the best method of lighting those rocks was to take his splendid crown for a beacon. He spoke warmly of the Convention. Cavaignac said, " You forget that my father was of the Convention !" " And mine also," replied Louis Philippe. On dismissing them he asked them to return, and all answered " Never !" In fact, none of them came back till 24th February, 1848. The "Never!" of the Republicans already announced the fact of the fall of the monarchy. Thiers convinced himself that his synthesis was broken.

In reality Thiers was not a Minister. The triumphant Revolution named him First Councillor, and afterwards Under Secretary of State. When, four months later, Lafitte was raised to the Ministry, Thiers thought of retiring. An order from the King was necessary to detain him in his post. There he rendered eminent services, keeping off the financial crisis with skilful diplomacy in regard to the administration of State property and the regulation of taxes. This attention to business did not clash with the idealism which harmonizes with the nervous temperament and the restless character of all true children of the South. The man who afterwards desired to see Italy dismembered, Germany divided, absolute power in Rome, all nations on their knees, that France should seem greater and more exalted, then, with his mobility of opinions, spoke of a general crusade to restore liberty —in the name of the principles of the French Revolution—to the oppressed peoples.

But the policy of Louis Philippe was a mercantile policy. The King was not so much the chief of the citizens as the head of the merchants. The market was his battlefield, the Bourse his temple of glory, gold was his sole ambition, fortune and the riches of his children his most ardent desire. He separated his property from the Crown to place it far from the dangers of the Revolution. He dishonoured the beginning of his reign, accepting the heritage of Condé from the hands of his mistress. He mistrusted Lafitte, the banker, who had made him King, sooner than lose some thousands of francs in the cession made by him of the Wood of Branteuil. Louis Philippe was too much of a merchant, and Thiers too much of an orator for them to understand each other. The King should always have remembered the brilliant words and superior talents of Thiers. But it happened that the same qualities which were so useful for the foundation of the new dynasty were but of little value when that dynasty had fallen.

The last few months of the reign of Louis Philippe were marked by events which showed it was approaching its close. Thiers had impressed Lafitte with the policy of revolutionary propaganda against the remonstrances of European Courts. To this end he wrote an eloquent discourse, which the Minister was to read in the Chamber. This discourse was corrected by the King's orders. A crisis was necessary to restore the text. The political sentiment of the discourse of Thiers was summed up in this sentence of supreme eloquence. After saying that France could not interfere, except in the event of being threatened in its independence, and compelled to declare war, he exclaimed, " If tempests burst forth at beholding the tricoloured banner and become our auxiliaries shall we not be responsible before the universe?" These words proceeding from the mountain of tempests — the French tribune—were to pass like a breath of life over the face of a corpse, and that corpse to be reanimated, although over its mangled limbs hosts of Cossacks had held guard. It demanded its right, its place among nations, and for reply saw its useless martyrdom renewed, and the heralds of despotism, the exterminating angels of the North, announced to the world, that amid orgies of blood and the lurid splendour of fires, unhappy Poland had been again buried, with hecatombs of her sons barbarously immolated.

At last Thiers obtained power; he was appointed a Minister. A people has seldom been so much moved as France was at this period. The blood of Poland had dropped like molten lead upon the hearts of all Frenchmen; the Belgian insurrection, the work of France, found itself terribly threatened; La Vendée renewed her sinister oath to fight and die for conquered right; the Duchesse de Berri disembarked to excite civil war by her presence; the Republican Parliament, full of talent and vigour, pronounced discourses like those of Garnier Pagès. Articles appeared like those of Armand Carrel, pamphlets were issued like those of Carmenin, impressing the public mind with the idea that the days of July had been lost, and exciting a hope of redress in a new revolution. The temporal power of the Popes was shaken, Italy was distracted, socialism became converted into a species of religion, with an industrial church; the insurrections of Lyons and of Paris, so well overcome, showed with terrible aspect the bottom of the abyss; and on all sides it was evident that if the new *régime* aspired to be durable it must raise its foundations on burning lava.

Such were the perilous circumstances in which Thiers mounted to power. The King had beheld in the fall of Charles X. the consequence of following a personal policy, and, without doubt, he had also followed a personal policy. But the difference between both these policies was notable. Charles X. was inspired by his religion, and Louis Philippe by his cupidity. Charles X. defended ideas, and Louis Philippe interests. For the one politics were a holocaust to God and to His Church; for the other a dunghill, with which he manured his fields. So he would not have men of talent in his ministry, for talent was an obstacle to his personal policy; he would have men ignorant or servile. If he accepted the Ministry of Broglie, a kind of Stoic, and of Guizot, a man of clear intelligence, and of Thiers, a great orator, they entered to satisfy public opinion, to carry on the debates in Parliament, and to obtain (by exciting a rivalry between them) the exhaustion of their politics in contrary efforts, so as to admit the ascendancy of the real policy—the will of the Sovereign. Both fell into the snare, both struggled in the Council of the Crown and in the Assembly, both broke their arms a thousand times in their disputes, but in the end their projectiles wounded Louis Philippe, and hurled him from the throne.

One of the most solemn acts of the Ministry of Thiers was the arrest of the Duchesse de Berri, mother of the legitimate King of France, of the poor Dauphin, upon whom had fallen the right to a crown, thanks to two abdications. The Duchess had shown great courage in landing in France to defend a cause which had in her eyes the double prestige of historic right and of maternal love. Thiers, in order to discover the refuge of the Princess, bought a traitor, easily met with at a time when everything had a price, and politics were a marketable commodity. Beust, who had always passed for a Legitimist, sold him the secret, and took the police even to the asylum of the unfortunate Duchess. Flying from the police, the Duchess was sixteen hours confined, with a few loyal persons, in the aperture of a wall by the side of a chimney, where the air scarcely entered, and they feared dying of asphyxia, till at length, a fire having been lighted in the chimney, and being nearly roasted alive, they went out and gave themselves up to their persecutors, victims of one of those infamous treasons of which Governments approve, but which history will for ever reprobate. Louis Blanc relates, in his " History of the Ten Years," that Thiers knew the traitor. One day he received a mysterious communication, giving him a *rendezvous* in the Champs Elysées, in a spot clearly indicated, and at an advanced hour of the night, when a great project would be made known to him. Thiers hesitated, but, taking two loaded pistols, he went to the place. There he met Beust, and there they decided on the betrayal. A proceeding of Government was prepared, like a crime, secretly, but the criminal who escaped the light of day did not elude the stings of conscience. When the Princess was captured Beust demanded her death with loud voice. Thiers, who was capable of her arrest, was not the man to follow on to the natural consequence of this proceeding. On this account he passed from the political Ministry of the Interior to the economic Ministry of Commerce.

These acts of Thiers proved that the predominating trait in his character was indecision. There were two courses—either not to take the Duchesse de Berri, or, having made her a prisoner, to place her on her trial. To keep her in the fortress of Blaze without a trial was for the Orleanists to compromise the new dynasty with a perilous possession ; for the Republicans to infringe the equality of the law, declaring there was not in France a tribunal capable of judging the head of a bloody civil war ; while to the Legitimists it was a crime of unlawful arrest, another insult added to those of legitimate sovereigns, another page to the history of their martyrdoms.

Thiers pronounced one of those clever and sentimental discourses, in which he is an adept, to avoid the trial of the Duchesse de Berri. In truth there were serious obstacles : the interest of the subject; the exalted position of the prisoner ; the threefold prestige of her sex, her rank and her maternity; the strengthening of the monarchical idea by the renewal of Royal martyrdoms; the European potentates all relatives of the accused, and all interested in her fate; the reigning family compromised by the ties of blood; La Vendée again in revolt, conquered but not tranquillized; eighty or a hundred thousand men of the army from Bordeaux to Paris, occupied by the custody of a woman, who was like the shadow of fifteen ages of monarchy; the Chamber of Peers in the presence of the daughter of one king, and the mother of another, who represented such great interests, and called forth such glorious *souvenirs*, the impossible condemnation, and the perilous acquittal; Europe excited by the affecting spectacle, and dreading to see the Convention arise behind the judges of Majesty (fallen in the background of the picture) with the flames of the Revolution.

But anything was better than the infamous cabal which decided to dishonour her in the eyes of Europe and in the estimation of her family. The Duchess had been privately married. That Joan of Arc of the monarchy for whom Chateaubriand sounded the funeral trumpet of the legitimist epopee, had returned to France to fight for the restoration of her throne, and was compelled to be delivered, in the presence of her gaolers, who neither respected the modesty of the woman nor the anguish of childbirth. The Orleans family were implacable towards the Princess, with whom they were united by so many ties. To save the Crown they did not hesitate to dishonour their blood.   And this is called political ability!

Examples of this kind must be productive of great immorality, and in fact France was rotten to the bones. *La Tribune,* a liberal journal, was summoned for raising a fold of the veil which shaded so much misery.   Lafitte loved the new King, and the King allowed him to fail.   The only thing which occurred to Thiers was to raise the fortifications of Paris; this was both expensive and useless, and the scheme was afterwards reduced to a circle of forts and bastions, which proved that feeble tactics were practised by the man who had studied so many works and written so many pages upon strategy.   The fortifications were made against the Revolution which passed over them like the wind and lightning.   No doubt Paris felt that those fortresses were insults, and did not forget the injury.

Thiers wished to be considered a defender of liberty. But the man who has passed his life in approval of the extremes of despotism is incapable of comprehending the sublime simplicity of liberty.   He defended the liberty of the press, though in the Government he was the author of the ferocious laws of September, which to save the majesty of power, violated the majesty of right.   He defended the right of public meeting, but when in power he declared France incapable of exercising it, and then suppressed all political associations.   At one time he admitted the people's right to self-government, and at another declared them subjects under perpetual tutelage. He opposed personal government, and no man ever carried his prejudices or his vanity to such an extreme, for in 1834 he denied himself an amnesty which he greatly desired, from the puerile weakness of not confessing himself vanquished in the Council of Ministers. To these he had added instances of ingratitude which history will never pardon. After the explosion of Fieschi's machine, he allowed Armand Carrel to be prosecuted, though he had known his generosity of character, and his clearness of conscience in the times of struggle against another dynasty, in days in which they were companion journalists and bosom friends. Even in external politics he contradicted himself, for though he had frequently declared that the Spanish war was as fatal to Napoleon as the intervention in Spain was to the Bourbons, yet to please the Liberals he would have risked a new intervention in our country, thinking her an exhausted Vendée, while our vital force is so great that our blood always burns in our veins to defend or to re-conquer our liberties. And afterwards, great statesman as he was, his vanity concealed from him the fact, that in the theatre of the Court, Louis Philippe moved him, like a Polchinello, by the cord of this vanity, and awakened all his evil instincts to make him the enemy of Guizot, and to render impossible the only Ministry that was powerful—a Ministry including the two rivals, who brought to the King the opinions of the nation, and did not suffer the nation to submit herself to the opinions of the King. And on the 11th October, 1836, he received the portfolio of Foreign Affairs and the Presidency of the Council of Ministers; both dignities offered by the Citizen King, and accepted by the parliamentary orator without even taking into account the will of the Parliament. His ambition was realized, he was not a *parvenu*, as Talleyrand observed, but an *arrivé*; the greatest diplomatic ladies smiled upon him, kings treated him as an equal; but the personal government of Louis Philippe was erected upon the shoulders of Thiers. Vanity is the greatest enemy of statesmen.

His foreign policy was fatal. Austria despised him ; England almost separated herself from the French alliance ; Switzerland cursed him ; Spain, for whose cause he fell, did not thank him for his services ; and the three allied northern potentates renewed before his face, and against the general wish of France, the sacrifice of Poland with the suppression of the Republic of Cracow. In the interior, the only thing he accomplished through his political incapacity was to place the decision of the King above that of his Ministers, and the will of the King above that of Parliament ; therefore he fell.

From that time Thiers presided over the Left Centre of the Chamber. The King never thanked him for the revolutionary ability which had raised

him to the throne, nor for the services he had rendered in founding his personal government. Because
the pressure of circumstances had drawn him to give
a liberal colour to his opposition, the aversion of the
King made him give a suspicious appearance to the
monarchy. When he went to the palace, when he
passed before those Princes to whom the 29th July
had, for the first time, presented the rich gift of the
most brilliant, if the most fragile of earthly diadems,
they looked upon him as a conspirator, as a shadow
of the societies which had been dissolved, as a remnant of the Revolution which had been stifled in
blood. The year 1835 gave him and three times took
from him in three days the Ministry. They wished to
make him an ambassador, to send him into exile with
a salary, for Louis Philippe thought all wounds could
be cured by a gilded plaster. He was considered a
fatality who, with his nervous character, active ambition, sparkling eloquence and parliamentary ability,
gave more embarrassment than service to authority,
and more annoyance than glory to the new dynasty.
Becoming aware of this opinion, he went to the King
to say that if his presence in France made one more
political combination, added to the many against which
the monarchy had to struggle, he had decided, on the
slightest word or indication to that effect, to condemn
himself to a perpetual banishment; so he naturally
brought with him to the tribune, with ideas of a
lively opposition, troubles which were often intense.

The ill-will persistently manifested towards him by the King gave him prestige in the Senate; and as the people are always generous, they soon forgot his lukewarm zeal in their cause, and heaped upon him popularity—always too much disregarded by power, to which it is most necessary, and always sought where it is so much needed—in the Opposition; so he exclaimed from the benches of the Left, " Shall we be so reduced as not to have even the fiction of a representative government? If such was our idea, why did you not say so during the three days of July?"

Things began to alter; the doctrinaire policy had borne its fruit. The middle class had become exhausted and corrupt during eighteen years of oligarchical domination. France, as in the worst days of the former reign, on all sides represented reaction. Every day the parliamentary rule pressed with more and more force upon the lower classes. Thiers rudely combated these politics. Guizot treated him with great harshness, saying, " Everything depends on the place where you find yourself. If you had been in mine, you would do what I do."

At last came the 24th February. The Citizen-Monarchy crumbled away like the legitimate monarchy. The King did not hear the warnings which sounded under his feet. At the beginning of the outbreak he said to his sons, " We will not act like the princes of the elder branch; we shall fight in the streets." And he called the first announcement of the commotions "a fire of straw." Electoral banquets were prohibited. The Opposition wished to celebrate them, notwithstanding the prohibition. Thiers opposed this, representing, as in 1830, legal resistance. An accusation was drawn up against the Government, and deposited upon the table of the Assembly. Guizot read it, and flung it contemptuously upon the table. But in the Ministry of Foreign Affairs, and on the steps of the Madeleine, the combatants fell wounded. Louis Philippe promoted Bugeaud, the Military Governor of Paris, a warrior famous for his victories, but very unpopular on account of his ferocity. This nomination exasperated the people. The King began to fear, and told Guizot to dismiss him. This display of weakness increased the boldness of the insurgents. Molé was summoned to the Tuileries. On his way, the mob took possession of his coach to put it upon a barricade. Molé arrived on foot. He heard the order to form a Ministry, and said that he, as a Conservative, was not equal to the gravity of the occasion, and that Thiers was the one suited to the occasion. "What will Europe say?" exclaimed Louis Philippe. "Do not think of that, your Majesty, when the throne is tottering." The King agreed, but with the condition that Molé should be included in the Ministry. Louis Philippe much enjoyed the ministerial crisis, which gave all the power to the Sovereign, with the prerogative of appointing his Ministers. And whilst Paris burned, they formed a Ministry as in times of peace. When Molé went to offer Thiers the chief place, he found him in his house in the little Place St. George. The dynastic opposition surrounded him, and the multitude saluted him as in his days of popularity. They imagined that the King would give him real power, that his name would still the disturbance, being absolute master of the situation by the ruin of Guizot, and the timidity of Louis Philippe. Molé set forth his programme. His first article was the dissolution of the Chamber. The King refused his consent. Thiers went to the Tuileries. The streets were piled with barricades. The fire of the insurgents resounded from all quarters. "You shall not go," cried the people; "they are deceiving you." Thiers entered, and presented his propositions. The King moved about with much agitation. He went to consult Guizot, shut up in a cabinet close by. When, however, a Liberal Ministry was decided on, it was too late. The King abdicated—it was too late. The Regency of the Duchess of Orleans was proclaimed—too late—too late. When the Duchess went to the Assembly she heard the cry, "Vive la République!" The monarchy of July found its grave and its cradle on the barricades. Louis Philippe and all his family fled to England. Thiers no longer formed part of the Government, but did not cease to shine in the tribune.

Let us pause a moment and contemplate, under its

different aspects, the life of this man, which we have slightly sketched. Born among the lower ranks of society, he raised himself to the highest by the brilliancy of his talents and his immense perseverance. But once in the highest he forgot his origin, which imposed upon him the imperious duty of defending the privileges of the least, to establish the right of all. If he had done this he might not have had a high position, nor a great fortune, but as it is, the fatigues of labour have been the lot of his life, and exile will perhaps be his end. Sorrow is the shade which follows genius, for there cannot be genius unaccompanied in some measure by the gift of prophecy; and there cannot be a prophet without labour for the ideas of the future, without drawing upon himself the hatred of the present. All the Hebrew prophets, those severe judges of tyrants, wrote their terrible sentences in the solitude of the desert. The most elevated intelligence, like the most gigantic tree, attracts the lightning.

But Thiers was not before his time; he followed it, and at times from afar. To found the oligarchy of the middle classes was his sole idea; to retard the entrance of the people into public life was his sole employment. He knew that the middle class is too proud to support all the ancient monarchical institutions, and too utilitarian and selfish to pass to new republican institutions. And so he became one of the founders of the hybrid Monarchy of the eighteen years—a Monarchy born of a revolution, but unfaithful to its origin, raised on the cash boxes of bankers, and mistaking them for a throne of divine right—a Monarchy composed of a little of everything —little statesmen, little philosophers, little generals, a little sovereign—a Monarchy which founded doctrinairism, that chaos of sterility in politics; eclecticism, that negation of all principles in philosophy; fatalism, that scaffold of all great characters in history; and public corruption, that cancer of declining epochs, as the only means of government.

Thiers was not a man of the Monarchy of July. Thiers propelled it towards the abyss during the last year of its existence, and when he tried to save it, it was too late. But certainly he had contributed to found it. Neither was Thiers the man of the Republic of February. But without doubt he had helped to bring it about. During the Republic he employed all his talent of oratory to overturn democracy, and all his skill to restore the Monarchy. One day there entered the doors of the National Assembly an obscure youth, pale and silent, who had, if not the air of his Olympian race, ambition in his soul, and the reflection of glory on his forehead. It was Louis Bonaparte. And Thiers, who had so much contributed by his History—his monumental work—to restore the prestige of the Empire, carrying it to the homes of the middle classes, as Béranger had brought it to the rude dwellings of the people, did he not behold the Empire come from its sepulchre in that pale face? Thiers did not wish for an Imperial restoration. An Empire means personal government, and this is not agreeable to a parliamentary orator. This was unforeseen. The young Bonaparte was his candidate for the post of President of the Republic. The motive of this election was told in a scornful sentence—" He has a wooden head." On such a head Thiers might very easily spread his own brain. One day the candidate became President. Speaking was a necessity with Thiers, and he had the habit of writing long documents on all critical occasions. He had written the protests against orders, the first proclamations of the Orleans family, the discourse in which Lafitte set forth the external policy of the Monarchy of July. A new document for the new Chief of the State was a basis of power, and of fortune for himself. And he sought this in mature years with the same intensity as in his early days. He carried the speech to Bonaparte. The President read it, and returning it to him, said, " I have already written the speech; for I wish to be myself." The personal government was founded. The wooden head (as Thiers called it) became the cerebrum of France. Thiers considered himself a statesman; but he had not foreseen this. When he uttered the sentence " *L'Empire est fait,*" the world already knew that the Empire was made, and probably by his fault.

In his hatred of the people, in his enthusiasm for the restoration of the oligarchy, he laboured in the Assembly to prevent universal [male] suffrage. And either the Revolution of February was nothing, or it was the entry of the people to the electorate. What happened in this imprudent retrogression, this restriction of the suffrage? He gave the President an arm for the *coup d'état.* Bonaparte desired universal suffrage. The deputies of the school of Thiers wished it when the Imperial legions murdered the Republic in the name of the rights of the people. This also was too late. One of the deputies of the majority who had met together in a quarter of Paris, came out upon the balcony to proclaim the principle upon which they had before trampled. The people laughed, and a sergeant was put in prison. The policy of Thiers led to this. We may say that he was from the tribune the Polignac of the Republic, as in the monument raised by his History to military genius he was the restorer of the Empire.

His History! This is indeed his chief monument, and it well merits this name. It shows art in the grouping of facts, warmth and movement in the narration, the profound erudition of an economist, and stranger than all, skilful tactics. But imagination—that great stamp of reason and intelligence, by which history may be elevated into a science—is not visible in any of its pages. Philosophy is wanting. Thiers saw admirably, as if he had accompanied and followed the marches and counter-marches of armies, the evolutions of the different divisions, and even the spot on which the soldiers stood. Thiers beheld the terrible encounters, the battles; heard the words of command, and minutely criticised them; counted the dead, examined all, from the plan of the engagement to its close, and understood all from the military administration to the strategy of the field. But Thiers did not perceive, did not follow the waves of ideas, which pass like the movements of the air, over great armies, and which involve them in an impassible atmosphere in what is called the spirit of their time, the life of their age. Thiers is no philosopher, with talents essentially analytic; the great general laws of life and of history are too high for his mental vision. Thiers feels the trembling of the earth, the shaking of societies, but he neither sees nor knows aught of the central fire of ideas. That his book is so deficient in great philosophical teaching can only be explained by the philosophical sterility of the Empire. This might find compensation in the presence of moral teaching. But conscience is also absent from this great work. Thiers did not wish to be in his book a philosopher, like some great modern historians; nor a judge, like some great historians of antiquity.

He manifests more admiration towards the mechanical forces of society than towards the spiritual forces of ideas. This is why he has been seen in the tribune, when European politics were discussed, less in advance than the Empire, less idealistic than the military, praising the antique European equilibrium, which is the chain of the peoples; and permitting the destruction of nations that France might be more exalted, although at the price of the unhappiness and degradation of all. We find this narrow and classic patriotism, which places the country above the whole human race, and the welfare of a few above justice for all, above generosity engendered by a philosophy superior to all interests, that desires to behold each individual in his right of citizen, each nation in her independence, all men united in the holy equality of justice, all nations friends in the bosom of humanity, mistresses of nature by their labours, and reflections of God by their virtues and their sciences. "Poetic Utopia!" cry the utilitarians, those who would give the swan to Socrates to benefit the gods, the cross to Christ to save the Cæsars, the inquisition to Galileo for the advantage of scholars, and who yet suffer, feeling the stings of falsehood and evil; whilst these Utopians, who appear as stars in the darkest nights of history, are the life of the age, the bases of society.

The French Republic charged the Ministry to make peace; and entrusted the task of infusing this idea into foreign Governments to the great orator, Thiers. He was liked in the different Courts of Europe, but he belonged to the ancient diplomacy, so admirably laid aside in the simple, energetic, and truthful manifestoes of Jules Favre.

And Thiers contributed more to the war than any other. His former disclosures were designed to wound the fibre of French patriotism, and to show war as a necessity for her greatness and her influence in the world, the destruction of Germanic and of Italian unity. Thiers said that France should be surrounded by small, dismembered, and feeble nations, incapable of opposing their forces to those of the French people—always powerful from their glorious history— the universality of her language, and her thirty-eight millions of citizens.

With these ideas of exclusiveness and supremacy, it was difficult to make way with foreign Governments, and they now behold the fate of France with indifference. Selfishness, which is repugnant in individuals, is still more repugnant in peoples. Man does not exist if he does not live in his family, in his country, in humanity, where his heart and his conscience expand. And peoples do not really exist when they are separated from communion with other peoples. A people shut up in selfishness is as useless as a polypus upon its rock, devoted solely to the labour of nutrition.

It is a sad pity that such a man as Thiers, a man of remarkable eloquence, should belong to the reactionaries of history. His oratory is certainly enchanting. Small and slender, of mediocre features, of sharp voice, of unpleasing gestures, and of a vivacity and mobility which prevent him from being grave and solemn; without the superior understanding of a philosopher, without the brilliant imagination of a poet, it is strange that he should produce immense effects and obtain incalculable victories by the marvels of that speech, which, fluid, connected, light, and graceful, flows like conversation, yet has at times the intonation and the grandeur which belongs to the art of elocution.

And do you seek to know why this personage has dominated less than he should have done in his time, having been placed in the most favourable circumstances in which a man could find himself? He has not possessed all the moral power he should have had, to which those exalted intelligences aspire, who from their ætherial elevation despise low, worldly grandeur; he has had not this, because his ideas are not progressive, because his character is moveable and changeful as a flood, and a name cannot be graven on the eternal bronze of history which is not chiselled by the force of a great character and of a powerful imagination.

THE END.